A BRIEF ILLUSTRATED HISTORY OF ROMANIANS

Neagu M. Djuvara was born in 1916 in Bucharest to a family of Aromanian descent that settled there in the late 18th century and gave Romania several notable figures. He obtained a degree in history from the Sorbonne (1937) and became a doctor of law (Paris, 1940). Between June and November 1941, he took part in the Romanian army's campaign in Bessarabia and Transnistria, and was wounded close to Odessa. Admitted to the Ministry of Foreign Affairs in 1943, he was sent to Stockholm on a diplomatic mission related to the peace negotiations with the USSR on the morning of 23 August 1944, hours before Romania changed sides in the WW2. He worked as a legation secretary in the Swedish capital until September 1947, when the Communists took control of Romanian diplomacy. Djuvara chose to remain in exile, where he was active in various diaspora organisations. In 1961, he left for the Republic of Niger, where he would work for the next 23 years as a diplomatic and legal advisor to the country's Foreign Affairs ministry, while also teaching international law and the history of economics at the University of Niamey. In 1972, he obtained a state doctorate from the Sorbonne with a thesis on the philosophy of history, under the supervision of philosopher Raymond Aron; this was followed by a degree in philology from INALCO (Paris). From 1984 to 1990 he served as the secretary general of the *Casa Românească* cultural association in Paris. Following the fall of communism in Romania, he returned home and became an honorary member of the "A.D. Xenopol" Institute of History in Iași and the "N. Iorga" Institute of History in Bucharest.

His major works include: *On Romanian Nationality Law* (doctoral thesis); *Civilisations and Historical Patterns. A Comparative Study of Civilisations* (recipient of a French Academy prize); *Between East and West. The Romanian Principalities at the Beginning of the Modern Age*; *A Brief History of Romanians*; *The Genesis of the Romanian People*; *Mircea the Elder and His Wars Against the Turks*; *From Vlad the Impaler to Dracula the Vampire*; *The Journal of Georges Milesco* (autobiographical novel); *Somewhat Irreverent Memoirs and Stories*; *Bucharest–Paris–Niamey and Return or Memoirs of 42 Years in Exile (1948-1990)*; *Is There Such a Thing as True History?*; *Thocomerius – Negru-Vodă. A Voivode of Cuman Descent and the Beginnings of Wallachia*; *The Seventy-Seven Years' War (1914-1991) and the Premises of American Hegemony. An Essay in Political Science*; *Who Were Wallachia's Great Boyars? The Grădișteanu Family Saga (16th-20th Century)*; *A Reply to My Critics and the Foes of Negru-Vodă*; *The Mystery of the Stockholm Telegram of 23 August 1944 and Several Incredible Details Regarding Our Capitulation.*

NEAGU
DJUVARA

A BRIEF ILLUSTRATED HISTORY OF ROMANIANS

Translation by Cristian Anton

HUMANITAS
BUCUREȘTI

Illustration research: Cătălin Strat
Cover design: Angela Rotaru
Layout: Manuela Măxineanu
DTP: Iuliana Constantinescu, Andreea Dobreci,
Dan Dulgheru

Printed by Monitorul Oficial R.A.

This book features photographs by Marius Amarie that were kindly offered by the National History Museum of Romania (pages 23 and 41 – Gepidic artefacts from Apahida; pages 27 and 39 – Artefacts from the Pietroasele hoard; page 35 – Inscribed 9th century ceramic vessel; page 270 – Sword of King Carol I; page 273 – Sword of Edhem Pasha; page 276 – The Steel Crown of Romania) as well as photographs offered by the National History Museum of Transylvania (page 12 – Dacian silver fibula and a bronze sword discovered at Benești). Humanitas would like to thank the two institutions for their support. We have also used images of charters and seals found in the National Historical Archives and photographs from the online archive of communism in Romania (IICCR).

Descrierea CIP a Bibliotecii Naționale a României
DJUVARA, NEAGU
A brief illustrated history of Romanians / Neagu Djuvara;
trad.: Cristian Anton. – București: Humanitas, 2014
ISBN 978-973-50-4334-6
I. Anton, Cristian (trad.)
94(498)

HUMANITAS PUBLISHING HOUSE
Piața Presei Libere 1, 013701 București, România
tel. 021/408 83 50, fax 021/408 83 51
www.humanitas.ro

Online bookstore: www.libhumanitas.ro

FOREWORD

This book is not an ordinary history book; it is not a textbook, and it does not profess to replace school textbooks. The idea for it came to me a few years ago, when Mrs Irina Nicolau, a specialist in ethnology and oral history, voiced her exasperation about the fact that our school textbooks – even after the revolution of December 1989 – were continuing to disseminate the same version of history, intentionally deformed over the past decades, and written in the same pretentious, dead language of officialdom, dressed up to disguise the poverty of thought and often the absence of any real meaning. It was she who persuaded me to summarise our country's past in the simplest and most fluent manner on audio tapes for today's younger generation. The present title is the transcription of those recordings, "purged" of the errors inherent to improvised speech and complemented where it seemed to me that the misgivings were too obvious – within limits, of course. I therefore let the story flow, free of interruptions, explanatory notes and citations – in short, avoiding the style which scholars call "academic" – to make it comprehensible to all, from history enthusiasts to those who have chosen to remain indifferent to our past.

It is a very abridged story; for example, I did not list the names of all the voivodes (or princes) who were fighting for the throne during the 15th or 16th century, nor those of the Phanariote princes replaced by the sultan in Constantinople once every two or three years (when they were not beheaded or hanged at his orders) throughout the 18th century. It should not be mistaken for a work of *vulgarisation*. I am not fond of the word "vulgar" used as a derogatory term, which would suggest that the story is not only simple, but also simplistic or puerile.

The reader will quickly realise that, under the guise of light storytelling, I had the audacity to tackle the most delicate and controversial issues in our history, under the assumption that the high school student too has an adult mind, instead of a fragile one that should be spared and offered a sweetened, rosy image of our past. Nothing serves our country better than knowing (or acknowledging) the truth, as much of it as we mortals can perceive – as God alone knows *the whole truth*. For that reason, do not be surprised if I sometimes happen to say "some authors believe that..." or "I believe that..." etc.

It is often said that one must be *objective* in searching for the truth. I am not fond of this word either: if you look it up in a dictionary, you will find that "objective" used to mean "outside consciousness" and therefore, logically, can only be applied to the study of inanimate objects. Yet historians primarily deal with *people* – individuals or groups, therefore subjects, not objects, and in order to understand these subjects they too have to be subjective. They will be trying very hard to relate with various mentalities and opinions, one after the other, some of them contradictory (individual, national, religious, doctrinal etc.). Their impartiality can only stem from a succession of partialities, constructed as honestly as possible. If we proceed in this manner, not only will we not be able to pursue an alleged "national" agenda in describing and explaining the past, but we will not be tempted to hide some facts or manipulate others in the name of this false patriotism, under the pretext that we must respond to the fabrications of our Hungarian, Bulgarian, Greek or Russian neighbours, and of others. *Lies should not be met with more lies.* The only rational answer is complete academic integrity. This is the only way we will assert ourselves before the international scientific community and take our rightful place in Europe and the world.

I have kept the somewhat ambiguous title of "The History of Romanians" – as opposed to "The History of Romania" of which we tend to speak more and more nowadays – firstly because it is traditional; secondly, because "Romania" is a term applied to the country inhabited by Romanians only after the Union of 1859 –

therefore, can we really call our territory in the Middle Ages "Romania"?; and finally, because it enables me to briefly mention other branches of the Eastern Roman world found outside the territory of present-day Romania, such as the Aromanians or the Vlachs that founded the Second Bulgarian Tsardom, the Asen dynasty (Romanian: *Asănești*).

However, the scope of the book goes beyond the history of "Romanians" in its strictest sense, both ethnically and temporally. Temporally, because we will be going further back in time, before the human group speaking the Romanian language was formed, and getting closer to the peoples who mixed to form this group, meaning the Romanian people; this was a long process, very difficult to follow and explain because of the scarcity of documents. We must briefly mention the Geto-Dacians, then the Romanised Italic and Mediterranean peoples brought by Roman colonisation; perhaps even some remains of Germanic barbarians (Goths, Gepids etc.) but most importantly the great Slavic migration, which left deep traces in our language, customs and institutions, and which must be seen as the third major component in the ethnogenesis of the Romanian people. I also see a fourth significant component, namely the *Turkic* peoples arriving from Central Asia in successive waves, such as the Avars, the Pechenegs, the Oghuz Turks and the Cumans, most of whom spoke Turkic languages, related to Ottoman Turkish. For example, the Pechenegs and the Cumans ruled over our territory east and south of the Carpathians for 350 years, and it was there, in the lands which our neighbours called "Cumania" up to that time, that the first organised Romanian state appeared at the turn of the 13th and 14th centuries, namely Wallachia (Romanian: *Țara Românească*). I will try to demonstrate why I believe that the Turkic component has not been sufficiently explored until now. In any case, it is only *after* this complex mix of peoples and the formation of the language we call "Romanian" that we can speak of a Romanian people. Therefore, we have to begin telling the story over one thousand years before this process was completed.

Secondly, from an ethnic point of view, we have to speak about the peoples that not only did not mix with the Romanians (such as the Hungarians, Saxons, Ruthenians) but became the dominant and privileged groups across wide areas of our territory until recent times. Other foreign elements were added later on, some of whom were easily assimilated into the Romanian majority – like the Greeks and other Balkan peoples – but also others who were more difficult to assimilate, whether we have kept them at a distance, or they have sought to preserve their individuality – such as the Gypsies, Armenians and Jews. We must mention all of them, for they have shared the same territory with the Romanians, and the influences of one group over the others are countless and difficult to quantify.

Lastly, I will emphasise the impact which our neighbours have had on the founding of the Romanian states and the birth of the Romanian nation. One by one or simultaneously, the Bulgarian Tsardom, the Byzantine Empire, the Kingdom of Hungary, the Serbian Despotate, the Kingdom of Poland, the Ottoman Turks, the Austrians and finally, the Russians have played a part in the destiny of our people. This will provide us with almost concentric views over larger and larger areas – South-Eastern Europe, Central and Eastern Europe, and Europe as a whole – for we must even mention faraway France, whose role was crucial to our adoption of Western views, customs and institutions during the past century, and which made an overwhelming impact on the modern Romanian language. Without a broader perspective, without including Romanians in the broader history of Europe and the world, their history will remain *incomprehensible*.

One final remark: no author should imagine that the history that he or she is writing is the definitive one, which future generations will identify with. Every generation forms a new vision of the past and may uncover unexpected things from that past which could change its vision yet again.

Aware of the volatile and precarious nature of historical writing, I now leave these preliminary observations aside to begin the story of our people, *as I see it at the end of this century and millennium.*

Bucharest, October 1999

NEAGU DJUVARA

The lines above have told you the story of how the book called *A Brief History of Romanians* came to be, back in the late 1990s. Since then it has sold tens of thousands of copies and became very well known in Romania, as well as having been translated into six languages, including English and French. It made our history more accessible to others and, I hope, offered a vision free of the constraints of academic writing, which would spark more interest in our past.

Then some time ago, Humanitas Publishing House proposed an illustrated version of the book, which sounded like an excellent idea from the start. When accompanied by illustrations, a history book becomes even better and easier to understand, for we are offered the chance to see how ancient artefacts discovered by archaeologists actually look like, or catch a glimpse into how the authors of the wonderful illuminated manuscripts saw the barbarians or medieval warriors. As we get nearer to the modern age, the iconography becomes even richer and we get to know Romania's princes and monarchs, their allies and their enemies, the politicians – good and bad – their triumphs, tribulations or even tragedies, and sometimes even the common people going about their daily lives. The photographic discourse focuses on the most important documents, even if their condition is not optimal. But you will also find images of wonderful artefacts: pieces of pottery, jewellery and weaponry. Some of them come from unexpected sources, often unknown to the public, and are accompanied by detailed captions that complement the information provided in the text itself. Together, the text and illustrations that accompany it intertwine to form a new, enhanced historical account – and hopefully, one not lacking in originality.

Bucharest, May 2013

I. THE BEGINNINGS

Pottery of the Cucuteni culture (4800 to 3000 BC)

If you look at a physical map of Romania, observe the shape of the Transylvanian Plateau: you could say that our country forms a great circle around Transylvania. Well, that was where the Romanian nation was born.

But who were the inhabitants of the Transylvanian Plateau 2,500 years ago? For trying to find who lived there before that time is far too difficult an undertaking. We cannot push this study into prehistory as part of such a condensed account; it is true that archaeology has revealed very ancient traces of human habitation in our present-day territory, going back thousands, even tens of thousands of years. However, we currently lack any means of identifying the race or races of those ancient inhabitants, or of understanding the least bit about their customs and beliefs, and even less about the languages they spoke. Describing those civilisations, lost in the mists of time, would serve us little in trying to understand how those whom it is safer to consider our ancestors have appeared in this space. From the many archaeological remains found all over the country, it is only certain that wave after wave of successive migrations came in from the south, from the west and from the east, and it is impossible to tell what race they were, and how they mixed or wiped each other out just by looking at the shape of dwellings and graves, or the style of tools and ceramics. Let us limit our account to those peoples whom scientists of the previous century have called "Indo-European", for they spread westwards across the whole of Europe, as well as south and east, all the way to India.

Around four or five thousand years ago, starting from the present day territories of Belarus, Western Ukraine and Poland, peoples speaking the same language started to spread slowly but relentlessly across our continent, and over time came to rule it all. They were not of a single race (meaning that, in anthropological terms, they did not all belong to the same physical type). It was thought during the past century that all Indo-Europeans originally resembled modern-day Scandinavians, and that they were tall, blonde and dolichocephalic (that is, their skulls looked egg-shaped when seen from above). This was a mistaken conception: Indo-European was only a language. Archaeology has proven that all kinds of peoples could be found in this original crucible, and that they ended up speaking the same language after living together or near one another for thousands of years. It is from these Indo-European-speaking peoples, who colonised Europe in successive waves, some at rather long intervals, that almost all of the peoples living in Europe today are descended.

Bronze ritual chariot from Bujoru, Teleorman County, belonging to the Basarabi culture. It dates back to the 8th century BC, two centuries before the first mention of the Getae in the Histories *of Herodotus.*

Sword discovered at Benești, Sibiu County, dating from the late Bronze Age. The marks on its edge reveal that it was used in battle.

I say *almost all* because small enclaves were left unchanged by the Indo-European migrations, and following these, came several other peoples speaking entirely different languages. Of the latter, the Finns, the Estonians, the Hungarians and the Turks are the foremost examples, while of the remaining pre-Indo-Europeans, only the Basques form a distinct ethnic and linguistic group to this day, in the north of Spain and south-west of France. Some anthropologists claim that Sicily too was mainly populated with pre-Indo-European peoples; the Sicilians, however, have adopted the language of their Roman rulers and no traces were left of any language that preceded Indo-European idioms.

Dacian silver fibula from Transylvania, where other similar pieces of jewellery were found. Fibulae were used by both women and men to fasten various items of clothing.

The Geto-Dacians

Dacian silver ring from the 1st century AD, part of the hoard found at Măgura, Teleorman County

Let us return to the territory defined by the Carpathian Mountains and the river Danube. Here, archaeological and documentary sources reveal the presence of an Indo-European people who had probably arrived during the second or third millennium BC. Some called them *Dacians* (especially in Transylvania) others *Getae* (in Wallachia, Dobruja and Bessarabia).

To the south there lived the Thracians. Many historians believe that the Geto-Dacians were in fact a Thracian tribe, relying on a single sentence from the Greek historian Herodotus (5th century BC). Today it seems that this is not exactly true. They may have been close relatives of the Thracians, but their languages (or what little we can make of them) were not very similar, for in the Geto-Dacian language we do not find the same place names, nor the same royal names as in Thracian, and

Prehistoric Dacia, from the Paleolithic until 512 BC

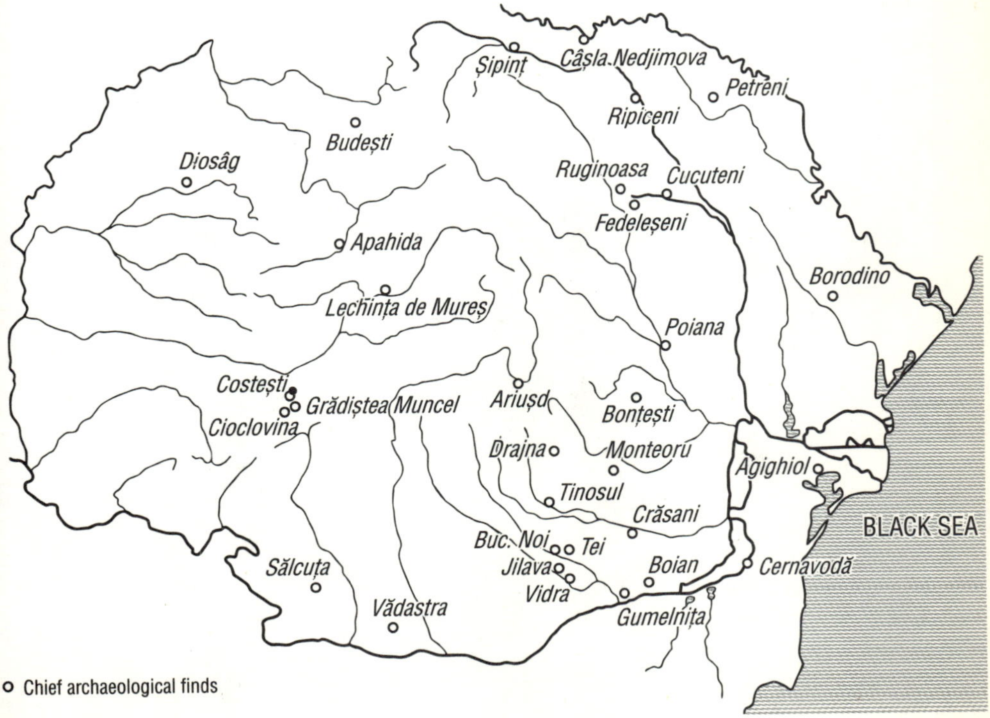

Bust of a Dacian nobleman (tarabostes)

most importantly, we know of dozens, if not hundreds of names of Thracian deities, whereas the Geto-Dacians seem to have only worshipped one god: *Zalmoxis*. Therefore, the Geto-Dacians were one people; the Thracians were another, living to the south, in present-day Bulgaria and European Turkey; while the Illyrians inhabited areas further to the west, in what is now Albania and parts of the former Yugoslavia.

In the 1st century BC, Geto-Dacian tribes were united under one king, named Burebista. This is the first time in history that our ancestors appear united, led by a single ruler, who dared to take on Rome itself. Burebista reigned over many other tribes, from beyond the Dniester River in the east, all the way to Pannonia in the west – but he died assassinated, in the same year as Julius Caesar (44 BC).

Rome

The Romans were another Indo-European people, who had settled present-day Italy. They began with one town, Rome, which was one of many in a region called Latium (hence the word "Latin"); over the course of three to four hundred years, starting with the area around Rome, they slowly began to build a vast empire. First, they con-

The Capitoline Wolf, symbol of the legendary origin of Rome and the eternal nature of the City and its empire. The statue dates from the 6th century BC, but the twins – Romulus and Remus – were only added in the 15th century. Numerous copies of the statue are displayed across Romania.

quered all of Italy, then Spain, then Gaul (modern France) and then all of North Africa.

You may have heard of the wars between the Romans and the Carthaginians. The Carthaginians were *Semites*, closely related to the Arabs or the Jews, and were a nation of skilled merchants who had settled in modern Tunisia. These wars lasted for decades and nearly ended in Carthaginian general Hannibal conquering Italy itself, but eventually the Romans prevailed and ruthlessly razed the once-mighty city of Carthage from the face of the earth.

That is how the Romans gained a foothold in Africa. By the time we are concerned with, meaning the time when Rome also showed an interest in the lands inhabited by the Geto-Dacians, the Romans were the world's greatest super-power, except perhaps for Han China in the Far East, which was established at about the same time as the Roman Empire. Take a look at the map of Europe: the Romans were the masters of all the lands around the Mediterranean. Their empire was like an enormous ring surrounding the Mediterranean Sea: Italy, Spain, Gaul, the whole of North Africa; they also conquered Greece, Asia Minor, Syria and the Balkans, reaching the Danube and becoming neighbours with the Dacians.

So why did the Romans start to attack the Dacians? To begin with, it must be said that the Dacians were an aggressive people. With their eyes on the riches of the Roman Empire, they frequently launched devastating raids across the Danube, into lands that were now ruled by the Romans, and which for centuries had been under the civilising influence of Greece. As a matter of fact, the Romans themselves had been heavily influenced by Hellenic culture – which is why we speak of the "Greco-Roman civilisation". The Romans were, first and foremost, warriors, while the more refined elements of their culture came from the Greeks. The Greeks had commercial "outposts" on our territory as well, in Dobruja; these were harbours with small colonies around them. You may have heard of Tomis, the old name of Constanța, and of Histria, further to the north. There were other colonies along the Black Sea coast, to the south, in modern Bulgaria, and to the north, all the way to the Crimea.

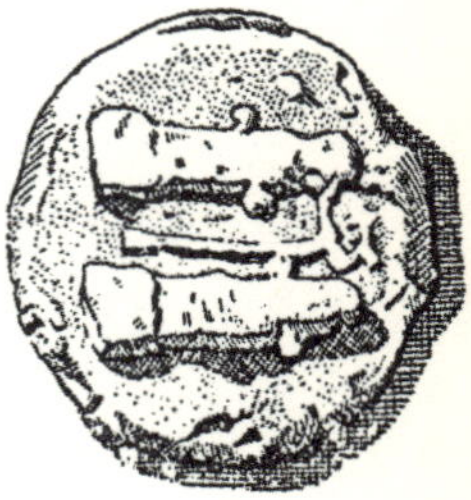

Two weights found at Callatis (modern Mangalia) a Greek colony on the Black Sea coast. The bronze rectangular piece bears the symbols of Hercules; the round one is made of lead and has decorative elements on both sides, as shown above.

Silver denarius with the effigy of Titus Flavius Domitianus, the Roman emperor who fought a war against the Dacians in 86-88 AD

Therefore, to some extent, Greek influence had also reached the Dacians.

Before long, conflict and enmity broke out between the Dacians and the Romans. This first happened before the birth of Christ, in the time of Burebista. Hostilities would then erupt again at the end of the 1st century AD, when the legions of Rome were actually defeated at one point, under the weak emperor Domitian. But the tables turned when Trajan, one of the greatest Roman emperors of all time, came to power. By that time, another king had succeeded in uniting all Dacians, but he ruled over a smaller territory, no further than the river Tisza to the west and the river Siret to the east. His name was Decebalus (Romanian: *Decebal*) – a name he had taken, and which probably had a special significance in the Dacian language (we now pronounce the *c* softly but at that time it was pronounced as *k*; the name was spelled "Dekebalos" in both Greek and Latin script). Decebalus did not accept Roman influence – in effect, he would have become a client king – and continued to conspire against Rome.

The Roman province of Dacia

Emperor Trajan decided to go to war and bring Dacia under Roman rule. Have another look at the map. The Roman Empire surrounded the Mediterranean, but Dacia seems to be somewhat further from the centre, to the north, outside this "ring". Both Dacia and Britain look like "appendixes" of imperial power, which is why they

Golden aureus *issued by Emperor Trajan between 112 and 117 AD. The obverse shows the effigy of the emperor, with the inscription stating "Emperor Trajan Augustus, conqueror of Germania and Dacia, high priest, tribune and six-time consul, father of the country". On the reverse, we see Trajan's Column and an inscription that reads "From the Senate and people of Rome to the first among rulers".*

were the first to be abandoned when barbarian pressure started to build up.

Battle scene from the First Dacian War, as depicted on Trajan's Column

Trajan personally led the first war (101-102 AD), defeated Decebalus and imposed on him a treaty by which the Dacian king promised not to ally himself to the enemies of Rome, to destroy his own fortresses, to accept Roman architects and engineers, as well as a certain degree of supervision etc. In short, he agreed to become a client of Rome. But Decebalus did not keep his promises; instead, he rebuilt his fortresses and looked to form alliances with faraway enemies of Rome. In response, Trajan ordered a second campaign of conquest against Dacia and the removal of Decebalus.

The war took place during 105-106 AD. Trajan instructed Apollodorus of Damascus, a very famous Greek architect from Syria, to build a bridge across the Danube at Drobeta (modern-day Turnu-Severin) which, when completed, was regarded as a marvel of its time. The emperor invaded Dacia with his legions, while another army corps crossed the Danube from Scythia Minor (modern Dobruja). After fierce fighting, the Romans finally took the capital, Sarmizegetusa, while Decebalus took his own life to escape the victor and the humiliation of adorning his triumphal parade in Rome as a slave.

Bas-relief of King Decebalus from Trajan's Column

To piece together the events of this war between the Romans and the Dacians, we need look no further than an iconic monument in Rome, which has miraculously

remained intact to this day – *Trajan's Column*. On it, swirling from bottom to top, are bas-reliefs that tell the full story of the conquest of Dacia, as if in a comic strip; they not only allow us to follow the phases of the war, but also to discover what kind of clothes both sides were wearing (including Dacian women); what weapons they were using; and even what breeds of cattle were farmed in the country etc. Trajan's Column is a veritable treasure trove for historians and ethnologists.

Thus, the large and previously well-populated kingdom of Dacia became a Roman province. But what exactly did that mean for the country? It meant that the realm of Decebalus came under the direct rule of Rome. The new province of "Dacia" did not incorporate all the territories that would later be inhabited by Romanians, but was limited to present-day Oltenia and about two thirds of Transylvania. Scythia Minor was already included in the Roman province of Moesia, along with the northeast of what is now Bulgaria. Fortified outposts were built to the east of the river Olt and the Carpathian Mountains to fend off the raids of the free Dacians and

Decebalus, shown here as he is about to be captured by his Roman pursuers, killed himself rather than be captured and paraded through Rome as part of Trajan's triumph. This is undoubtedly one of the most moving scenes on Trajan's Column.

of other tribes. In the province itself, an entire administrative apparatus was installed alongside the legions which kept the peace within and outside the borders. Towns and cities were built following the Roman model, along with a network of roads to connect them. Most importantly, however, the Romans started an intense colonisation process using elements from outside the province; indeed, after killing thousands of Dacian warriors – with thousands more fleeing across the mountains, unable to take everyone with them, thus leaving women, children and elders behind – and taking thousands more captive, the Romans began to re-populate the province with Roman colonists. The question is, who were they?

Here is an explanation that was suggested to me by Jerome Carcopino, a French professor of ancient history who discovered something that no one had thought about before. Why did so many people rush to Dacia in such a short period of time? Because it had *gold*, and plenty of it.

King Decebalus possessed colossal riches, which he had hidden underneath a riverbed; but one of the prisoners taken by the legions revealed the secret location,

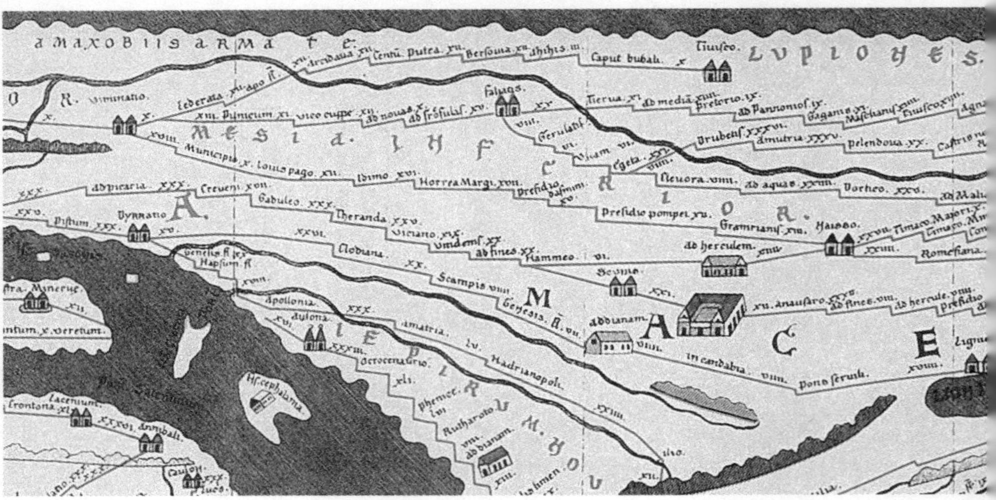

and there the Romans found gold in enormous quantities. It is also known that gold could be mined from the Apuseni Mountains (also known as the Western Romanian Carpathians).

Carcopino had a very simple idea: he wanted to compare the typical Roman coin before Trajan with that issued during his reign, and found that, whereas gold Roman coins before Trajan were as thin as cigarette foil, by the end of his rule they were considerably thicker. This means that Trajan re-valued the Roman gold coin based on the gold plundered from or mined in Dacia. To compare with events in recent history, what happened after the Dacian wars of conquest was similar to the discovery of gold in California during the previous century, which triggered a "gold rush" in the United States. That would is the most likely reason why tens of thousands of colonists from all over the empire arrived in Dacia in the space of just a few generations. Nothing else would explain how the population was completely Romanised during the short lifespan of this Roman colony.

Of course, this was not a disorganised free-for-all, a mass of individual initiatives like there were in America. This was an organised colonisation process, run by the empire. Records speak of "multitudes from the entire Roman world" (*ex toto orbe romano*) brought in by the emperor. However, the fact that there was gold to be

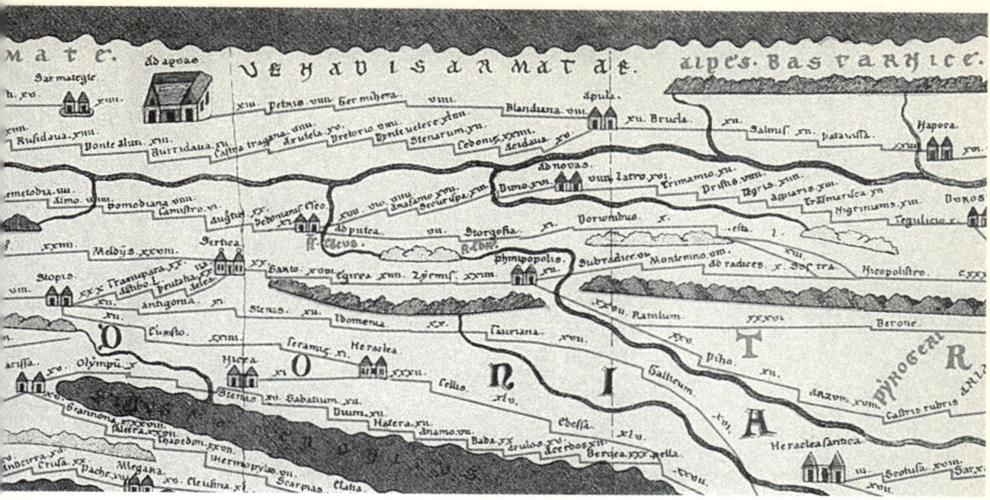

Tabula Peutingeriana, *a map drawn on a sheet of parchment measuring 34 cm in width and 6.8 m in length. Judging by the toponymy, the map was made around the 3rd century AD. The illustration above, which is in fact a copy made in the 11th or 12th century, includes the Roman province of Dacia* (top right).

found in the new province was undoubtedly a boon for the recruitment of colonists.

Nevertheless, some archaeologists have doubted Carcopino's theory because no evidence was ever found to support the hypothesis that gold had been mined in the Apuseni Mountains from the time of the Dacian kingdom; only after the Roman province was established do we find evidence of mining tools, as well as documentary evidence regarding the arrival of miners from other Roman provinces. This example shows how difficult it is to establish the accuracy of historical facts.

Colonists came from all over the empire, but mostly from neighbouring provinces, such as Illyria, which had been a Roman colony for hundreds of years – therefore the Illyrians were already Romanised. Of course, colonists came from Italy too. And here is an interesting phenomenon: as endless wars expanded the Roman Empire, the number of slaves and prisoners of war brought to Italy increased. What were the social consequences of such vast numbers of slaves? Peasants in Italy grew poorer because landowners were working the land using slaves, instead of the locals. That explains why so many peasants from Italy were joining the legions or leaving their homelands to colonise Illyria, Gaul or Dacia. Language-wise, it appears that Romanian closely resembles one of the Southern Italian dialects. Many must have come from there to seek gold in Dacia.

Funerary medallion from Roman Dacia, dating back to the 3rd century AD, discovered at Aiud. It depicts a young girl and her parents above the head of a Gorgon (a monster from Greek mythology).

Over the space of just a few generations, Dacia became a very prosperous Roman colony – so prosperous, in fact, that it became known as *Dacia Felix*, or "Dacia the Fortunate". Regrettably, her fortunes did not last for long. A few cities were built: Ulpia Traiana, named after the emperor, was developed on the site of Sarmizegetusa, and the city of Napoca was founded on the site of present-day Cluj. Dacia became a well-organised province, like the rest of the empire, with a high degree of urban civilisation, including public baths, arenas for games etc. Roads were laid down throughout the province, and as a testimony to their engineering talent, stretches of road built by the Romans across the Carpathians can be found to this day.

Finally, let us quickly mention what happened to that bridge over the Danube, a true wonder of its time: it was actually one of Trajan's successors who ordered that it be demolished. The Romans built it and the Romans took it down – but why would they do that? Because when the first large-scale barbarian invasions began, they feared that the bridge would be used by the invaders to penetrate even deeper within the empire. So they dismantled the entire carriageway and took away the crossbeams of the bridge, leaving just the pylons, which were still visible centuries later.

The barbarian invasions

Decorative harness piece from the grave of a Gepidic chieftain, discovered at Apahida, Cluj County

The fate of Dacia Felix was decided by what we now call the barbarian invasions. Let us first determine who these barbarians were and what "barbarian" means in the first place. In the eyes of the ancient Greeks (and then the Romans) the word meant "uncivilised". Rome was a marvel of the world and it is hard for us to imagine what it meant for the people of those times. What little is left of the ancient city commands our respect and admiration, while for people who lived two thousand years ago it must have been a true wonder of the world, heaven on earth.

However, do not take the words "barbarian invasion" literally. The Germans have a better word for this historic phenomenon: they call it *Völkerwanderung*, which means "the migration of peoples", because true invasions, with hordes of horsemen laying waste to everything, plundering cities and slaughtering their inhabitants, only happened every two or three hundred years, such as when the Huns, the Avars, and then the Hungarians arrived in Europe, as well as some Germanic tribes, like the Vandals (whose name entered modern languages with the meaning

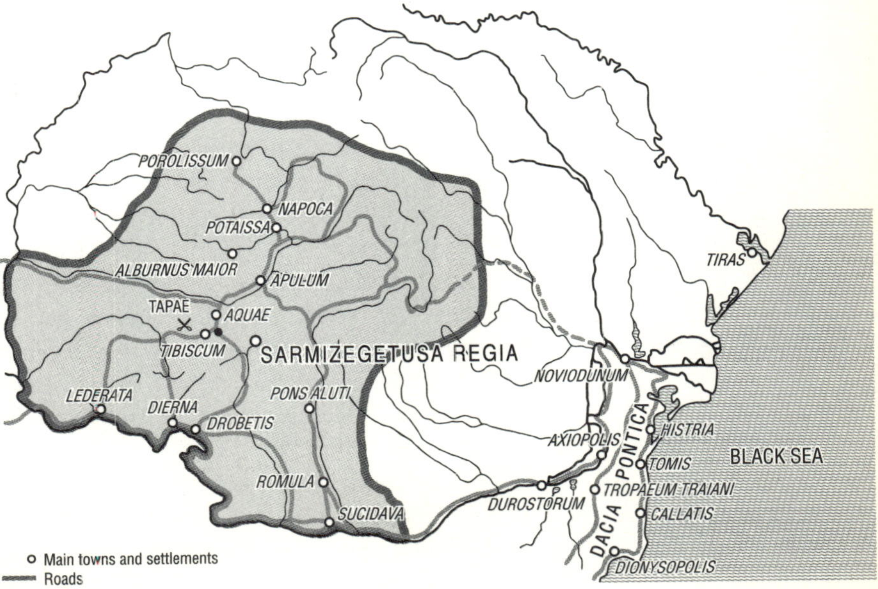

Dacia, province of the Roman Empire. Starting with 117 AD, the south of Moldavia and present day Muntenia were placed under the control of another Roman province, Moesia Inferior.

of "savages who destroy for the sake of destroying"). But the Goths (actually, the Visigoths and Ostrogoths) the Gepids and other Germanic peoples, who had come from modern-day Southern Russia, although just as aggressive, initially sought to settle imperial territories, while some even presented themselves as potential allies to defend the empire against other enemies. Because you know what happens in time with overly rich, overly fortunate countries, such as the Roman Empire in the early centuries AD: citizens no longer want to serve in the army; then these Germanic tribesmen, who were more or less "savage", put themselves forward as potential allies, or additional soldiers for defending the empire. They were called *foederati*, meaning allies of Rome, and kept their organisation and chieftains.

These barbarians arrived in Dacia in the same way. But behind them came others, even more savage, hellbent on plunder and destruction, so the Romans decided that Dacia, beyond the Danube, was too far from the centre and too hard to defend, and that it was better to withdraw their legions south of the great river. In 271-272 AD, Emperor Aurelian (Trajan's twenty-seventh successor) ordered the evacuation of the province.

The Roman legions withdraw from Dacia

Along with the army and local administration, it is likely that a part of the Roman population, certainly the wealthiest one, inhabiting cities and villas – the "country mansions" of rich landowners – who were afraid to live without the protection of the legions, will have left the province north of the Danube to take refuge on the right bank of the river, where Emperor Aurelian had established a new province in present-day Eastern Serbia and North-Western Bulgaria, which he also named Dacia – but which would be mentioned in later records as "Aurelian Dacia".

Effigy of Emperor Lucius Domitius Aurelianus Augustus, during whose reign the Romans retreated from Dacia (271 AD).

Some German historians, and later the official Hungarian historiography have maintained that the entire population of Dacia was evacuated at that time, and that this large territory north of the Danube was suddenly

emptied of all its Latin-speaking inhabitants. But this theory only appeared about two hundred years ago, along with the emergence of national consciences and nationalistic ambitions across Europe. That is when the "continuity question" was first raised in European historiography and, of course, mostly in Romanian-Hungarian academic disputes: did a Latin-speaking people continue to inhabit the former province of Dacia? Or, as most Hungarian historians claim, was Transylvania uninhabited – or inhabited at most by small, dispersed pockets of Slavs – when the Magyars (or Hungarians) arrived in Europe at the end of the 9th century and the beginning of the 10th?

Ceramic mould of the terra sigillata *type, with decorative pattern. It dates back to the 2nd or 3rd century AD and must have belonged to a master potter from Apulum (modern day Alba Iulia).*

One more remark before I explain my views on the "continuity question": this issue no longer has any political importance. Even if Hungarian historians could miraculously prove that the Magyars were the first inhabitants of Transylvania, the fact that Hungarian-speakers today make up just 7% of our country's total population means that historical precedence would have no legal or political consequences. Modern international law does not take into account any alleged "historical rights". The only thing that matters is the current demographic (see the recent drama in Kosovo). Again, we must realise that

Traianus Decius, Roman emperor (249-251 AD). Bronze bust found at Ulpia Traiana Sarmizegetusa

Statuary from Ulpia Traiana Sarmizegetusa, evidence that the cult of the god Mithras was practiced in the capital of Roman Dacia.

the "continuity question" does not carry any practical significance anymore. It is only from the passion of trying to get to the bottom of a thorny question that I briefly summarise our arguments below.

First, here are the arguments brought forward by the partisans of non-continuity, or "Roesler's theory" as it has been called – after the 19th century German author (who did not invent it, but gave it its most categorical form):

– The evacuation of the Daco-Roman population was total; there are no local documents to prove the existence of Latin-speaking inhabitants north of the Danube between the 4th and 13th century AD – a silence of about 900 years, almost a millennium; Latin-speakers (henceforth called Vlachs or Wallachians for reasons I will explain shortly) start to appear in documents only around the 10th century, but only *south* of the Danube – in Thessaly, Epirus, Macedonia and then Bulgaria. They only appear north of the Danube around the year 1200, in official documents of the Hungarian kingdom – so it can be concluded that they are migrants from the south, nomadic shepherds following their herds, encouraged by Hungarian kings to colonise a scarcely populated Transylvania;

Pottery decorated by stamping, discovered at Potaissa (present day Turda) dating from the 3rd century AD

– When the Magyars arrived in Transylvania – which translates to "the land beyond the forest" (of the Apuseni Mountains) from the Latin words *trans* (beyond) and *sylva*

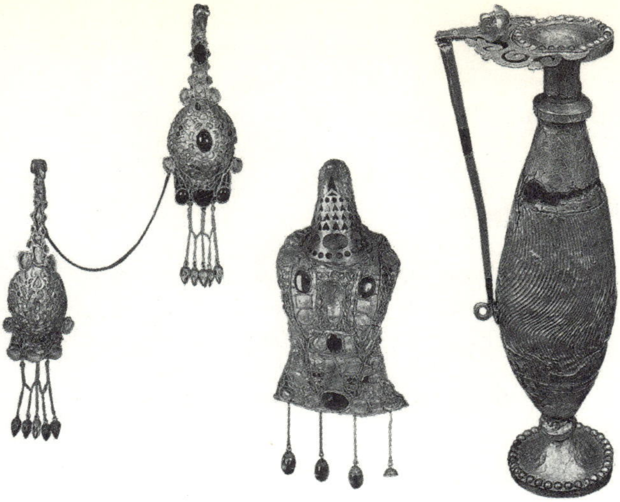

Several pieces from the famous hoard known as "The Golden Hen and Chicks" found at Pietroasele, Buzău County. The style of decoration is Germanic, from the 4th century AD. The hoard itself had a turbulent history: it was hastily buried, bent out of shape, stolen, divided up, confiscated by the Bolsheviks and finally returned to Romania in 1956.

(forest) – the land was both uninhabited and uninhabitable, since over 90% of it was covered in dense forests;

– Had the Vlachs north of the Danube not lived around Aromanians and Albanians for a few centuries, there would have not been such a strong correlation between Daco-Romanian (Romanian spoken north of the Danube) and the Aromanian and Megleno-Romanian dialects spoken south of the Danube (the latter being spoken around Thessaloniki) and there would not be several dozen words (allegedly) borrowed from Albanian in the Romanian language; this theory was supported by the work of two Romanian philologists,

Christian ritual oil lamp discovered in Dej, dating from the 5th or 6th century AD

namely Ovid Densusianu and Alexandru Philippide, who were convinced – on the basis of what I believe are erroneous arguments – that the cradle of the Romanian language must be pursued south of the Danube.

Ovid Densusianu (1873-1938)

Alexandru Philippide (1859-1933)

Vasile Pârvan (1882-1927)

"The Continuity Decalogue"

Now, here is how we can organise our arguments in favour of continuity:

1. There are barely any instances of total evacuations of a territory which were not caused by a major military defeat; in fact, the Goths (on account of whom Aurelian had ordered the withdrawal) had not proven to be that destructive no matter where they had passed through or settled, and we actually have proof that, in Dacia, it was the locals who were guiding them through the mountain passes to attack the Roman army. In one document, a bishop claims that the local population often preferred the rule of barbarian chieftains, who were content to get a share of the food they produced, while the Roman administration and taxes would crush them mercilessly.

2. Our great archaeologist, Vasile Pârvan, discovered two documents from the 4th century AD in which a "king" of the Goths from our parts, north of the Danube, calls himself a *jude* – which is not a title that the emperor in Constantinople could have conferred on him (unlike those of "patrician", "despot" or "caesar") but merely what Daco-Romanians called the rulers of a group of villages or a valley, their judges and administrators (a term that will survive until much later); it follows that this barbarian king from north of the Danube ruled over a Latin-speaking population and wanted to call himself by the name that his subjects would normally give to their rulers.

3. The statement that all traces of Latin inscriptions in Dacia disappeared after the withdrawal of the legions and administration is incorrect. A few were found, from the 4th and 5th centuries, very few indeed – which can be explained by the near-total desertion of the cities and a complete regression towards rurality. The few written documents dating from the following centuries that were discovered only mention the various barbarian ruling

elements, who played a role in wars and politics, and not the local peasantry (whom the barbarians would still have needed to provide them with food); this is a constant in universal history: no one talks about the populations of fallen empires, only about the new masters.

4. The silence of documents (the *a silentio* argument) is not a valid argument. Let us set aside our exclusive, almost superstitious trust in the written document. History is not only reconstructed with written documents; the Latin-speakers of Switzerland (Rhetia) are not mentioned in any such documents, yet they speak their Romansh language to this day; and closer to home, there are no written documents about the Albanians for over a thousand years (an even longer silence than in our case) yet their Greek or Slavic neighbours could not argue that the Albanians simply fell from the skies where we find them today and where they have been mentioned in antiquity.

5. The late mentions of Romanians in official Hungarian documents has a simple explanation: it was only around the 12th or 13th centuries that Hungarian feudal structures and royal authority became sufficiently present to govern; that was when Romanian villages, rulers and nobles, either pressured by Hungarian tax collectors or called before a court, began to need the royal chancellery or some local authority to have their ancestral rights recognised. Observe, if you will, how a series of Romanian words that can have distant legal connotations are of Hungarian origin: to promise – *a făgădui*, to delay – *a tăgădui*, to settle a score – *a se răfui*, to suspect – *a bănui*, to ponder – *a chibzui*, to allow – *a îngădui*, to redeem – *a mântui*... we even venerate Christ as the "Redeemer" (*Mântuitorul*) using a word coming from a Hungarian

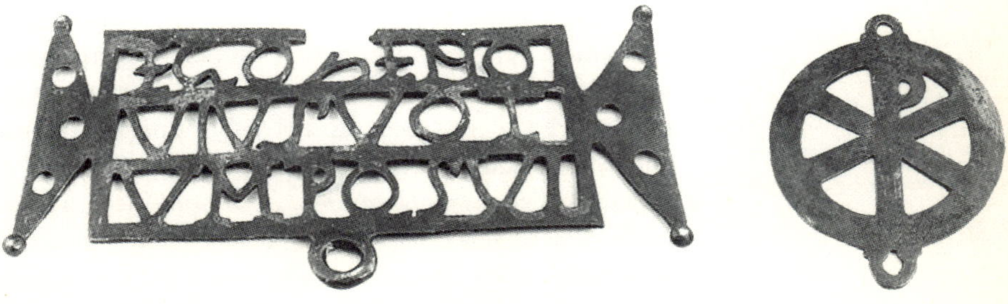

Ego Zenovius votum posui – *"I, Zenovius, have brought this gift". This inscription attests to the use of Latin and the presence of Christianity in 4th century Dacia.*

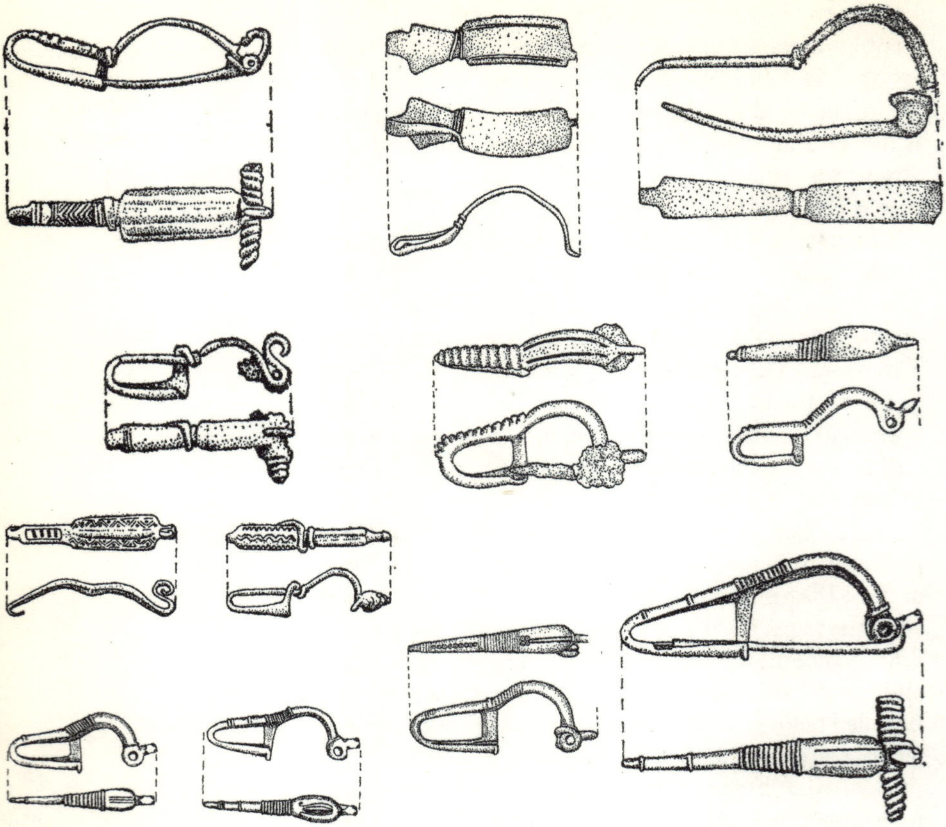

Archaeological drawings of Romano-Byzantine fibulae dating from the 5th to the 7th centuries, discovered on the present day territory of Romania

root. If Romanians had only arrived in Transylvania during the 12th and 13th century, it is hard to imagine that they would have assimilated such essential notions without having already lived around the Hungarians for several centuries, and then spread them across all the territories they inhabited.

6. It is quite typical that in the first documents, Romanians (Vlachs) are located in "woods", meaning vast, forested areas, because there, in clearings surrounded by dense forest, it was easier to defend against enemy cavalry. For example, shortly after 1200, the region of Făgăraș is called "*silva blacorum et bissenorum*" (the woods of the Vlachs and Pechenegs) in a royal charter granting that land to German (Saxon) colonists. If the Romanians

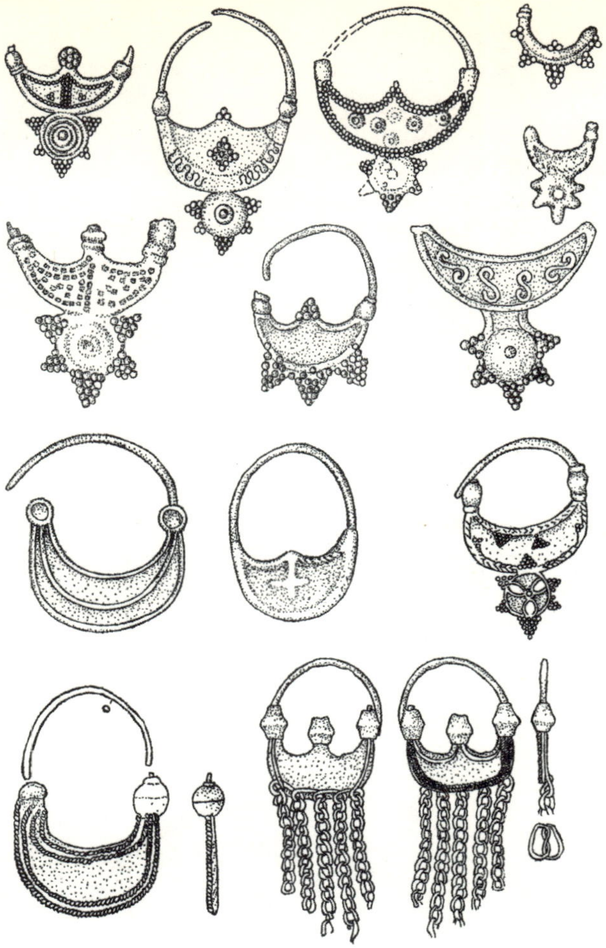

Jewellery items dating from the 8th to the 11th centuries, discovered on the present day territory of Romania

were recently colonised nomadic shepherds from the south, as Roesler's theory claims, would they have taken flocks of sheep into the woods?

The archaeologist Radu Popa – who died before his time – has located other regions in Transylvania that were first called *silvae* (or *sylvae*) before they were turned into administrative "counties", ruled by Hungarian counts.

Furthermore, the association between heavily wooded areas and Vlachs is also found south of the Carpathians, in modern Wallachia. Do you know what the name of *Vlașca* county means? In the Old Slavic language it meant "land of the Vlachs". How about *Codrul Vlăsiei*? (an ancient woodland in Wallachia, of which only a very small portion survives to this day, north-west of Bucharest, but which covered an enormous area in the Middle Ages). *Vlasie* is the Slavic plural of "Vlach" (meaning Wallachian or Romanian) so it literally means "the woods of the Romanians". Even the name of modern-day Teleorman county is proof of a dense woodland which once existed there, inhabited by the natives, since *deli orman* means "mad forest" in the Turkic languages spoken by both Pechenegs and Cumans. So it was not just the Transylvanian forests, but also those in the Wallachian lowlands that were inhabited by the ancestors of Romanians in the early Middle Ages, even before they mixed with the Slavs, otherwise they would not have called them *Vlasie*.

Let us be clear: when I say "woods" (*sylvae*) you must imagine immense wooded areas, the size of a county or two, in the depths of which could be found naturally empty spaces, or large areas cleared by man, deforested and grubbed up, where entire communities lived off the cultivation of millet, onions and cabbage, the herding of cattle and the farming of pigs and poultry. In these clearings, people were relatively more protected from

Victorious warrior, probably a Bulgarian, as represented on a gold vessel from the Sânnicolaul Mare hoard, from the 9th or 10th century

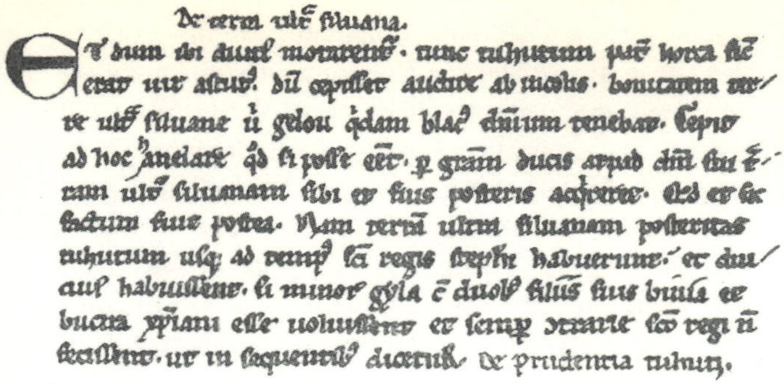

Paragraph of the Gesta Hungarorum, *a chronicle by an anonymous notary of the Hungarian king Béla III*

marauding nomadic cavalry. Yet we have sources which reveal how the nomads still managed to detect these inhabited "oases": from afar, they simply observed the flight of circling birds. If the birds kept hovering over a particular spot, the nomads would know they were looking for leftovers or rotting corpses – and headed straight for that place.

7. As to the alleged Bulgarian or Macedonian words found in the Romanian language, our ancestors did not need to live in the Balkans to adopt them: they were common words among the Slavic tribes across the south-east of Europe, many of which must have settled north of the Danube, all over the territory of our country (documents mention Slavic enclaves up until the 13th century).

In fact, the former Aurelian Dacia, which the ancestors of the Romanians allegedly abandoned, was overrun by West [hic] Slavic tribes, who produced the Serbian and Croatian languages, whereas the Slavic words in Romanian belong to the East [hic] Slavic group, which includes the closely related Bulgarian and Macedonian languages. In the territories north of the Danube, the Slavs mainly settled in fertile valleys, where they left traces in the names of rivers (found relatively close together): Dâmbovița, Ialomița, Prahova, Neajlov, Milcov, Bistrița etc. Only gradually did they mix with their local Vlach neighbours and let themselves be Romanianised.

Relying on the rules of language evolution, linguists believe that the fusion between the Late Latin of the Vlachs and the Slavic language of the newcomers only began around the 9th century, when the transformation of Late Latin into "Proto-Romanian" was almost complete; that is why Slavic influence on the grammatical structure (syntax) and the form of words (morphology) in our language is almost non-existent, yet massive on the vocabulary (lexicon); compare with French, for example: the mix between Gallo-Romans and Germanic peoples – Franks, Burundians etc. – happened much earlier on, and thus the impact on the new Romance language, especially in relation to morphology and phonetics, was far greater.

8. As to the so-called borrowed words from Albanian, modern linguists tend to explain the similarities between the two languages – amounting to just a few dozen words – through a common Indo-European origin. Why would a Romanised (and thus more culturally advanced) population have to borrow words from its Albanian, un-Romanised, less civilised neighbours in the first place?

Similarly, we do not need to imagine our ancestors living south of the Danube to explain why Daco-Romanian, Aromanian and Megleno-Romanian are cognates, since the same mix of peoples, speaking the same

Pages from a 14th century copy of Nestor's Chronicle *or the* Tale of Bygone Years, *a compilation of older chronicles that mentions the "Vlachs" or Romanians.*

Late Eastern Latin can yield the same results, even one thousand kilometres apart.

In fact, in Daco-Romanian we have a few examples of words for plants and materials which are not found south of the Danube – how could they have been preserved in the language for a thousand years if our ancestors had all migrated south? I will provide just one example, yet quite a relevant one: how could the word *păcură* (from *picula*, Latin for "crude oil") have been preserved south of the Danube, if crude oil only naturally surged from the ground at the foothills of the Carpathians?

Inscribed 9th century ceramic vessel displaying the name "Petre" ("Peter")

9. Hungarian historians are now trying to deny the historical value of a crucial document, the chronicle written in Latin by an unknown "clerk" of King Béla of Hungary – known to history only as Anonymous. This document, probably based on an earlier chronicle, is of an absolutely capital importance to our history, because it tells of how the Hungarians, who first invaded Transylvania from the west, encountered three voivodeships inhabited by Romanians and Slavs. This piece of information, namely that the Magyars came across the Vlachs after crossing the Northern Carpathians, is also found in an even older Kievan Rus chronicle, known as Nestor's Chronicle, a completely independent source. There is just one strong argument in favour of these critics: it is the mention Anonymous makes of the Cumans among the peoples found in Transylvania at that time, yet we know that they did not arrive north of the Danube until about 150 years after the Pechenegs and Hungarians. Nevertheless, such "time warps" are often to be found in chronicles (and to add to the confusion, the Pechenegs and the Cumans spoke roughly the same language).

The names of the three "voivodes" – Glad, Menumorut and Gelou – are a source of debate in themselves. Only the latter is presented as a Vlach, so Hungarian historians tried very hard to find a Hungarian origin for his name, while at the same time drawing attention to the poverty of his people and the poor quality of the weapons used by his warriors. We are used to writing his name as "Gelu" and pronounce it the way we do in modern Romanian: *djé-loo*. But in the Classical Latin of the chronicler, the *g* must have been hard (as in the English word *geese*) and the diphthong *ou* (as in the English word *show*) would be preserved – which gives us Gelou (pronounced *geh-low*) probably a deformation of the Romanian name Ghelău.

And it is precisely in the region of Cluj, where the chronicler located the voivodeship of this Gelou, that we have a mountain, a river and a settlement called either Ghilău or Gilău throughout the ages; I believe these have kept the name of that first Romanian voivode. The proof that this is an authentic Romanian name, maybe even an ancient one, comes from an ancient Greek text that mentions a settlement in Thrace called Geloupara, which means "Gelou's village" and is spelled in exactly the same way.

Glad must be a Slavic name distorted by the chronicler, who also added that this voivode came from Vidin and so was probably Bulgarian; finally, Menumorut is obviously a Hungarian variant for the name of a Turkic chieftain – perhaps a Bulgarian, or rather Proto-Bulgarian – ruling over a Vlach and Slavic population.

10. In my view, however, the decisive argument in favour of continuity is the preservation of the ancient names of the Carpathian Mountains and of all the major rivers north of the Danube – Nistru (Dniester) Prut, Siret, Buzău, Argeș, Olt, Timiș, Mureș, Criș, Someș, Tisa etc. all of which had been attested even before the Roman conquest – and, most importantly, that of the Danube itself (Romanian: *Dunărea*) which, in Romanian, has maintained a different form from the Latin *Danubius*, in fact one that is closer to river names found in the Baltic languages. Who else could have passed these ancient names onto migratory peoples like the Hungarians, other than a people who had stayed put despite endless waves of new arrivals?

That is why I am absolutely convinced that a great number of Romance-speaking enclaves survived uninterruptedly, through the Dark and Middle Ages, in the lands north of the Danube, with continuous links to populations living to the south (for the great river has never been a barrier to communication and movement).

The arrival of the first barbarians

Let us now take a closer look at the barbarians who invaded Daco-Roman territory.

First there came the Goths, which were divided in two branches – the Ostrogoths and the Visigoths, meaning the East Goths and West Goths respectively. They did not settle in our lands – they were far more interested in the riches of Italy or Constantinople, the second Roman capital since Emperor Constantine, which later became the capital of the Byzantine Empire. Both branches eventually migrated westwards – the Ostrogoths settling in Italy, while the Visigoths went as far as Gaul and Spain.

A Germanic people that did spend a few hundred years on our territory were the Gepids, who were related to the Goths and were present in the Banat and Western Transylvania for at least 200 years. Some of their lingering kinsmen may have been pushed westwards by a bizarre coalition of Avars and Lombards (I call it bizarre because the Lombards were a Germanic people, like the Gepids, while the Avars were probably an Asian steppe

Charlemagne, conqueror of the Avars, king of the Franks and emperor of the Holy Roman Empire, as this coin proclaims: "Karolus Imp Aug" *(which stands for* "Karolus Imperator Augustus"*).*

Daco-Roman territory during the Migration Period

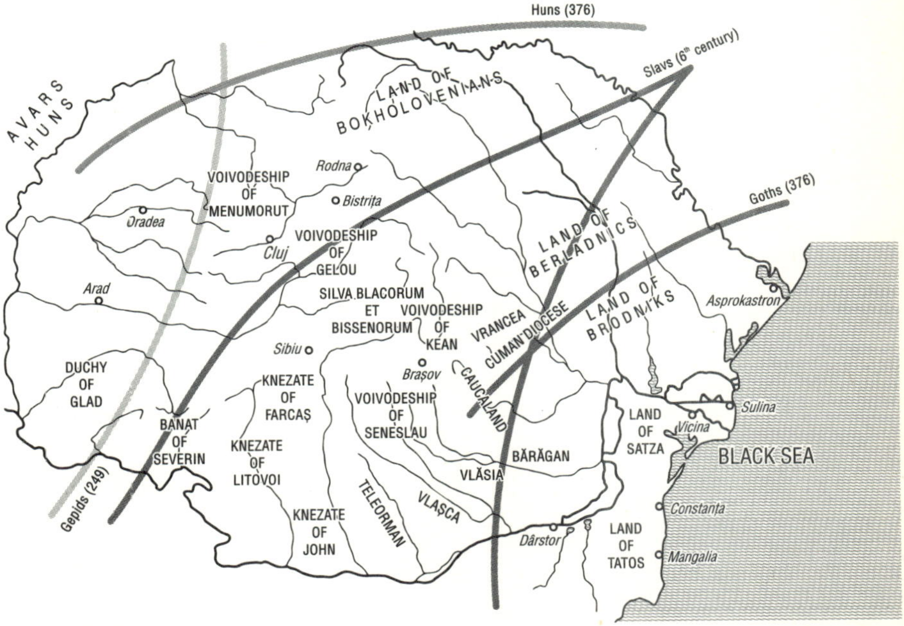

Patera (a bowl used for libations) from the Pietroasele hoard, left behind by Germanic migrators

people); yet it seems they did not leave any traces in our language – but neither did the Lombards leave any in Italian, after dominating the north of Italy for centuries.

The Gepids were replaced by the Avars, who belonged to that Asian group of peoples that scholars call *Turkic*, and who spoke a Turkic language – they are called that to differentiate them from Ottoman Turkish. This was at the end of the 6th century. And along with the Avars came a very numerous people, who were not as organised as the Germans, and as yet had neither aristocracy, nor kings, nor any political structures. These were the Slavs.

They too came from modern day Ukraine, from Poland and modern European Russia, and slowly migrated south, attracted by the riches of the Roman Empire. Even before 500 AD they began to cross into the empire, mostly westwards into Italy, but were so poorly organised that most of them ended up as slaves. This has led some philologists to believe that "Slav" was the origin of the word *sclavus* (slave) in Late Latin.

It is likely that they arrived in Transylvania, Wallachia and Moldova around the same time, but from now on we find them allied to the Avars.

In the first few centuries after 500 AD, the Slavs preferred to settle valleys and open plains, whereas the descendants of Daco-Romans took shelter in the woodlands and mountains.

The text of a 12th century Croat priest, known to history as the Priest of Dioclea, suggests another reason why the "Roman" population of Dalmatia was retreating to the mountains before the Slavs: the fear of persecution by these pagans against them, as Christians. Which would also explain why the mix between the Vlachs and the Slavs was accelerated after the Bulgarians and the Slavs they were ruling over were converted to Christianity in the 9th century. Nevertheless, let us not call the descendants of the Daco-Romans "Romanians" just yet – we can only do that when we have a Romanian language, and that only took place when there was symbiosis, mutual influence, and eventually fusion between the former Daco-Romans and the Slavs. But if we cannot call them "Romanians", then what should we call them? Let us continue to call them "Vlachs".

Why is that? You see, "Vlach" is not a derogative term, like the Hungarians or other foreigners, such as the Greeks, would like to think of it. "Vlach" is a very noble name, given by Germanic peoples to the Romans, originating from the name of a Celtic tribe called the *Volcae*, who lived in present day Switzerland and Austria. This tribe was Romanised, so that the Germans, their neighbours, in time began to refer to all those who spoke Latin by the name Volcae.

That is why, from the British Isles to the Black Sea, along the borders of the Roman Empire, there are regions

Dodecagonal bowl from the Pietroasele hoard, destroyed and restored several times over its tumultuous history

Nicolaus Olahus (1493-1568) or Oláh Miklós in Hungarian, was archbishop of Strigonium and primate of Hungary (the highest Catholic clergyman in a country). His father, Ștefan, was Romanian, and so it would be better to call him Nicolae Valahul in Romanian.

that still bear names coming from the word Volcae. You know of Wales in Great Britain, a region which, like Scotland, is on the fringes of England, both inhabited by the remnants of the island's Celtic population. Well, the English word *Wales* has the same root as Wallachia (Romanian: *Valahia*). And if we go further south into Europe, the French-speaking half of the population of Belgium, that is the Walloons, also bear a name that comes from Volcae, given to them by the Flemish, who speak Dutch – a Germanic language.

The French are derogatively called *Welsche* by the Germans (just as the French gave the Germans their own insulting nickname, *Boches*) who also used to call the Italians *Wahlen* during the Middle Ages. The Poles and other Slavs call the Italians "Vlachs", which is what they called Romance language speakers in the Balkans and north of the Danube. The Slavs borrowed the word from the Germans, but with a shift from "Valch" to "Vlach". It was from the Slavs that the Greeks got the word later on during the Dark Ages, which goes to show how deep the Slavs had penetrated continental Greece. And as V is spelled B in the Greek alphabet, the term had morphed into "Blach" by the time it reached the "Franks" and the West during the crusades. To conclude, the name "Vlach" was given to speakers of Romance languages by Germanic and Slavic peoples, and then by the Greeks. So from now on, when I say "Vlachs" this means the forebears of Romanians. And for a long time, that is what other peoples called us. We, however, called ourselves Romanians (*români*) or Rumanians (*rumâni*) or, further to the south, Aromanians (*armâni*) – with the "prosthetic A" characteristic to the Aromanian dialect.

To sum up, the locals kept their Roman name, while foreigners called them Vlachs or Wallachians. I will therefore use the terms Romanian and Vlach interchangeably – but find that it is better to make the difference and keep the term "Romanian" for a later period, after 1000 AD, when the symbiosis between Vlachs and Slavs had started and we can begin to call their language Romanian.

The centre of Avar power was somewhere in Pannonia (now the Hungarian *Puszta*) and it seems to have been some sort of huge encampment called the Ring.

Golden belt buckle, inlaid with garnets in the cloisonné *technique, part of the burial treasure of a Gepidic princess at Apahida*

For over 200 years (cca. 550-780 AD) the Avars were a major power in central Europe, somehow ruling over the Slavs. Though a fearsome tribe of mounted warriors, the Avars were few in number, but lead huge numbers of Slavs into savage attacks on the Byzantine Empire, besieging Thessaloniki and Constantinople – with the end result that the Slavic tribes, who had become used to war and plunder by that time, pushed deep into the provinces of the empire and settled there, even as far as the Peloponnese, in Southern Greece. And even though the Byzantines, in their pathetic attempts to rebuild the empire during the 10th and 11th centuries, managed to "re-colonise" the Peloponnese and parts of continental Greece with Greeks, places that had been heavily settled by Slavs, Albanians and Vlachs – like the whole of Macedonia – would forever remain predominantly Slavic, as would Moesia, Aurelian Dacia and all of Illyria, where the former Romanised population was gradually reduced to mere enclaves, like islets getting smaller and smaller as waters rise around them.

The Avars collapsed by 797-805 AD under a double blow: in the west, from the emperor of the Franks, Charlemagne (*Karl der Grosse* in German) and in the south, from the Bulgarian khan Krum. The fall of this short-lived great power was to be so complete and sudden, that there is still a Russian saying that says, "*they perished like the Obri*" – the Russian name for the Avars.

The Slavs

Slavic fibula

At the time of the Avar collapse, the Slavs, who had spread across our country and the entire Balkan Peninsula, became independent. By this time, they had learned the art of war from the Avars – and to some extent, how to be their own masters, from them and their Germanic neighbours.

In this respect, it is interesting to look at the terms that the Slavs will use for their leaders, their hierarchy and political structures, many of which we, in turn, borrowed from them: the king will be called *kral* – from the name of the great Frankish king and later emperor Charlemagne, whose name was pronounced "Karl" by the Germans and "Kral" by the Slavs (from the same name come the words *király* – king in Hungarian and *crai* – prince in Romanian); yet two other important titles, *ban* and *jupan* (Romanian: *jupân*) are inherited from the Avars; *boyar* (Romanian: *boier*) is also Turkic, either Pecheneg or Proto-Bulgarian (this is what historians call the Turkic people who conquered modern day Bulgaria from the Byzantines in the 7th century and who were gradually absorbed by the majority Slavic population); two other terms, the titles of *knyaz* (Romanian: *cneaz*) and *vitez* (Romanian: *viteaz*) could be of German origin, stemming from *könig* (king) and *viking* respectively (this was a generic name for the Scandinavian raiders who started to attack Northern Europe in the 9th century, going as far west as France, England and Iceland, and as far east as Russia, where they founded the first Russian state, and where they were known as Varangians).

The only authentic Slavic word for "leader" is *voivod* (Romanian: *voievod*) which originally meant "warlord", while in our country – *and only in our country*, in Wallachia, Moldova and Transylvania (where the Hungarians kept the title for their representative there) – it came to mean "overlord", chief of state or ruler of a region; yet miraculously, alongside the Slavic term, we also have the name *domn* (from the Latin *dominus* – lord) which the Romans gave even to the emperor during the last few centuries of their empire, and which the Romanians will later use to name God (Romanian: *Dumnezeu* – from Latin *dominus* and *deus*). The word *domn* will be almost synonymous to voivode, just as *jude* (from Latin *jus* – justice) will be equivalent with *cneaz*.

But we also have an even more admirable remnant of the old Roman structures: the survival of the word for "emperor" (Romanian: *împărat*, from the Latin *imperator*) in our vocabulary, when the Romanians had had no emperor for hundreds of years, neither north nor south of the Danube, where the great ruler of Constantinople was now being called by the Greek name *basileus* or *tsar* in the Slavic languages (which comes from Caesar, originally pronounced "Kaisar", also leading to the German word *kaiser*).

Generally, however, almost all the words in our language that refer to the local medieval nobility are borrowed from the Slavs. Which leads us to the conclusion that, around the time they began to be assimilated by the majority Vlach population in the ancient territory of Dacia, these Slavs were in a dominant position, at least for a while (we will learn further on another meaning for the word *rumân*). Since the leader of a Vlach community was called a *jude* (pl. *juzi*) the Slavic word *cneaz* will come to mean more or less the same thing (I will point out a possible difference later) so for centuries we had either a *cneaz* or a *jude*, depending on whether the community he was leading was predominantly Slavic or Vlach.

One of the oldest Slavic inscriptions (dating back to 943) that mentions Dimitrie, a local chieftain (Romanian: jupân*) from Dobruja, who was killed in a battle against the Byzantines*

Byzantium's Varangian Guard, as seen in a miniature from the chronicle of John Skylitzes. From Russia, the Vikings reached Constantinople in the 9th century, when Emperor Theophilos recruited some of them into his army. Over time, the Scandinavian mercenaries developed into an elite corps.

It would take a good few hundred years for these Slavs to be assimilated. What happened on the territory of ancient Dacia was the exact opposite of what happened south and south-west of the Danube, in present day Bulgaria, Serbia and Croatia, where Romanised populations were assimilated by the Slavs. It is apparently quite a strange phenomenon, as it could mean that fewer Slavs settled in our lands than in others, enabling the Vlachs to assimilate them, so to speak, and give them a Romance language, whereas south of the Danube it was the Vlachs who were assimilated by the Slavs or the Greeks, with fewer and fewer remaining over the centuries.

Did the rule of the First Bulgarian Empire extend to our territory?

Earlier we made a mention of the Bulgarians – or rather the Bulgars – who were a Turkic people, like the Avars; their last known homeland before the migration was the central Volga basin, from where some of them were pushed westwards by other Central Asian peoples in the 7th century AD, crossing the Danube through Southern Bessarabia. After fierce clashes with the Byzantines, they forced their way into Dobruja and present day Northern Bulgaria around 670-680, where they would soon be assimilated by a Slavic majority. And there these warlike,

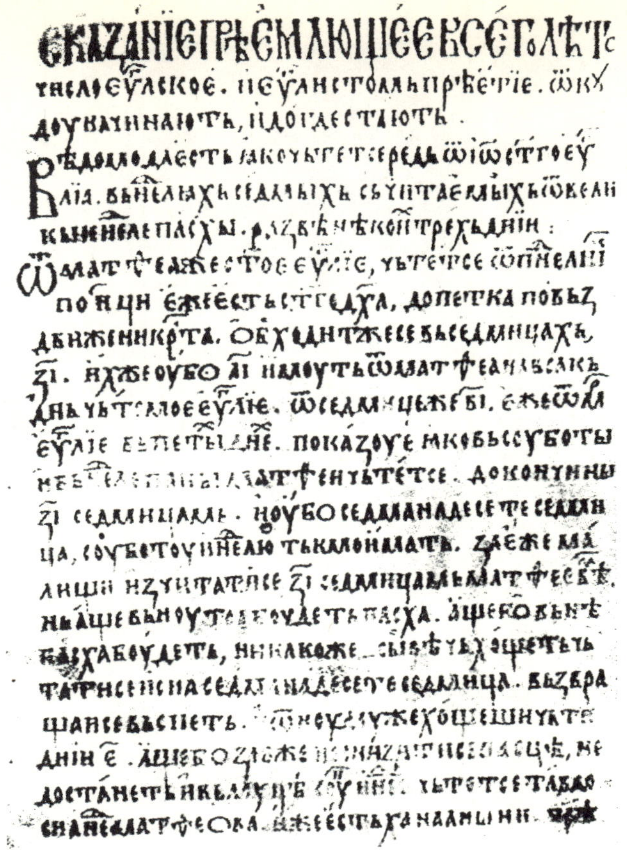

Page from Nicodim's Tetraevangelion (Greek for "Book of Four Gospels") of 1404, one of the oldest Slavonic manuscripts in our country

well-organised horsemen founded a powerful state, constantly at war with the Byzantine Empire, besieging the capital Constantinople several times. Yet at the same time they were fascinated by the great imperial city, by the efficiency of the empire and the pomp and influence of the Christian Church, and so their khan Boris, in a move inspired by both religious fervour and political acumen, became a Christian in the year 865, along with thousands of his warriors and boyars, and started to call himself *tsar*. A few years before that event, two Byzantine missionaries from Thessaloniki, the brothers Constantine (whose monastic name was Cyril) and Methodius – it is unclear whether they were Slavs born in Greece, as the Bulgarians claim, or Greeks speaking Slavic, according to the Greek version – set out to convert the Slavs in

The baptism of Tsar Boris I, illustrated in the chronicle of John Skylitzes

Moravia, translating the Holy Scriptures in what is now called Old Church Slavic (or Slavonic) and inventing an alphabet adapted to Slavic phonetics in the process; we now know it as the Cyrillic alphabet, after Constantine-Cyril – in use to this day in Bulgaria, Serbia and Russia, as well as in our principalities until the 1860s.

How did we get the Cyrillic alphabet? And not only the alphabet, but also the Slavonic liturgy and Holy Scriptures, and our entire Eastern Orthodox Church hierarchy? The most natural explanation is to acknowledge that at its greatest extent, following the collapse of the Avar Ring, the First Bulgarian Empire ruled over large parts of our country. They were present in the east, in Dobruja and Bessarabia, and they bordered the Franks on the Tisza River in the west – why would they avoid Wallachia and Transylvania, when those regions had small emerging polities led by knyazes speaking their language?

Nevertheless, most Romanian historians, led by the great Nicolae Iorga, vehemently opposed this theory. Since that time, however, archaeological evidence has surfaced in support of the logical arguments: Slon fortress in Prahova County (both Slavic names) is typically Bulgarian, while graves characteristic of Bulgarian chieftains were discovered in Sibiu county. That is why I believe we have to imagine a Bulgarian presence of about one and a half centuries in our territory, between the end of the 8th century (after the Avars were wiped out) and the beginning of the 10th century (when the Magyars arrived in the Tisza River basin and the Pechenegs invaded our territory).

The relative calm of this interval is the most logical explanation for the assimilation of the Slavs by the Vlach majority, the emergence of a ruling class (the future boyars) born from the *juzi* or knyazes, and the use – for many centuries – of the Cyrillic alphabet and Old Church Slavonic, which was also to become the language of our chancelleries later on, when we developed political structures.

It is true that Christianity did not really become established among the Bulgarians until after 864 (the year Tsar Boris was baptised) but it is likely that the new religious structures, brought in by the Byzantines, spread simultaneously across their empire, including the lands inhabited by Vlachs and the Slavs they were about to assimilate.

The two phases of our conversion to Christianity

While speaking about the new church hierarchy we got from the Bulgarians, I realise I have not yet mentioned the question of our ancestors' conversion to Christianity. Were they converted at the same time as the Bulgarians, or maybe even after them? Our language – as well as substantial archaeological evidence, especially in Dobruja, but in other areas of the country as well – is proof that Christianity arrived in Dacia and Moesia very early

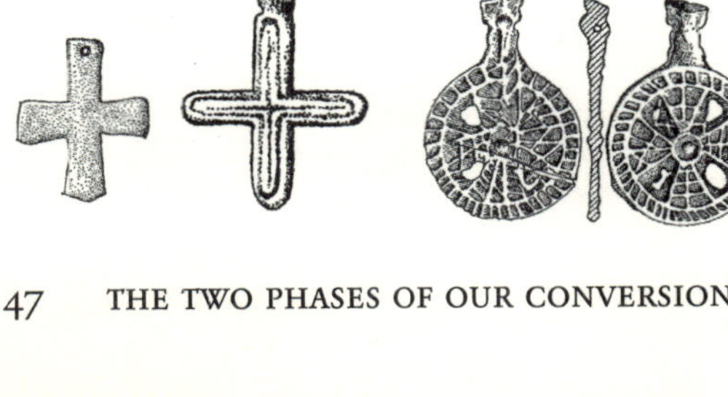

Christian ritual items discovered on the territory of Romania, dating from the 6th to the 11th centuries

on, perhaps even before the Roman legions and administration left, probably brought in by legionnaires born in the Orient, by merchants, travellers, and even missionaries – after all, were not Greece and Macedonia among the first apostolic journeys that Saint Paul made in the west? However, in establishing the most likely period of our conversion, it is linguistic evidence that is the most compelling; the fundamental words of the Christian religion all come from Latin: God – *Dumnezeu*, cross – *cruce*, Christian – *creștin*, faith – *credință*, church – *biserică*, prayer – *rugă*, communion – *cuminecare*, to baptise – *a boteza*, angel – *înger*, pagan – *păgân* and saint – *sfânt* (preserved in its old form for holy days: *Sân Petru – Saint Peter, Sân Nicoară* – Saint Nicholas, *Sân Toader* – Saint Theodore, *Sânta Măria* – Saint Mary) as well as Easter – *Paște* and Pentecost – *Rusalii*.

Perhaps you will wonder how the Christian faith endured in the province of Dacia, now isolated from the empire, as well as the newly emerging Church structures, organised after Constantine the Great ended the persecution of Christians in the year 313 AD. A difficult question. We can only imagine that the small Christian communities of the former province managed to stay in contact with the nascent ecclesiastic hierarchy across the Danube. In fact, until the Bulgarians arrived, the Eastern Roman Empire maintained an active presence along the

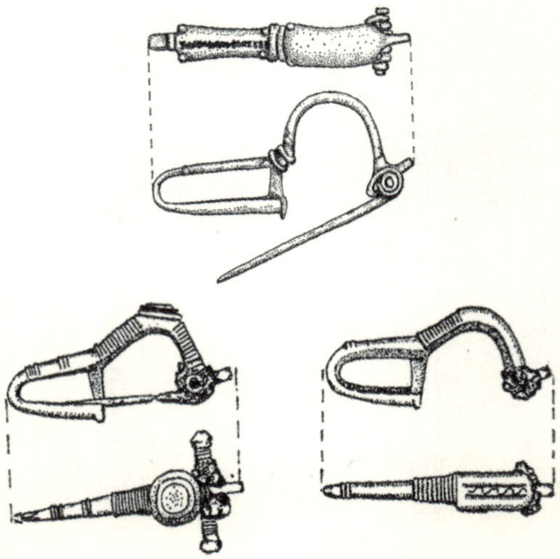

Romano-Byzantine fibulae, dating from the 5th to the 7th centuries

Danube, at times even holding bridgeheads on the left bank of the river. On the other hand, we know of some Gothic and Gepidic chieftains who were not only Christian, but were spreading Christianity in its Western form, which they had received from Rome.

At this point it is important to mention a crucial event in Roman history, which happened two centuries before the Empire collapsed: the division of 395 AD, when the realm was split in two, with two emperors and two capitals, in Rome and Constantinople, and which had incalculable consequences still affecting us to this day. The two halves of the empire – the Western one adopting Latin as its language, the Eastern officially choosing Greek in the 7th century – saw the development of two different forms of Christianity, as the rivalry between the Pope in Rome and the Patriarch in Constantinople resulted in increasingly frequent and serious conflicts, and eventually lead to a schism (or separation) between the two heads of the Church in 1054 – when they excommunicated each other – a wound that has not healed since.

The Western Church then called itself "Catholic" – which means universal in Greek – while the Eastern Church took the name "Orthodox", or the one that interprets the dogmas correctly. And just so you can appreciate the endless nature of the consequences of the 395 AD East-West split of the Roman Empire, note that the frontier

Pope Leon IX and Patriarch Michael I Keroularios, in a miniature from a Greek 15th century manuscript. The Great Schism happened on 16 July 1054, when a Papal legate placed the bull decreeing the excommunication of the Patriarch on the altar of Hagia Sophia in Constantinople.

Church of Saint Nicholas in Densuș, Hunedoara County, one of the oldest Orthodox churches in Romania. It dates back to the 13th century and was built with stones from the ancient ruins of nearby Ulpia Traiana Sarmizegetusa.

The death of Tsar Samuel of Bulgaria, following the disastrous battle at Kleidion (modern day Klyuḉh) in 1014, in which the Bulgarian army was annihilated by the Byzantines.

between the two halves of the empire coincides almost perfectly, after more than a millennium and a half, with the present day borders between Catholic Croatians and Orthodox Serbs. This goes to show how a seemingly casual or arbitrary decision in history can have unforeseen repercussions that continue throughout the ages.

To come back to the question of Christianity in forsaken Dacia, we can assume that the faith was preserved in rather less "Orthodox" forms in some of the more isolated regions, where priests were probably handed down the gestures and mysteries of the religion from generation to generation, often without the confirmation required by canonical tradition for passing down the apostolic attributes of priesthood. That is why most of the words we use in our church hierarchy belong to a second wave, meaning they are of Bulgarian or Greek origin (yet even these would come from the Bulgarians).

Words such as *mitropolit* – patriarch, *vlădică* – Catholic priest, *popă* – priest, *diacon* – deacon, *stareț* – prior, *duhovnic* – confessor; some terms naming places of worship: *schit* – hermitage, *strană* – choir, *clopot* – bell, *hram* – patronage; liturgic elements such as *utrenie* – matins, *vecernie* – vespers, *sfeștanie* – blessing ceremony, *prohod* – funeral service, *nedeie* – celebration, *prescură* – consecrated bread, *spovedanie* – confession, *post* – lent, *blagoslovenie* – an old word for "blessing"; as well as theological terms: *Maica Precista* – Mother of God, *duh* – spirit, *rai* – heaven, *iad* – hell, and many names of holy days.

Christian ritual oil lamp from the 4th century

The old word (interestingly, *cuvânt* – meaning "word" in Romanian comes from the Latin *conventum*, which meant religious gathering, and is also the origin of the word *convent* in English) *sânt*, which is derived from *sanctus* in Latin, has been altered by the Slavic *sventu*, resulting in the Romanian *sfânt*. And so, only after this prolonged contact with the Bulgarian church hierarchy (itself only recently organised by the Byzantines, using Byzantine clerics) did the Church begin to establish itself north of the Danube in a more disciplined, more "orthodox" form – even though many old customs of decidedly pagan origin, either born or kept during the centuries of isolation, were maintained, and still endure to this day in our folk traditions.

Expelled from north of the Danube by the Hungarian and Pecheneg invasions, weakened by infighting and attacked from the south by the Byzantines, now led by an emperor of exceptional energy, Basil II Boulgaroktonos (meaning "Slayer of Bulgars") the First Bulgarian Empire collapsed altogether in 1018, when its territory became a Byzantine province once more, for over one and a half centuries.

History remembers a horrifying episode from the 20-year struggle of Basil II against the Bulgarian tsar Samuel: after winning a last battle (at Kleidion) and taking 14,000 prisoners, the emperor had their eyes gouged out with hot irons – all but one man in every hundred, who was left with just one eye to guide the others back home; one can only wonder how many Vlachs were among those 14,000. The wretched column would march for hundreds of kilometres until the defeated were returned to their homes, terrifying the entire country and posterity on the way.

Stephen I of Hungary, also called "Saint Stephen" for being the first Christian king of the Magyars. This depiction is posthumous and comes from in the Vienna Illuminated Chronicle.

The Hungarians

Saint Stephen's crown, which, according to legend, is even more important than the person of the king himself. Historians have not been able to ascertain the exact date it was made, but agree that its current appearance is a result of successive additions; the style and craftsmanship are Byzantine.

The last of the barbarians to settle north of the Danube before the establishment of the first Romanian states were Turkic, like the Avars before them: these were the Hungarians (who call themselves Magyars) the Pechenegs, the Oghuz Turks (for a shorter time) and the Cumans. The Pechenegs arrived at the same time as the Hungarians, during the last few years of the 9th century, after pushing them westwards, from present-day Russia.

The Hungarians crossed the Carpathians through the valley of the river Tisza, in the north, and settled in the Pannonian Plain, which was favourable for their horse herds. Some chronicles say the region was still inhabited by speakers of an early Romance language (*pastores romanorum*). For decades after their arrival, the Hungarians, who were a nation of formidable horsemen, mounted scourging raids into modern Germany and throughout France, until the German king Otto I the Great (who would later become emperor) halted their expansion in 955 at the battle of Lechfeld, in Bavaria – and so they settled in Pannonia permanently. The Hungarians were fortunate to have an exceptional personality very early on in the Arpadian dynasty (named after Árpád, the first

Magyar chieftain to lead his people westwards) in Stephen I (1000-1038) later sanctified by the Papacy as Saint Stephen. He introduced Christianity of the Western rite to his realm (thus becoming the first king of Hungary) after wavering for a while between Rome and Constantinople, and integrated his multi-ethnic state into the Western feudal system, which was only just beginning to coalesce. Among others, he favoured the influence of the German Church and began to colonise the entire kingdom with German settlers – from knights to ploughmen, miners, craftsmen and tradesmen etc.

The capture of Gyula, "dux magnus et potens" *(Latin for "great and powerful lord") in Transylvania, by his nephew Stephen I. Scene from the* Vienna Illuminated Chronicle.

Their westwards expansion halted, the kings of Hungary would henceforth seek to expand the kingdom to the south and east, encroaching on the Slavs and Romanians, even attacking the Byzantine Empire. And, either through force or political marriages, they seized the Slavic kingdom of Croatia during the last years of the 12th century, which would belong to the Hungarian crown from then on, but will not lose its language and identity, and would be led by a *ban* chosen from the Croatian nobility for most of the time.

German engraving of Sibiu in the 16th century

In Transylvania (also called *Ardeal* in Romanian, from the Hungarian *Erdély*) they expanded slowly, from the west, both into and around the Carpathian arc. Here they clashed with the Pechenegs, the same people they had faced in the steppes of Ukraine around two centuries earlier.

To strengthen their rule over Transylvania, the kings of Hungary applied the same policy of intense colonisation here, as they had done in Hungary proper. To defend against the Pechenegs, and then the Cumans, they settled a people called the Székelys to guard the frontier at the foot of the Eastern Carpathians. In Latin they are called *Siculi* (we call them *secui*) and they were originally a distinct ethnic group that arrived in Europe with the Magyars. Their precise origins are unknown, but what is certain is that the Hungarians assimilated them early on. They were given two counties which formed a kind of march, which enjoyed a special status and was ruled by a *comes siculorum* – a count chosen from amongst their chieftains.

Another important colonisation was that of the Germans, who were settled in compact groups across Transylvania. This process, initiated by the kings of Hungary, had a decisive impact on the future of the province and, it might be argued, on that of our entire country. The colonists, who were originally drawn from the left bank of the Rhine and the region of Mosel, were identified as *Flandrenses* or *Teutonici* in the early documents. However, from the early 13th century onwards, as their recruitment moved more towards the easterly regions inhabited by Germans, the term *Saxones* quickly became generalised and remained affixed to them for centuries. The chronicles – both Western and Oriental – were already calling them "Saxons", including a Persian account of the advance of Mongol armies through Transylvania during the great Mongol invasion (1241-1242) led by the sons and grandsons of Genghis Khan.

The initial purpose of the Hungarian king was to utilise the land more effectively, to settle the underpopulated areas and introduce a more advanced type of agriculture to the province. Four areas were designated for the settlement of Saxons, the principal of which was that around Sibiu; another was on the Târnava Mică and Târnava Mare river valleys; the third, around modern-day Bistrița; and finally, that which centred around Brașov. Therefore, their initial livelihood was agriculture. But as the craftsmen and merchants they brought with them began to establish market towns, which then developed into *burgs*, they began to play an increasingly important role in the trade between Western and South-Eastern Europe – and even the Near East – which passed through Hungary at the time. Thus, both Sibiu and Brașov (or *Hermannstadt* and *Kronstadt* in German, though both originally had Romanian or Slavo-Romanian names) became important centres of trade (with Wallachia) and transit towards the Orient.

There were seven chief Saxon *burgs* in Transylvania, hence the name *Siebenbürgen* (literally meaning "seven cities" in German) by which the province was known across the German-speaking world for centuries. And it was through the exploits of this community that Transylvania became known further afield, all the way to Shakespeare's England.

We must also emphasise the spread of a particular form of civilisation from the Saxons to the surrounding peoples – the Romanians and Hungarians. Later on, in the early 16th century, when Protestantism erupted from Germany (I only dare use this term because of the sudden and ample nature of its expansion) and spread to Eastern Europe, the Saxons adopted Lutheran doctrine en masse. One of the most noticeable consequences of this phenomenon was the translation of the Bible and of other

The coats of arms of the seven Saxon burgs of Transylvania, as seen in the 1550 Chorographia Transylvaniae, quae Dacia olim appellate *(Latin for "The Description of Transylvania, Once Called Dacia") by Georg von Reichersdorff*

Johannes Honterus, humanist scholar and theologian, born in Brașov (German: Kronstadt, or "City of the Crown"; Latin: Corona)

sacred texts from Latin into German (as well as other languages). In this respect, the great Protestant humanist Johannes Honterus (1498-1549) played a crucial role through his efforts to advance and disseminate culture (he worked as a translator, founded schools, libraries, as well as one of the most important printing press in Transylvania and the first paper mill, in Brașov) and became a key figure of the Renaissance in Transylvania. This widespread cultural movement of the time also reached Wallachia, where our first great typographer, deacon Coresi, received both encouragement and financial support from the Saxons of Brașov for the translation of religious texts into Romanian – that is, until his superiors in the Orthodox church determined that heretical elements had been subtly introduced to the Romanian translation and restricted the production of sacred texts in Transylvania. The decisive first steps had nevertheless been made.

From a demographic point of view, we must note one aspect that was characteristic to the Saxon population (as opposed to the Romanians, Hungarians or Székelys). This was *birth control* – an extremely rare phenomenon in Europe before the contemporary period – which was practiced in order to avoid splitting up the properties granted to them or which they had acquired over time; thus, every family made efforts to limit the number of children they produced to two, which explains why the Saxon population, initially comparable to those of the other nations, remained at a level of about 350,000 until the 20th century.

When the history of Romania is written, there is never enough emphasis on the role played by the Saxon community not only in Transylvania, but also throughout the territories defined by the Carpathian Mountains and the river Danube. In the aftermath of the tragic events of World War II, it was not only the German people living within Germany's borders which suffered the consequences of Hitler's madness, but also those German communities who had spread across Europe over the centuries. For present day Romania, the deportation of hundreds of thousands of Transylvanian Saxons to Russia and their subsequent repatriation to Germany is an irreparable loss and a real tragedy. Un-

The fortified church in Prejmer (German: Tartlau) a settlement that dates back to the 13th century. Repeated invasions forced the inhabitants to turn their churches into strongholds.

fortunately, all that remains of this once thriving community are the tourist attractions: medieval towns such as Sighișoara, Sibiu, Brașov and the fortified village churches of Transylvania.

Let us now go back to the Pechenegs from across the Carpathians. They ruled for almost 200 years and were very aggressive; we find them in constant conflict with either the Russians, or the Hungarians, and even with the Byzantines, until emperor Alexios I Komnenos crushed them in 1091 at the great battle of Levounion, after one of their incursions into the empire. He enrolled some of the captives into his army, and settled the others, with their women and children, in various corners of the empire.

Could all the Pechenegs have disappeared from our country at that time? I find that hard to believe. They left place names (toponyms) in at least all of the villages called Peceneaga; perhaps they left traces in our language too, but they are hard to identify, not least because theirs was very close to the language of the Cumans, who replaced them – half brothers and half enemies, who lent a hand in their destruction by the Byzantines.

The Cumans

The Cumans too came from the Eastern steppes, from present day Ukraine, where, for several centuries, they were a real power, constantly at war with the Kievan Rus principalities (many old Russian folk songs, miraculously discovered all the way up north, near the lakes, refer to the struggle against the Polovtsy – the Russian name for the Cumans, or "the people of the steppe", from the root *kum*). The bulk of the Cumans lived in Southern Ukraine, and were called the White Cumans, while those who reached as far as Southern Moldavia, Wallachia and even Bulgaria were called the Black Cumans (or what we might nowadays call a "lesser" branch of the Cuman people). The Cumans replaced the Pechenegs and were somewhat less nomadic than them; we can picture how, for about 150 years between the end of the 11th century (around 1090) and the mid-13th century (around 1240) when they fled before the great Mongol wave, the Cumans formed a relatively stable, organised polity, enough for Wallachia to appear as "Cumania" in the Byzantine and Western chronicles of the time. And for the first time, under the rule of these barbarians, we sense a political presence from the Romanians. Nicolae Iorga spoke of the "Cuman-Romanian symbiosis". For example, it is certain that it was from them that Romanians learned the art of war in the Middle Ages (especially cavalry tactics); we have a few words left from their language, often with a military connotation, such as beci – cellar (originally "fortified

Pecheneg warriors slaying Sviatoslav I of Kiev and his retinue in an ambush. The Cumans pushed the Pechenegs westwards in the late 11th century.

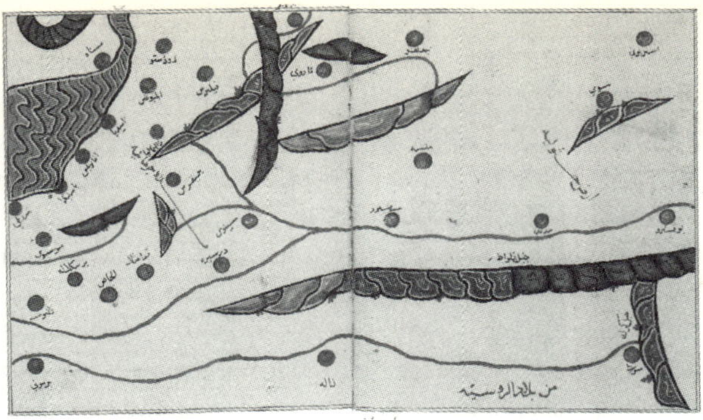

Map from Al-Idrisi's Tabula Rogeriana (1154) which shows North-Western Bulgaria and present day Romanian Banat.

enclosure", hence the Ottoman Turkish name Beç, given to Vienna) *bir* – tax, *ceată* – armed group, *olat* – region, *toi* – scuffle, probably even *odaie* – room; most of them are place names, incidentally very numerous, such as Comana and Comarnic, but especially all toponyms ending in *-ui* (like Vaslui, Covurlui and others); we mentioned Teleorman earlier. Just as significant is Bărăgan, the great steppe of South-Eastern Romania.

The Asen uprising and the "Kingdom of Vlachs and Bulgarians"

The Cumans went as far south as Bulgaria – which ceased to exist as an independent state since the fierce repression of emperor Basil II Boulgaroktonos (for example, one of the traces they left was the name Kumanovo, the place where Yugoslav and NATO military negotiators have recently met). Yet the region still had an important Romanian-speaking population, which had undoubtedly kept in contact with Romanians north of the Danube. These Vlachs were mainly sheepherders, which is probably why the word "Vlach" has, over time, become synonymous with "shepherd" for Bulgarians and Greeks.

In the year 1185, two brothers from the region of Tarnovo, Peter and Asen, who had had a fiscal dispute with the Byzantine emperor Isaac II Angelos, and were refused military service in the imperial army, incited both Vlachs and Bulgarians to a rebellion against the empire. And as things were not going their way militarily, the brothers crossed the Danube and returned with more

Coin issued in 1981 to commemorate "1,300 years since the founding of Bulgaria", imitating a gold coin from the time of Ivan Asen II. At the same time, the regime in Bucharest was celebrating "2,500 years since the first mention of a centralised Dacian state".

Tsar Kaloyan, on a fresco found at Boian Monastery (nowadays Bulgaria)

Romanians and Cuman cavalry, defeating the Byzantines after a while. This Cumano-Romanian alliance leads me to believe that the two Vlach brothers from Tarnovo shared a more ancient bond with the Cuman chieftains, perhaps even a blood relation, since the name Asen is actually Cuman. Peter and Asen will take up the crown of the former Bulgarian tsars, as that was tradition of the land, which the Byzantines had interrupted 200 years before them. A third brother, Ioniță, nicknamed *Kaloioannes* in Greek (meaning "John the Fair" or perhaps "the Brave") took the family ambition even further, and managed to obtain a royal crown from the great Pope Innocent III. The correspondence between Ioniță and the Pope clearly proves that he was claiming *Roman* origins, which the Pope recognised (one knows how well-informed the Papacy has always been).

Nevertheless, things would become complicated after the sacking of Constantinople in 1204 by the knights of the Fourth Crusade, diverted from its path by the greed and trickery of the Venetians (a dramatic event, of incalculable consequences, because in its aftermath, the Catholic and Orthodox Churches became such bitter enemies that they were unable to reconcile to this day).

Ioniță abandoned the Catholic faith for the influence of the Greek Patriarch (who had taken refuge in Asia Minor, at Nicaea) and waged war on the "Frankish" crusaders; in 1205, he defeated Emperor Baldwin I of Flanders with Cuman support, and then imprisoned him in the dungeons of Tarnovo, where he eventually perished. But after Ioniță's reign, the state of the Asens,

The siege of Constantinople in 1204, as depicted in a 1330 Venetian manuscript On the Conquest of Constantinople, *written by the French knight and historian Geoffroy de Villehardouin. The miniature shows the crusaders attacking the city from both land and sea.*

established within the political and cultural tradition of the First Bulgarian Empire, will no longer be known as the "Kingdom of the Vlachs and Bulgarians", as the Frankish chroniclers called it, but simply as the "Second Bulgarian Empire" – while the initial contribution of Romanians to this great achievement would be diminished over time, enabling some Bulgarian historians to make the ridiculous claim that this state was, in fact, a "kingdom of Bulgarians and shepherds".

The Mongol invasion

During the first decades of the 13th century, a formidable power, of unprecedented violence, suddenly appeared at the other end of Europe, originating in the steppes of Mongolia – that of Genghis Khan's Mongol horsemen. We have to stop for a moment and consider the Mongol phenomenon, not just because it is a crucial moment in world history, but also because it had consequences of

Mongol cavalry in battle (illustration from an early 14th century Persian manuscript)

The burning of Suzdal in 1238, depicted in a miniature from a 16th century manuscript. The Mongol armies of Batu Khan destroyed the Russian city while on their way to Europe.

paramount importance for us – thousands and thousands of kilometres away. The enormous and well-organised army of Genghis Khan, built around the horsemen of his tribe and incorporating many other Mongol or Turkic peoples over time, started to advance around 1206 and began by conquering all of Northern China. The Mongols then made their way westwards, destroying many Asian states along the way – the Persian kingdom among them, leaving a trail of inconceivably gruesome massacres behind them – historians spoke of pyramids of hundreds of thousands of heads after the fall of each great city.

Their fame and terror spread like wildfire throughout the known world. When the Great Khan died in 1227, his vast empire was divided between his sons, one of which was elected Great Khan in his place; yet even before the succession, a great army the likes of which the Earth had never seen before was heading west through Siberia and towards Europe, under the command of Batu Khan, a grandson of Genghis Khan. North of the Sea of Azov, on the Kalka River, they delivered a crushing defeat to a coalition of White Cumans and Rus-

Tatar incursion into Transylvania, from a 1488 edition of János Thuróczi's Chronicle of the Hungarians

sians – reconciled on this occasion – led by the Great Knyaz of Kiev. The news soon reached the Black Cumans, north of the Danube. For fear of the Mongols, the Black Cumans, who had previously resisted all attempts to convert them to Christianity – killing several missionaries and Catholic monks – now asked their chieftain to request the protection of the king of Hungary and a bishop to baptise their entire people. An impressive delegation, led by the king's son himself, the future King Béla IV, and the Archbishop of Strigonium (Esztergom) promptly crossed the Carpathians in 1228, somewhere near the border between Moldova and Wallachia. Tens of thousands of Cumans were baptised along with their chieftain, and a bishopric of the Cumans was hastily established on the river Milcov (*episcopatus Milcovensis*) where a church, palace and fortress were built soon after – though none of it would survive the Mongol wave that hit 13 years later.

In 1241, three Mongol columns advanced from Russia westwards, destroying the Russian states one by one, devastating the kingdom of Poland, supported by German knights, and then our country – where they would encounter resistance from the Saxons in the north,

Ögedei Khan (1186-1241). His death caused the Mongols to retreat from Europe and provided Béla IV with a respite to strengthen the Hungarian kingdom.

recently settled in the mining region of Rodna, and from a "Vlach" polity in the south – before joining forces in Hungary, where they destroyed the army of King Béla (who would only find refuge on an island in the Adriatic). The Mongol hordes were now expected to strike at the great Western nations. However, in 1242, they suddenly retreated, not because of some Christian counter-attack, but because of the news that the Great Khan had died, and all of his brothers, sons and grandsons rushed to Karakorum to elect the new Khan. As an afterthought, we should mention that Western rulers – the Pope, the king of France and the king of England – believed for a while that they could use these fearsome newcomers against the power of the Muslims, which, to them, remained the greatest enemies of Christianity.

Central and Western Europe would have time to recover and gain strength. Yet the Mongols did not pull out of Europe completely, and instead established a powerful state in Southern Russia, on the lower Volga, known as the Golden Horde, which dominated the vassal Russian principalities for the next 200 years and expanded westwards, to the shores of the Black Sea and the Crimea, where the Mongols mixed with the White Cumans, whose language they adopted. They would henceforth be known as the Tatars, and through their savage raids, they will constitute a constant threat to our principalities for many centuries to come. As early as the first decades of the 14th century, we find that the Bulgarian, Serbian and Romanian political entities have become the vassals of these Tatar khans that settled north of the Black Sea. Nevertheless, the formidable Mongol expansion will also have some positive consequences, at least for the Romanians, as we will discover further on.

The Charter of the Knights Hospitaller (1247) – A "snapshot" of Oltenia and Wallachia before the "dismounting"

The Hungarians, who already ruled Croatia, the city of Belgrade and its surroundings, and the future Banat of Temeswar, had managed to cross the Carpathians into modern Oltenia during the last quarter of the 13th century and establish a march, or buffer province, called the Banat of Severin (Hungarian: *Szörény*) in which a Hungarian *ban* ruled over several Romanian voivodeships, some of which were "transalpine" – that is, partly in Oltenia and partly in present-day Hațeg region, across the Carpathians.

A document of exceptional importance allows us to form an idea of the political and social situation in those regions around the time of the Mongol invasion: it is the charter that King Béla IV of Hungary granted in 1247 to the Knights Hospitaller (also known as the Knights of Saint John of Jerusalem, or *cavalerii ioaniți* in Romanian) in order to settle the Banat of Severin, to colonise and defend it as vassals of the king of Hungary. The document is known to history as the Charter of Hospitallers.

Let us talk about this document for a moment, because it provides us with a sort of "snapshot" of this region just a few decades before the "dismounting" of the voivodeship of Wallachia (the traditional term used for the establishment of the two Romanian medieval states). But first, who were the Knights Hospitaller?

Soon after the First Crusade, at the end of the 11th century, a religious and military order was formed in the new Christian kingdom of Jerusalem – warrior monks whose mission was to care for the wounded and always be ready to take up arms against the "heathens" or "non-believers", meaning the Muslims. It was called the Order of Saint John of Jerusalem and initially the majority of its members were Frenchmen. More orders will appear later, of which it is important to remember the Knights Templar, who will become the great "bankers" of Western

Portrait of Guillaume de Chateauneuf, Grand Master of the Order of Saint John, from a history of the Order. King Béla IV granted the Banat of Severin to the Knights Hospitaller.

Denár from the reign of King Béla IV (1235-1270). In 1241, the Kingdom of Hungary was very close to disappearing from history on account of the Mongol invasion.

The Battle of Mohi, of 11 April 1241. Béla IV found himself without the support of his ally, the Cuman khan Kuthen, who had been killed by Hungarian magnates on the eve of the Mongol invasion.

Europe and the Teutonic (i.e. German) Knights who, after leaving Palestine and a brief presence in South-Eastern Transylvania (Romanian: *Țara Bârsei*, German: *Burzenland*) will colonise Northern Poland and create a large enclave around the port of Danzig (Polish: *Gdańsk*) called East Prussia, which the Germans will rule until the German disaster of World War II.

After their expulsion from Palestine at the end of the 13th century, the Hospitallers settled in Cyprus, then on the island of Rhodes, and finally, pushed out by the Ottoman Turks, on the island of Malta. Since then, they were known as the Knights of Malta. Eminescu uses an anachronism when he places them under that name at the battle of Nicopolis, in the time of Mircea the Elder, in his famous lines of the poem *Epistle III*:

> *Gleaming mail did the Knights of Malta don*
> *The Pope put all his three crowns on...*

In 1247, six years after the catastrophic Mongol invasion, King Béla IV of Hungary made a deal with the Grand Master of the Hospitallers, bestowing onto the Order the Banat of Severin, that is, Oltenia and a small part

Béla IV fleeing after the Mongols crossed the Danube in the winter of 1242.

of present-day Banat, to defend as vassals. The "contract" they drew up on this occasion reveals some extremely interesting details that help us put together a picture of this part of our country about half a century prior to the establishment of a state comparable in size to the great duchies of the feudal age, which will be called Wallachia (Romanian: *Țara Românească*; Slavic: *Vlașca Zemlia*).

It is surprising to discover the number of knights who were supposed to arrive – just a few dozen. Let us not forget that, at that time, Western knights wearing armour as heavy as they were, riding the largest war-horses in Europe (also covered in mail) each accompanied by about ten squires, were the equivalent of today's tanks in the tactics of their age. Moreover, the crusading knights from Palestine had established a reputation as the world's best fortification builders. That is precisely what the king of Hungary was expecting from them, as well as organising colonisation – on condition they would not accept any settlers from Transylvania, proof that people had begun to seep out from Transylvania towards the plains of the south and east even before the drafting of the Charter.

Here is some of the information revealed in the Charter:

– We learn about the existence of a Romanian voivodeship ruled by a certain Litovoi, to which the king had granted special status within the province, and which extended across the Carpathians, into Hațeg – an area that the king did not include in the territory given

Princess Elizabeth the Cuman (Hungarian: Kun Erzsébet) who married the son of Béla IV, the future King Stephen V

to the Order. Two knyazes, Ioan and Farcaş, are also mentioned. The name "Ioan" is spelled the way Romanians would pronounce it, and not as Johann (German) or Janos (Hungarian) or Iovan (Slavic); Farcaş means "wolf" in Hungarian, so the Hungarians claim that he might have been a Magyar chieftain. More likely, he was a Romanian knyaz who had come south from Transylvania, where his name, or that of his ancestors, had been changed from Lupu (Romanian) or Vîlcu (Slavic) to Farcaş. Litovoi is a Slavic name. Interestingly, 25 years later, another Litovoi (or perhaps the same?) from the same area rebels against the Hungarian suzerain and dies in battle; he is succeeded by a brother of his called Bărbat, a decidedly Romanian name;

– The Order was encouraged to claim land beyond the former "Cumania", where the king granted special status to another voivodeship, that of Seneslav, probably situated in the Argeş region; this name is Slavo-Romanian, perhaps deformed by the Hungarian chancellery – could he have been the Vlach lord that resisted the Southern prong of the Mongol attack in 1241?

– From the financial clauses of the charter it can be inferred that tithes and taxes were being levied on harvests and fishing in the march, and therefore, that an organised peasantry and economy were in place, even if somewhat dispersed;

– The country was nevertheless sufficiently populated to have its own levy (*apparatu suo bellico*) which the Order had to raise in aid of the king should he have been at war with his neighbours;

– Finally, the charter reveals that alongside the voivodes and knyazes mentioned by name, there were other "lords of the land" (*maiores terrae*) to whom the king granted substantial privileges, such as the right to appeal to the king's court in case they disputed the verdict of his vassal (the Grand Master of the Order) and were allowed death by beheading if found guilty. It follows that these lords made up a rather important local power, enough for the king to take them under his protection in some circumstances, extending his jurisdiction from a thousand kilometres away; so the country must have had political and military leaders from before that time – they were the future boyars we will find around the voivode a few decades later.

Ladislaus IV the Cuman (1272-1290) son of Stephen V and Princess Elizabeth the Cuman

Whatever became of the Cuman masses baptised in 1228? When the Mongol wave was approaching, their leader requested safe passage over the Carpathians and shelter for his people from the king of Hungary. The king settled them along the valley of the Tisza, where they would cause much trouble to royal officials for generations to come. Moreover, the king married a Cuman princess – Cuman women were famous for their beauty and such noble unions had been made with Russian knyazes, and even with Byzantium's imperial family – and it was from this marriage that the last king of the Arpadian dynasty would be born, Ladislaus IV (Hungarian: *László*) nicknamed "the Cuman", because of his love for his maternal heritage (he would adopt Cuman dress and hairstyle, to the dismay of his Hungarian subjects).

And so again I wonder: could all the Cumans have fled from our country at that time? There are many signs that this was not the case. Later Hungarian documents from Transylvania tell of the presence of some Cumans in the province around the 14th century, and there are a great deal of Cuman names in the regions of Făgăraș and Hațeg, as well as toponyms in Wallachia – secluded places, high up in the mountains, very typical of our ancestral traditions, such as Loviștea. It is not a trivial matter that in the early Wallachian documents of the 14th and 15th century we find a fairly large proportion of Cuman names among the country's boyars – which does not necessarily mean they were all of Cuman descent, but shows how profound the Cuman influence had been.

Detail from the Codex Cumanicus, *a manuscript that was most likely written in the early 14th century. The first part of the Codex consists of a vocabulary of Latin, Persian and Cuman words.*

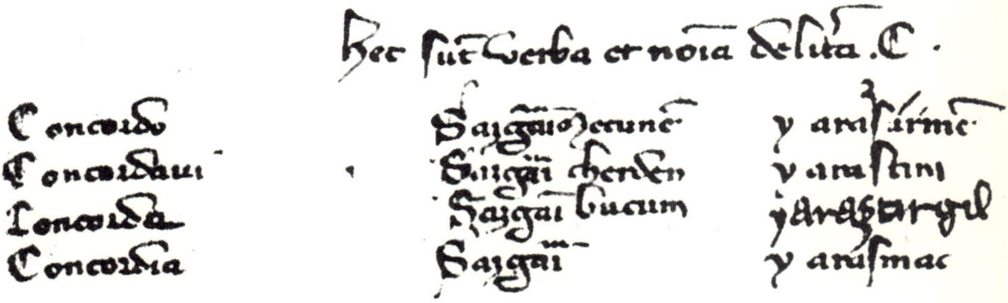

II. THE DAWN OF THE ROMANIAN MEDIEVAL STATES

Was there a "dismounting"?

Stamp of the "Radu Negru" High School in Făgăraş. The school's curriculum was taught exclusively in Hungarian up to 1919, when it was renamed after the Romanian voivode. The legend of the dismounting was so influential in the collective imagination of Romanians that the Dobrujan town of Caraomer was renamed Negru Vodă in 1927.

And so we find ourselves at the end of the 13th century, the crucial moment when the first organised Romanian state emerged between the Carpathians and the Danube: Wallachia. It may seem strange, but the circumstances surrounding this major event have remained obscured enough to cause serious controversy between historians: was there a "dismounting" like tradition demands, of the legendary Negru Vodă* from the land of Făgăraş? Or was the unification of the voivodeships south of the Carpathians a local phenomenon? Also, who was Basarab I the Founder, Great Voivode?

I mentioned earlier that the avalanche that was the Mongol invasion, which had destroyed or severely weakened almost every polity in central and Eastern Europe, had also created favourable conditions for the voivodeships in Wallachia to shrug off some of the Hungarian pressure and achieve the political unity of all those speaking Romanian between the mountains and the Danube for the very first time. This happened around the year 1300. Later chronicles, from the 16th and 17th centuries, mention the traditional date of 1290. However, most contemporary historians tend to indicate a later date, after 1300; there is even a group of historians, unfortunately in the majority, who claim that the dismounting tradition, with Negru Vodă crossing over from Făgăraş,

* *Vodă* is another Romanian word for voivode, usually appended to the name of a ruler, but also used on its own.

Basarab I, voivode of Wallachia (1324-1342), and his consort, depicted in a fresco inside the Princely Church at Curtea de Argeș.

is purely an invention from the 17th century, with no grounding in historical reality.

Nevertheless, a few outstanding historians, such as Gheorghe Brătianu or Șerban Papacostea, have recently spoken against this theory, asserting that oral tradition contains a grain of truth. I definitely stand with them in this attempt to rehabilitate the old legend, and moreover, I am convinced that Basarab the Founder, our first-ever recorded ruler, was descended from a lineage of Cuman chieftains.

Who was Basarab the Founder?

It has been proven that during the last quarter of the 13th century, despite the constant Mongol threat, there were

King Andrew III of Hungary (1290-1301). It was during his reign that Romanians in Transylvania lost the right to be represented in the Diet (miniature from the Vienna Illuminated Chronicle*)*

migrations of Romanian, Hungarian and Saxon groups from Transylvania into Wallachia, spurred by the rich plains and the trade there was to be made on the Danube and the Black Sea shore. Câmpulung was initially a Saxon trading post and in time it will have an important Catholic minority, with a beautiful church. Also, the nearby small cave church at Corbii de Piatră is built in a style from around 1290, and unusually, it has two altars, one Orthodox and one Catholic, side by side. On the other hand, Andrew III, the last Arpadian king, applied a discriminatory policy against the Romanians, whose nobility was no longer summoned to the Diet gatherings. The kings of Hungary, vassals of the Pope, began to see the expulsion of the "schismatic" Orthodox from their kingdom as a duty worthy of a veritable crusade. Therefore, Romanian nobles who refused to submit to Rome were excluded from the ranks of the nobility and gradually reduced to the state of simple peasants (unlike the Croatian nobles at the opposite end of the realm, who had received Western Christianity from the outset).

Nevertheless, the events around the year 1290 strangely confirm the traditional date of the legend as the time when Negru Vodă "dismounted" from the land of Făgăraș and settled in Câmpulung, and his descendants in Argeș, from where they would soon extend their authority south, to the Danube. This "alpine" origin of the dynasty is probably the source of the name "Muntenia" (an alternate name for Wallachia, from the Romanian *munte* – mountain) traditionally given to the entire country – which is mostly covered by plains.

Twenty years later, foreign sources (Hungarian, Papal, Serbian, Bulgarian etc.) speak of "Basarab, Great Voivode" reigning over all of Wallachia, the country between the Danube and the mountains – including Oltenia; note that Basarab is originally a first name.

But what does "Great Voivode" actually mean? It means that this leader, Voivode Basarab, came to dominate all the other Romanian knyazes and voivodes of that territory, the former "Cumania" and the Banat of Severin. It means that the descendants of Litovoi and possibly other knyazes from Oltenia submitted to Basarab. Thus, he is a *primus inter pares*, the first among equals. This is not unlike ancient Persia, where there was a High King, a king ruling over other kings; not unlike India, where the Maharaja ruled over all rajas; and not unlike Ethiopia, which had a King of Kings etc. This was the meaning of "Great Voivode", even if recently (intentionally or not) it was somehow altered to "Voivode Basarab the Great". Moreover, after his rule, when this supremacy was no longer disputed, the term "Great Voivode" went out of use.

The old seal of Câmpulung, Basarab's capital city

I have several reasons to believe that Basarab was descended from a line of Cuman chieftains. Nicolae

Coins in Wallachia came in two types: on some the legend was in Old Slavonic, others in Latin. The above is a silver ducat of Vladislav I Basarab, with the eagle shown regardant (as if looking over its shoulder) and the legend in Old Slavonic.

Silver ducat of Vladislav I Basarab (common type, with the legend in Old Slavonic)

Iorga wrote of him: "*The name is Cuman...* [and then underlined] *but perhaps not just the name?*" Yet not even the great Iorga dared to take this "investigation" any further, so deep is this pre-conception of ours that some things can be said about our national history, while others cannot. A contemporary historian who wanted to dismiss the idea that Basarab could have been of Cuman descent even writes that Basarab was undoubtedly Romanian – otherwise he would not have had the idea of uniting Romanian lands... Well then, how about a French historian, passionate about the Gallo-Roman origin of the French people, writing "*Clovis* (the Frankish king) *was surely Gallo-Roman, otherwise he would not have thought of unifying Gaul?*" I invite you to participate in the following exercise: try to find out who founded all the new European states in the Middle Ages after the collapse of the Roman Empire. In Gaul, it was the Franks, Burgundians and Visigoths; in Hispania, it was the Visigoths, Suebi and Vandals; in Italy, the Lombards. Some have lent their name to the lands: France, Burgundy, Lombardy, Andalusia.

I also believe this to be a constant in universal history: when empires collapse from within, the new states that are established in the same territory are never the initiative of the former citizens, who are left without elites and without momentum for a long time.

This observation is confirmed time and again in history, by examples such as ancient Egypt, Persia, China, India... again, this is a sort of natural law. So why does it matter if it were somehow proven that Basarab's ancestors were, in fact, Cumans? Far from being an abnormality, it would only be a natural consequence.

Here are a few arguments in support of my opinion (for we cannot digress too much within this particular volume):

– Not only is Basarab's name Cuman, but that of his father, Tocomerius (or Thoctomer) is Cuman as well; the late Orientalist Aurel Decei has proven this, and it must be said that the form "Tihomir", which is found in most books, is inaccurate. Would Slavo-Romanian knyazes have borne Cuman first names passed from father to son only 100-150 years after the Cuman invasion? Highly unlikely;

– The Papal chancellery regarded the first two voivodes, Basarab and Nicolae-Alexandru, as being faithful subjects of Rome, despite some "betrayals" which the Hungarian chancellery was quick to deem "schismatic"; but the Roman curia could not have been mistaken. Therefore, if they had originally been Catholics, they could not have been Slavo-Romanians, as that group had been looking to Constantinople for centuries; only the Cumans had been baptised in the Roman rite. Moreover, both Basarab and Nicolae-Alexandru had Catholic wives;

Silver ducat of Vladislav I Basarab (cross type, with the legend in Latin)

– Cozia and Horezu monasteries were two of the most prestigious establishments founded by the Basarab dynasty; both bear Cuman names (Romanian: *cozie* – walnut grove; *hurez* or *huhurez* – owl);

– It is often suggested that Basarab could have risen over other Romanian voivodes and knyazes as a leader against the Tatars, but this is not mentioned in any document; on the other hand, some Serbian and Hungarian sources indicate that he and the Bulgarians had in fact received Tatar support in a battle against the Serbians (at Velbujd in June 1330, when the allies were defeated by the Serbs) and in the famous battle of "Posada" (November 1330) against the Hungarians – an event which we will revisit, as it constitutes the "birth" of Wallachia as an autonomous entity in feudal Europe.

Thus, it is more likely that Basarab was accepted as "Great Voivode" not because he fought victorious battles against the Tatars, but because he was the most capable of dealing with them. A Cuman lineage could have been an advantage at a time when the Western Tatars (of Crimea and Budjak) were, for the most part, former Cumans.

Silver ducat of Vladislav I Basarab (cross type, with the legend in Latin)

In fact, the great Russian knyazes had done the same, which is to say they preferred the distant Mongol suzerainty that did not affect their faith and customs to the far more restrictive domination of Catholic power. Several decades before Basarab, the great hero of medieval Russia, Alexander Nevsky of Novgorod, then of Vladimir,

Charles Robert of Anjou or Charles I of Hungary (1312-1342) depicted in the Vienna Illuminated Chronicle *holding the cross-bearing orb, a symbol of power for Christian monarchs*

had chosen the same path: he fought heroically against westerners, defeating both the Swedes and the Teutonic Knights – yet also decided to humbly submit to the Great Khan of the Golden Horde. The same will be done by the great Muscovite knyazes the following century;

– We even have a rather strange document among early 14th century Transylvanian annals: it speaks of a Hungarian cleric who testified in 1325 that the son of a Cuman "count" dared to speak ill of the king before a young Hungarian nobleman, saying that "he did not even reach up to Bararab's ankle". Why would the young Cuman, if he wanted to humiliate the king of Hungary, not compare him to the king of Poland, the knyaz of Halych or some Serbian despot? Why compare him to Voivode Basarab, when he had not yet distinguished himself by defeating the arrogant king? Was it not because he was proud of him, knowing he was of his own people, or perhaps was even related to him?

– Finally, I wonder if the nickname "Negru Vodă", traditionally given to the "dismounting" voivode (or founder) for which many explanations have been found, some more creative than others, does not have a simpler meaning and if we should not stick to the explanation given by Paul of Aleppo, a famous Oriental traveller passing through our country three hundred years later: that he was called "Negru Vodă" because he was dark-skinned (*negru* means "black" in Romanian);

Indeed, Cumans would have looked dark-skinned to our Slavo-Romanian knyazes. In fact, several decades later, the Moldavian chronicler Miron Costin gives us the same explanation. This is a striking parallel to the case of an 11th century Byzantine writer, general Keukaménos, who was the first to speak of the Aromanians in more detail: his name means "charred face" or "the dark one" in Greek, a nickname that was given to his grandfather, who was Armenian, and was probably even darker-skinned than the Greeks in Constantinople.

Of course, none of these arguments are conclusive in themselves, but together, they form what is called in legal jargon a "body of assumptions" that is compelling, to say the least.

Consequently, we can imagine the following scenario for the "dismounting": when the Cumans in the bishopric of Milcov and those in Wallachia crossed the Carpathians in 1238-1240 to take shelter from the Mongol invasion under the protection of the Hungarian kingdom, not all of them accepted to be colonised in the Tisza river basin. Many who had already mixed with the Romanians or indeed, had *become* Romanian (for we must emphasise that all the sources we have on Basarab identify him as Wallachian) will have chosen to stay among the Romanians, both north and south of the Carpathians. As a descendant of these people, "Negru Vodă" (Basarab, or more likely his father, Tocomerius, inasmuch

Envoy of Basarab presenting Charles Robert with a letter in which the Wallachian voivode was proposing a very advantageous peace. But the proud king refused and headed towards the disaster known to historical tradition as Posada.

as a 17th century church document speaks of Nicolae-Alexandru as the "grandson" of Negru Vodă) who perhaps owned lands both north and south of the mountains, managed to impose his authority onto other Romanian chieftains, to set himself up at Câmpulung, a Saxon trading post, unify all the lands between the Carpathians and the Danube, and become recognised as "Great Voivode" – though still a vassal of the king of Hungary.

Throughout this period, that is between 1247 (when the Charter of Hospitallers was written) and the early 14th century (when we get the first information about Basarab) we know nothing about the voivode Seneslav from Argeș or any of his potential successors.

The year 1330

The Arpadian dynasty of Hungarian kings had died out on the paternal line several years before. After years of fighting between various pretenders, a maternal line descendant of the last Arpadian kings finally emerged victorious – he was Charles Robert of Anjou, from a branch of the French Angevin dynasty who had come to rule the kingdom of Naples in Southern Italy. The new king, who had strong links to the Papacy, would soon

The battle of Charles Robert against Basarab I (this representation, which is more "modern" is from a 1488 edition of János Thuróczi's Chronicle). The text says "On the unfortunate war of King Charles with Basarab, voivode across the mountains".

come into conflict with the "Great Voivode" Basarab, whom he would nevertheless recognise as a vassal ruling over all of Wallachia in 1324. However, in 1330, concerned by Basarab's unruly attitude, his links to the Bulgarians and the Tatars, as well as his defeat at Velbujd at the hands of the Serbs, Charles entered Wallachia with a great army, intending to re-establish his authority as suzerain in all respects. But on his return to Hungary, his force was ambushed by Basarab's army in a mountain pass (a place yet unidentified, but mistakenly known to history as "Posada") attacked from the flanks and rear by troops rolling enormous boulders from high above, their path ahead blocked by large tree trunks felled across the road. For three days, the flower of Hungarian nobility was slaughtered mercilessly. The disaster is mentioned by multiple sources, among them a chronicle illustrated with colourful miniatures (known as the Vienna Illuminated Chronicle or *Chronicon Hungariae Pictum*) where the king is depicted fleeing for his life, while Basarab's men, shown wearing sheepskin coats and hats, fire arrows from high ground and push large rocks down towards armoured knights. This famous miniature from the Vienna Illuminated Chronicle was at the origin of a mistaken assumption which not even Iorga escaped, that the armies of our

Two very similar representations of the Battle of Posada (both from the Vienna Illuminated Chronicle*) which have caused specialists to wonder whether or not they actually depict two different battles from Charles Robert's campaign in Wallachia. It has also been proven that the rocky appearance of the terrain is only a stylistic element inspired by Italian miniatures.*

first voivodes were only made up of peasants armed with bows and arrows, and that the dress and conduct of the voivode's court must have been somewhat rustic. But the discovery in 1920 of a miraculously well-preserved tomb at Curtea de Argeș, containing most likely a member of the ruling family, and the fact that this "Wallachian prince" was dressed in expensive clothes, inlaid with pearls and belt-buckles in Western style, like a Hungarian magnate or prince, brought about an otherwise logical revelation: that Romanian voivodes, boyars and knights (Romanian: *viteji*, meaning "braves") could not have dressed and armed themselves any differently to their neighbours, with whom they had close ties and interdependencies – the Bulgarian Tsardom, the Serbian Kingdom and the Kingdom of Hungary.

Nevertheless, if peasant archers played a crucial role in the battle of "Posada", this does not mean they made up all of Basarab's army, which could not have lacked cavalry armed with swords, spears and axes, and in the case of the richest, protected by plate or mail armour, as in the rest of medieval Europe.

Even at the battle of Agincourt, in 1415, where the English king Henry V defeated a far more numerous force of French knights, the decisive action belonged to

As at the Battle of Posada, archers played a decisive role at the Battle of Agincourt, which occurred on 25 October 1415, as part of the Hundred Years' War (illustration from a 15th century chronicle).

the English archers, firing volley after volley, protected by rows of sharpened stakes – but victory could not have been obtained without armoured knights. That was the tactic of the time. And that is how we must imagine the last phase of the battle of "Posada".

Nicolae Alexandru (1352-1364) in a 14th century fresco from Câmpulung Monastery (restored around 1820). Further down is the signature of his son, Vladislav Vlaicu, on a charter.

Therefore, 1330 was the moment when this principality (or voivodeship) of Wallachia became quasi-independent. But independence in the Middle Ages did not have the significance it has today. All the countries in Europe had rulers who are more or less the vassals of others. For example, the king of England was the vassal of the king of France because he owned some duchies and counties on French territory, for which he had to swear allegiance to the French king, who was his suzerain in those lands. But he may have been equally as powerful as his suzerain. Let us not think that to be the vassal of the king of Hungary was a humiliation. The fearsome Teutonic Knights were the vassals of the king of Poland. The king of Hungary is, in turn, the vassal of the Pope. The Wallachian prince had to be the vassal of the Hungarian king, and if Basarab rebelled against him at one point, it was to assert his autonomy, after which he made peace with the king and renewed his oaths of allegiance, together with his son, Nicolae-Alexandru; and as we will see further on, the voivode of Moldavia also swore an oath to the king of Poland, precisely in order to have a protector against Hungary.

It was no humiliation. That was how the feudal system worked.

Moreover, the king of Hungary and the Romanian voivode of Wallachia shared common economical interests: both needed free access to the Black Sea and trade from the Orient, which brought in handsome profits from taxes. Commercial routes led from Sibiu and

Braşov to the Genoese ports on the Danube and the Black Sea coast, at Vicina, Chilia, Cetatea Albă and all the way to Crimea. With the help of the king (and in his name) the Wallachian voivode turned against the Tatars and extended his dominion north of the Danube Delta for a few decades, in the territory between the Prut and Dniester rivers, which has since borne the name Bessarabia (Romanian: *Basarabia*, or the "country of Basarab") but was called Budjak (Romanian: *Bugeac*) by the Turks and Tatars. It is yet unclear what happened to this Romanian-Hungarian condominium until the next century, when it was conquered by the other Romanian voivodeship, Moldavia, which we will discuss shortly.

Before that, though, a quick word about Basarab's immediate successors, Nicolae-Alexandru and Vladislav, whose reigns have also witnessed events of great significance for the future of Wallachia and the Romanian people in general.

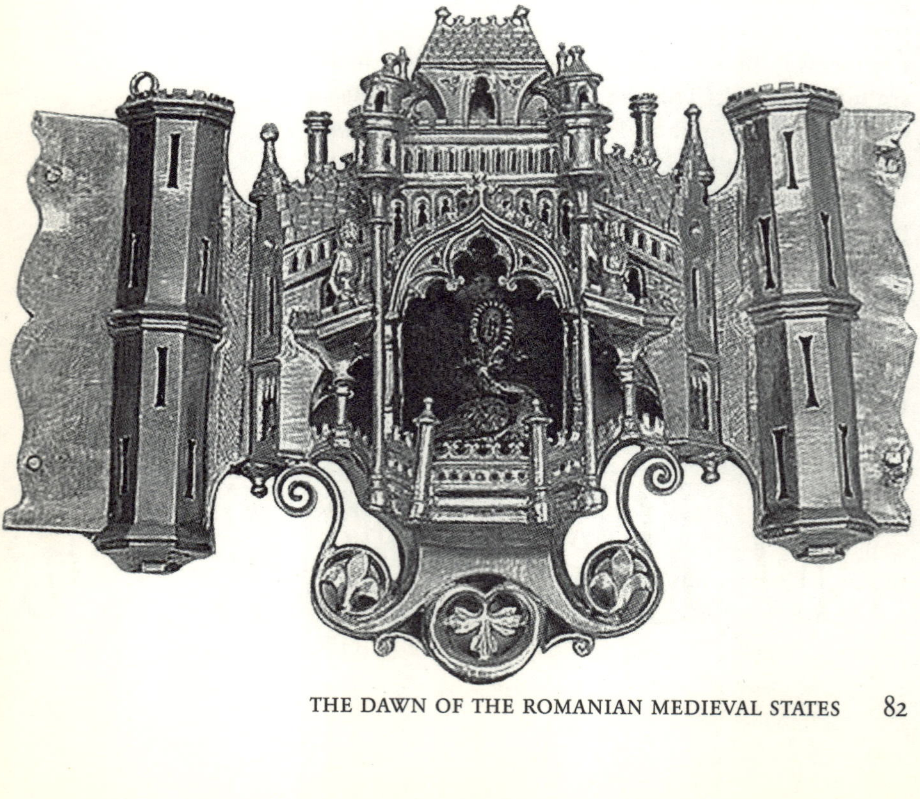

Golden belt buckle discovered in 1920 in a grave inside the Princely Church at Curtea de Argeş. It was most likely the work of a jeweller from Sibiu and belonged to a Wallachian voivode from the House of Basarab.

Detail of a fresco in Curtea de Argeș, probably representing Nicolae Alexandru, son of Basarab I.

1359 – Basarab's successors and the choice between Rome and Constantinople

After a long reign, Basarab was succeeded in 1352 by his son, Alexandru, whom external documents initially describe as being on good terms both with the Pope and the king of Hungary. But in 1359, furious at the king for intercepting his direct correspondence with the Pope, from whom he had hoped to get recognition as an "autocratic" prince – meaning a sovereign ruler anointed by God, not elected or appointed – the Wallachian voivode called upon the patriarch of Constantinople and the Byzantine emperor – who, by that time, was left with the prestige, but none of the power he had once held – and succeeded in having the metropolitan of Vicina, whose congregation was thinning because of Tatar invasions, moved to Argeș, where he held court as the "autocratic ruler of Wallachia" (*autokrat r* was the Greek word, but in Slavonic it was *samodržac*).

About the same time, Alexandru built the beautiful princely church of Curtea de Argeș, where we find him in the portico: a small, painted character, kneeling humbly before the sight of Christ, the Virgin Mary and Saint Nicholas, one of the most venerated saints of the Eastern Church; it is probably at this time that he started to appear in Greek documents with the double name Nicolae-Alexandru (historian Daniel Barbu has recently brought convincing arguments that, at the time, a name change during the course of a ruler's reign could only happen after a change of religion, and perhaps a new baptism). The year 1359 is thus another crucial date in our history, along with 1330, when the house of Basarab chose to bring the country definitively into the fold of the Eastern Church of Constantinople, to which the majority of their subjects had belonged for centuries, despite the best efforts of the Catholic Church and the Hungarian court to place Wallachia under the influence of Rome.

Understandably, this turn of events was not to the liking of King Louis I of Hungary, one of the great kings of the Angevin dynasty, who kept up the pressure during the reign of Nicolae-Alexandru's successor, Vladislav (whom the people remembered as Vlaicu Vodă). Yet he too stood firm, and even dared take up arms against the king, finally reaching a favourable compromise in 1386, when the king confirmed the voivode's rule over Wallachia (including Severin) and also gave him the duchy of Făgăraș across the mountains in exchange for an oath of loyalty.

Seal of the medieval city of Baia, the first capital of Moldavia and the seat of Dragoș Vodă and his heirs. The exergue says, in Latin: "Seal of the seat of Moldavia".

The "dismounting" of Moldavia

What happened in Moldavia at about the same time was similar, and yet different from that which I mentioned above about Wallachia. There was certainly a "dismounting" in Moldavia, that is, the arrival of a group from across the Carpathians, who conquered the present-day region.

How did this come about? First, the kings of Hungary, supported by their Romanian subjects, fought battles against the Tatars, trying to chase them away from the Carpathian border. Hungarians and Romanians crossed the mountains and beat the Tatars; thus, the king of Hungary, satisfied with the services of Dragoș, one of the voivodes in Maramureș, made him overlord of a territory in Moldavia where several small polities had previously formed, most likely in connection to the knezate of Halych. Therefore, Dragoș was initially the lord of a feudal "march" of the Hungarian kingdom, to the east of the Carpathians. However, a few years after Dragoș settled in Moldavia, a rival family from Maramureș, that of Bogdan, rebelled against the king of Hungary, crossed the mountains and deposed his descendants. A new dynasty emerged – the Bogdănești, though they are better known to modern historians as the Mușatini, from the name of Margareta Mușata, mother of Petru I. Historian Ștefan Gorovei has recently proven that the traditional date when Dragoș was known to have dismounted (1359) was wrong. Dragoș must have settled in Moldavia during King Louis' great campaigns of 1345-1347 against the Tatars, while his successors must have been ousted by Bogdan's clan around 1363.

And so it was Bogdan's descendants who became the true founders of the autonomous principality of Moldavia. The heartland of the new voivodeship was the Moldova river basin, which gave its name to the country; the first capital was at Baia, on the river Siret, and then moved to Suceava. The expansion of the voivode's authority over pre-existing polities happened gradually, but still at quite a fast pace, for around 1390 the lord of Suceava styled himself "ruler up to the sea" – meaning that he had taken Bessarabia from the Wallachians and Hungarians, save for one or two fortresses. It is certain though that, at the time, our neighbours were aware of there being two separate Romanian polities when they mentioned "Greater Wallachia" and "Lesser Wallachia" (Moldavia).

To maintain a relative autonomy, Moldavian voivodes took turns between accepting the protection of the Hungarian king, and submitting to his rival, the king of Poland.

Now is the time to say a few words about the structure of this small Romanian state – a rare subject in our

Unlike Wallachian voivodes, the rulers of Moldavia (up to Stephen the Great) only issued coins bearing legends in Latin. They were the symbols of the country's prosperity and prestige. At the top, a groș*; below it, a* ban *– both from the reign of Alexander the Good.*

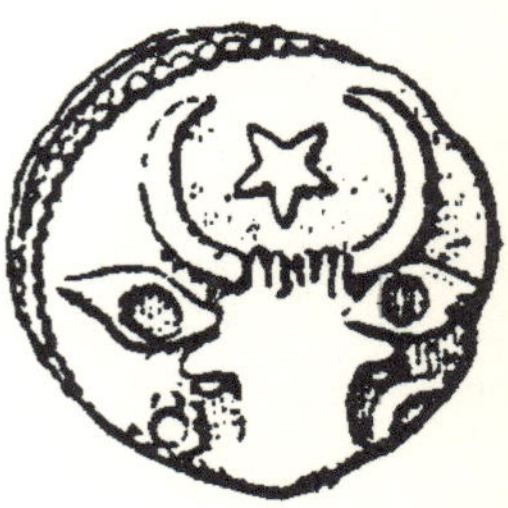

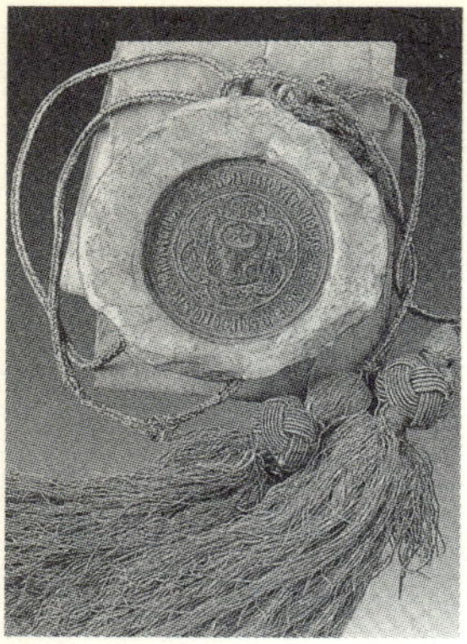

Seal of Alexandru Lăpușneanu, on a court document from 1560. The voivode was an illegitimate son of Bogdan III and only became voivode after seeing off another pretender, Joldea, by cutting off his nose (in order to be eligible, pretenders to the throne had to be "whole of body" and "of the blood" of voivodes).

history books. We find that power is divided between the voivode and the great boyars. For example, when a Moldavian voivode went to swear allegiance to his suzerain, the king of Poland, as princes did all over Europe, he signed a charter which said "*I promise to come with my host should your neighbours strike...*" yet the king insisted that the treaty also be signed by the great boyars. Sometimes, a separate treaty with the boyars was annexed to the main charter. The power of these nobles who elected the voivode was thus so great that a foreign suzerain deemed it necessary to secure their oaths alongside that of the voivode to ensure his authority over the land. We also find that, of the sixteen boyars who signed such treaties, only three or four were great courtiers – chancellors, castellans etc. The others only signed with their names, *jupân* this and *jupân* that – which means that they were noble by birth, and possessed large estates, and men to call to arms. Therefore, in early medieval Moldavia, the great boyars wielded almost as much power as the voivode. The same is valid for Wallachia, though there are fewer documents to support this.

Let us now analyse the structure of Romanian society in the 14th century: how succession to the throne occurred; where power was concentrated, apart from the voivode; what it meant to be a "great boyar" or a "great courtier"; who came next in the ranks; the role of the Church in the affairs of the state; and the status of burghers and peasants.

Succession to the throne

The system of succession to the throne was one of the most unfortunate of our medieval institutions. Despite the fact that the first two successions in Wallachia seem to have happened without difficulty, after the third generation – or the second, in Moldavia – we find that the throne was not automatically handed down to the eldest son of the defunct voivode (as the kings of France or England had managed) but that a successor was elected from his sons. It was as if the descendants of former knyazes, voivodes and other lords in the land wanted to revive the initial election of the Great Voivode. From that moment on, this would become the rule – with rare exceptions, such as the extraordinary figures of Mircea the Elder in Wallachia and Stephen the Great in Moldavia, who succeeded in placing their eldest sons on the throne before they died. When the throne became vacant, the "country" would elect a new voivode from the house of Basarab (in Wallachia) or Bogdan (in Moldavia). It was an elective hereditary system. Any member of the house was eligible if they were considered worthy, even illegitimate children (in fact, many of our greatest rulers were bastards, such as Stephen the Great, Petru Rareș, Neagoe Basarab and Michael the Brave). It was

Mircea the Elder and his son, the future voivode Mihail, whom he appointed co-ruler in 1409, while still on the throne. Mihail only ruled on his own for a brief time (1419-1420) before he was killed in battle, defending his throne and country from his cousin.

enough to be "of the blood" of voivodes – or, as it was said in Romanian, "from the bone" of voivodes.

It now becomes evident that competition, rivalry and intrigue were inherent to this system, which professed to elect the best candidate, but in reality was the origin of a never-ending string of internal power struggles and a constant pretext for foreign intervention. Where did this tradition come from? From the Slavs? From the Cumans? But then, why did it exist in Moldavia as well? Or was it just a consequence of the fact that the first voivodes had been elected?

The assembly of estates

Mary of Mangup, second wife of Stephen the Great. By taking a princess of Byzantium as his wife, Stephen secured a useful political alliance.

What did chroniclers mean when they said that the "country had chosen" the new voivode? Essentially, it meant that an "assembly of estates" was hastily convened, a sort of emergency council which included great boyars, high-ranking clergymen, burghers and courtiers (the household troops) representing "the people".

During the Middle Ages, such assemblies were an actual institution in Wallachia and Moldavia, as they were in the West. They were not only brought together to elect a new voivode, but also in times of difficulty, such as in 1456, when the Moldavian voivode Petru Aron (predecessor of Stephen the Great) needed to get the "country's permission" to pay tribute to the Turks, or else assume responsibility for war.

In practice, however, shortly after the throne became vacant following the death of the voivode – or sometimes, unfortunately, his overthrow – the estates assembly became little more than a formality to formalise a foregone choice made by a small circle of great boyars.

The great boyars

Since early times, the great boyars were at the side of the voivode, advising him in all state matters during both war and peace. They were the ones from amongst whom the voivode chose his ministers – the *dregători* who formed his council, or *Sfat* (a Slavic word related to "soviet"). The names of their commissions are mostly of Byzantine origin, but got to us through the Bulgarian language. Sometimes we find the old Latin form almost unchanged, for example *comis* (from the Latin *comes*, which is the origin of "count" in the Western feudal hierarchy) or *vistier* (from *vestiarius*, the one who held the key to the lord's wardrobe, where the treasury was); *spătar* (from *spatha*, Latin for broadsword) commander of the army; *logofăt* (from the name of a Byzantine official called the *logothelis*, literally "keeper of the laws") the equivalent of a chancellor in the West. The only title that seems to be a local, Romanian creation was the *vornic*, a high-ranking official that we would now call the minister of justice and internal affairs. The Slavic term *dvornik* (from *dvor* – palace) appears to be a literal translation of *palatinus*, a high-ranking official in the Hungarian and Western courts.

There were also the *paharnic*, who tasted the voivode's wine to ensure it was not poisoned; the *stolnic*, who was in charge of his table (the equivalent of a seneschal);

Romanian boyars from the 16th century

and the *postelnic*, who was the foreign minister. There were many others of lower rank, among whom the *pârcălab*, the castellan of a border fortress, whose name came through Hungarian from the German word *burggraf* – lord of a castle.

I wanted to save the best for last: the highest rank among Wallachia's boyars, the Great Ban of Craiova, which was not established immediately after the country's dismounting, but only starting with the 15th century; the title of "ban" (a legacy from the Avars) was the same as that given by Hungarian kings to the rulers of Severin,

Charter of Vladislav II, voivode of Wallachia, in which he granted several villages to a certain "jupân Mihail".

and also to the king's representative in Croatia. From the 15th century onwards, the highest ranks in Wallachia were the *Great Ban*, the *vornic* (interior minister) the *logofăt* (chancellor) and the *spătar* (army commander). In Moldavia, the order was different: there was no Great Ban (the *ban* was only a minor official later on) and so the highest rank was that of *logofăt*, while the commander of the army was not called *spătar*, but *hetman* (Romanian: *hatman*) – a term borrowed by the Poles and Cossacks from the Germans (*hauptmann* – captain). There was a *vornic* for the Highlands (Romanian: *Țara de Sus*) and one for the Lowlands (*Țara de Jos*) a remnant of the historical expansion process of the new state established in the mountainous north-west by the Drăgoșești and then gradually expanded by the Bogdănești towards the south, down the Siret and Moldova river valleys, engulfing the small polities of the plains, such as those around Bârlad, for instance. In Wallachia too the memory of the three main regions that formed Basarab's voivodeship lasted for a long time – the central region, around the river Argeș; to the west, Oltenia, aware of its former autonomy; and the three Eastern counties of Buzău, Râmnicu-Sărat and Brăila, tied to the Hungarian kingdom by their commercial interests on the Danube.

Detail from a 1587 charter of Mihnea II, voivode of Wallachia, in which he granted an estate and two mills to the Episcopate of Buzău. Charters were reserved for the voivode, who used them to grant donations, privileges and exemptions, or confirm property titles. Their authenticity was certified by pressing the seal of the voivode onto a wax pendant attached to the document.

I have mentioned a few titles of court officials, but let us recall what I said earlier about the oath of loyalty made before the king of Poland: in the beginning, boyars in our principalities were not "made" by their court rank, but the other way around, meaning that the voivode would chose his ministers from among the boyars. The boyars owned the great estates (Romanian: *moșii*) from where they could recruit men to serve in the army.

Only later on, during the 17th century, did nobility and court ranks begin to have interchangeable meanings, to a point where this equivalence was institutionalised under the Phanariote regime – long after the medieval age. The great boyars were therefore very few in number, and although bitter rivalries and bloody feuds existed between them, they formed a rather compact and solidary class, which, for several centuries, constantly tried to curb the authority of the voivode and force him to share power.

Seal of Mircea the Elder, on a treaty with Poland

For over a hundred years, our historians have debated the rise of this privileged class. In my opinion, if we consider the historical context, the vocabulary of "nobility" (*voivod*, *cneaz*, *ban*, *jupân*, *viteaz*, *voinic*, *boier* etc.) and the names of the first voivodes and boyars mentioned in documents, this echelon probably began to emerge during the rule of the first Bulgarian Tsardom (9th and 10th centuries) and was at first predominantly Slavic; later on, a significant Turkic element (of Pecheneg-Cuman blood) was added to it, and only after the fusion of Vlachs and Slavs was complete did it include more and more Vlach *juzi*. Later on, in the age of voivodeships, as this new social class evolved, the Vlachs must have become inevitably predominant. Nevertheless, the Slavic origin of the old nobility must have been culturally imprinted on this category for far longer. It is otherwise hard to explain how an exclusively Slavic literature was able to circulate for centuries, not to mention the language of the Church and the princely courts – could it have done so for the benefit of a handful of priests and clerks? All of nobility, high and low, must have had some command of it until late in the feudal age. We have documents that prove Stephen the Great and Neagoe Basarab still spoke it. It was the same case in Western Europe, where most clerics and educated people had some knowledge of Latin.

Here is another plausible example: a son of Mircea the Elder, Radu, the elder brother and predecessor of Vlad Dracul, is known to history as *Radu Prasnaglava*. In all our history books this became "Radu the Bald" (Romanian: *Radu cel Pleșuv*) but in my view this is a translation error that stems from the fact that the word *gol* in Romanian means both "uncovered" and "empty". Yet there are other words for "uncovered" (as in uncovered head) in Slavic languages, which closely resemble the Romanian *pleșuv*, while *prasno* only means "empty". In Serbian, *prasnoglavac* means "village idiot" and therefore, the nickname given to our voivode in no way meant "the Bald", but quite literally "the Fool". And since it is inconceivable that mere chancellery scribes would dare insult a voivode's descendant – even a deposed one – in such a gross manner, we may conclude that it could only have been those who saw themselves on much the same standing as the ruling family, and who still spoke the Slavonic language, who had bestowed such an epithet on him – the great boyars. In fact, the nickname given to his nephew, Radu the Fair (brother of Vlad Țepeș) was also ironic, because it seems sultan Mehmet II rather fancied him during the time he spent as a young hostage in Turkey. The story is told in great detail in the Byzantine chronicle of Laonikos Chalkokondyles.

Seal of Alexander the Good

A final piece of evidence that the boyars, the high clergy and perhaps some of the merchants must have understood Old Church Slavonic as late as the early 17th century is the fact that the erudite boyar Udriște Năsturel (brother-in-law of Matei Basarab) translated *Imitatio Christi*, the most popular mystical work in the West, into Old Church Slavonic instead of Romanian. Again, I ask: would he have done that for the benefit of a handful of priests and clerks? The nobility, despite its renewal over the course of three or four centuries, must have still had command of it as a language of culture, as will be the case with Greek during the 18th century and French throughout the 19th and 20th centuries.

The lesser boyars

Who was further down the hierarchy, behind the great boyars? The voivode is always addressing his "boyars, great and small" in written documents. So there was an entire category of lesser nobility who owned estates and enjoyed certain privileges in exchange for service in the army or at court. As we have already noted, the first Great Voivode came across an already established class of land and serf owners, and as soon as he consolidated his authority, he tried to fill their ranks with men who were loyal to him and who stood out through exceptional bravery in combat. This was achieved through grants of land in uninhabited or sparsely populated areas, or estates confiscated from other boyars, who had proven

Helmet from 1520, with visor, of the type used by Western European knights. In Moldavia and Wallachia, boyars played a crucial military role: it was their duty to equip their household troops for war and join the voivode's army when called upon to fight.

themselves unworthy or disloyal (they were called *haín* in Romanian, a word which has since taken on the meaning of "evil"). Hence, shortly after, a custom was created – the historical origins of which as yet unclear – whereby the voivode had a primary, overriding type of ownership right over all the land in the country, akin to Grotius' *dominus eminens* (supreme lordship) according to some jurists. This allowed him to distribute vacant or poorly managed lands to whomever he wished, to inherit lands or houses left behind by heirless owners, or to seize the property of treacherous boyars. This recognised right was a powerful means of putting pressure on boyars great and small, and was the cause of a constant renewal among the noble classes. The only limit to these arbitrary decisions was the risk of rebellion by the major

Charter of Alexander II dating from 1575, by which the voivode of Wallachia was confirming minister Stoico's ownership of the village of Bucovul, with its mills and orchards.

boyar parties, who either took up arms against the ruling voivode, or conspired against him from exile in Constantinople, Hungary or Poland, from where they often returned with military support.

The role of the Church

Perhaps it would have been more appropriate to discuss the role of the Church within the state before that of the boyars, yet in the context of our three countries, nobility has always been closer to power than the Church. To begin with, our first high-ranking clergymen were Greeks appointed by the Patriarch of Constantinople, as had been the case in Bulgaria and Russia. Later on, when we began to elect our own metropolitans, they hailed from the ranks of the nobility for a long time, because in medieval society the Church was an important way of both attaining and exercising power.

Ceremonial Orthodox object made of hammered silver, which was then filigreed and gilded. It was commissioned in 1457 by Stephen the Great, who bestowed it on Putna Monastery.

The establishment of monasteries and sketes long preceded political entities throughout the area inhabited by Romanians; we have proof of a monastic life in Transylvania, Wallachia and Moldavia long before the creation of voivodeships. Centuries later, documents are in abundance – especially organisational records and charters recording grants to the larger monasteries. Voivodes and boyars stumbled over each other in their generosity towards the Church – both out of religious fervour and for the absolution of sins. The documents even reveal endowments made by foreign rulers, such as Lazar of Serbia or Sigismund of Hungary, while our voivodes increasingly supported monasteries across the Orthodox world, especially those on Mount Athos in Greece, as one by one Orthodox princes began to disappear – Bulgarian tsars, Serbian and Greek despots, and of course, the Byzantine emperor.

The Orthodox Church of the Dormition in Strei, Hunedoara County, built in the late 13th century or early 14th century in a hybrid Romano-Gothic style.

In Wallachia, as I noted earlier in the account of the incident that occurred during Nicolae Alexandru's reign, we have a metropolitan (Romanian: *mitropolit*) at Argeș since 1359. In Moldavia too we have the seat of a metropolitan, but this followed the voivodes as they moved

The church of Snagov Monastery on a postcard from the inter-war period. The monastery, which housed a printing press and even a mint, was built during the last years of Mircea the Elder's reign and later renovated and extended by his successors.

their capital over time. This is symbolic for the strong ties between the voivode and metropolitan, following a Byzantine tradition that came to be known as "caesaro-papism", or the idea that secular power would always come before the authority of the Church, especially when conflicts arose. Such quarrels did occur between Wallachian or Moldavian voivodes and their metropolitans, the monasteries on Mount Athos and even the Patriarch in Constantinople – and it was always the will of the rulers that prevailed.

The lower clergy, especially in the rural areas, came almost entirely from the peasantry, and more often than not lacked dogmatic knowledge. However, in both Wallachia and Moldavia, it was in the great monasteries that cultural activity was concentrated – the creation and copying of illuminated manuscripts, some of real artistic beauty, and later on, Romanian translations of the Bible and other religious works, as well as embroidery and mural painting schools. For centuries, those who sought prayer and spiritual peace found shelter in the monasteries, far from the turmoil and horrors of the world.

The free peasants

Yet another social category was that of the free peasants who owned their own land. In Wallachia they were called *moșneni*, an ancient word that comes from the pre-Roman layer in our language, related to *moș* (which is Romanian for "old man" and also exists in Albanian). In Moldavia, the same people were called *răzeși*, the origins of which are still uncertain. First, it was believed it came from the Hungarian *reszes*, but that word has quite a different meaning and some linguists doubt it would have resulted in *răzeș* in Romanian; some found a Polish origin for it, others a Turkish one, and others one in Latin (from the root *rază*, Romanian for radius). I wonder though, since it denominates an archaic layer of rural society, whether it too could possibly have an

Charter of Gavril Movilă, voivode of Wallachia (1618-1620) by which he exempted the inhabitants of the village of Livezeni from paying taxes.

ancient local root, like the word *moșnean*. The matter is yet to be resolved.

The *răzeși* and *moșneni* were free men, owners of small farms worked by an extended family that allotted the land to its members each year. This type of organisation was unique to the Romanians, different from the Serbian *zadruga* or other structures found in Slavic peoples. Some of the oldest documents referring to these people reveal that the first known ancestor of a community had in fact held the rank of boyar. In time, however, their status had reverted to that of free landholders.

As the tribute to the Ottoman Turks grew over time, so did the tax burden on the peasant masses, whose condition worsened even further; during the 16th and 17th century, many were forced to sell their lands to a boyar, thus ending up on the same level as the serfs.

Small wooden vessel used for drinking water (Romanian: căuș*) from Transylvania. The handle of this item has been beautifully carved and decorated.*

The serfs

Lower down in the social hierarchy came the serfs – peasants who had fallen into the possession of a boyar or a monastery, and had to work on their lands to earn a living. They were called *rumâni* and did not own any land, but their masters had to let them work as much of it as they were able to manage.

The fact that the ethnonym *romanus*, which evolved into *rumân* in our language, came to mean landless peasant, I believe can only have one explanation: that when the Vlachs and Slavs began to mix, the Vlachs, who were coming out of their thick woods or the mountains to settle the more fertile valleys settled by the Slavs, were regarded by the latter as landless labourers, and so the social meaning of *rumân* and *rumânie* (almost synonymous with "serf" and "serfdom") was able to survive for centuries alongside the ethnic one. The fact that Romanians were called Vlachs in all Slavonic documents proves that the term had a primarily ethnic connotation. Of course, not all Vlachs became *rumâni*. The oldest communities of *răzeși* and *moșneni* were made up of free peasants, and court documents show they were even referred to as "boyars" when called before a judge as witnesses.

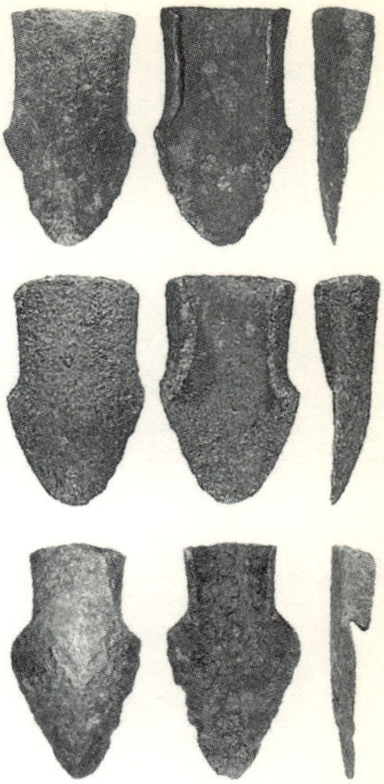

Medieval plough blades found in Dobruja

At the other end of the Roman world, in medieval France, we find a similar phenomenon – but with opposite results in the vocabulary. The ethnonym *francus*, of the Germanic people that became dominant in Gaul (the Franks) came to mean "free" – which in turn means that serfs were predominantly Gallo-Roman; it also meant "exempt from tax", hence all the towns called Villefranche, which were free from taxes – the equivalent of our towns called Slobozia, as the old Romanian word for "free" was *slobod* (a word of Slavic origin) and not the Latin-derived *liber*, which is a neologism from the 19th century (the Latin word *libertare* had led to *iertare* in Romanian, which means "forgiveness"). The term "franc" also entered our language two centuries ago, with the meaning of "honest" or "straight-talking".

In Moldavia, serfs were more often called vecini (today meaning "neighbour") a word coming from Late Latin and which meant a peasant living on a *latifundium*, a large villa estate.

The Gypsies

Starting with the late 14th century, an even more deprived social category emerged, made up of people who had no land, no houses and no freedom of movement – in a word, slaves. These were the Gypsies (Romanian: *ţigani*).

We can trace their exodus back hundreds of years and thousands of kilometres away. They were originally a tribe from northwest India, who could no longer bear the caste regime they had been subjected to by the upper classes. They were probably part of the Pariah caste, which members of the superior castes were not even supposed to touch – coincidentally (or perhaps not) their name appears as *aţigani* in our earliest documents, a word which was probably derived from the Greek verb *athinganoi*, which meant "untouchables".

The Gypsies wandered through the Middle East, expelled from one place to another, fighting the Persians and the Turks until they reached Europe and the Byzantine

Group of Gypsies before the gates of Bern, in the 15th century. The miniature is from an illustrated manuscript by Swiss chronicler Diebold Schilling the Elder.

Empire after being driven out of Asia Minor by the Ottomans. They did not get a respite there either; by the 14th century, the empire had been reduced to continental Greece and a strip of land roughly corresponding to modern European Turkey and Southern Bulgaria – a region that was actually called Románia, as the Byzantines, professing to be the successors of the Roman Empire for a thousand years, called themselves *Romiói*.

It was from their stay in Románia that the Gypsies got their name of "Romani". They arrived in our country in small groups, and as they crossed the Danube, our boyars and voivodes, who always needed more labourers, promptly enslaved them. They became slaves without any rights and were scattered across the boyars' estates, doing all sorts of household chores and trades; others were given to monasteries, while the "luckiest" few became slaves to the voivodes, looking for gold in rivers among other things – these became known as the *aurari* (from the Romanian *aur* – gold). Boyars allowed some of their Gypsies to roam the land freely and perform

"Walachia, Serbia, Bulgaria" and… "Romania", meaning the south of modern Bulgaria and the European part of Turkey (Rumelia) depicted in a Dutch map from 1650

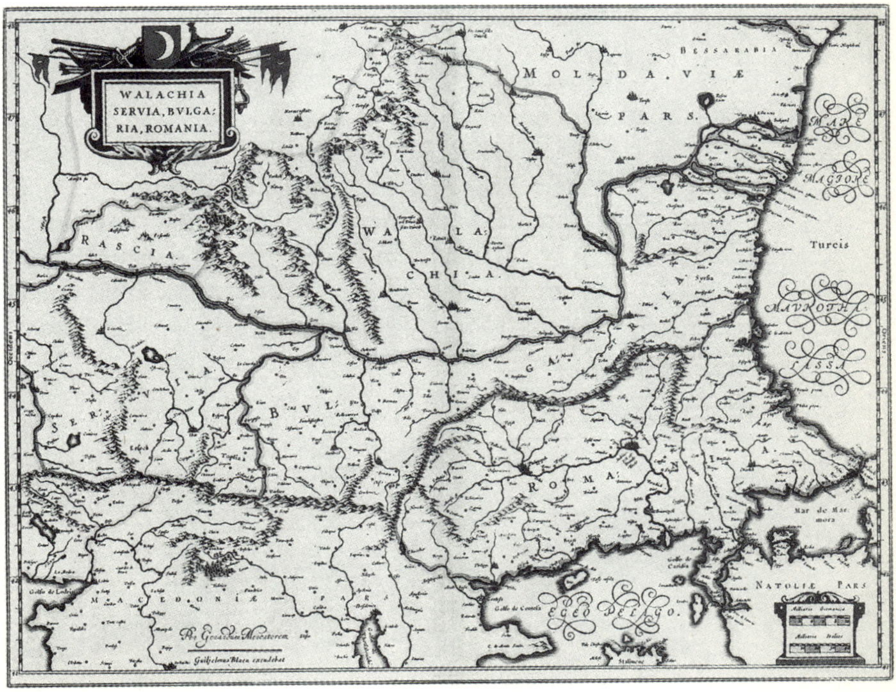

their trades, as they were extremely adept at metalworking. They were only supposed to return to their masters once a year, to be counted and arrange marriages. Small groups of free Gypsies survived for centuries in the thickest woods, but were so desperately poor and primitive that they were called *netoți* – fools. In Moldavia, Tatar slaves built their settlements close to Gypsy villages and sometimes mixed with them, so that over time only physical appearance set them apart.

The army

The army, or *oaste* in old Romanian (from Latin *hostis* – enemy) was raised by the voivode, who would call to arms the boyars, great and small, and all free peasants who were able to arm themselves as cavalrymen – which does not mean that boyars did not have serfs among their troops. This was more or less the "standing army", which the voivode could assemble quickly. However, when the greatest danger loomed, such as a Turkish invasion numbering "as many as leaves and blades of grass" as the old folk ballads go, the voivode would assemble the Great Army – or what we now call a general mobilisation – which meant every man capable of bearing arms. The burghers were on hand in case of emergency and usually were the first to answer the country's call to arms. Towns appeared at the same time as our two Danubian voivodeships, and sometimes even before their "dismounting". The first to establish them after the Roman towns ceased to exist were the Saxons, in Transylvania.

Bombard from the early 15th century

Ever interested as they were in new opportunities for commerce, the Saxons crossed the Carpathians over to Wallachia and Moldavia, apparently on their own initiative. That is how Câmpulung in Wallachia and Baia in Moldavia were founded, for example; Romanians promptly populated these towns, but the initial organisation was German. They had a sort of mayor (German: *Bürgermeister*; Romanian: *staroste*) who could be Saxon, Hungarian or Romanian, and we can still find Catholic churches from that time. As it turns out, we were not very far from having a Saxon urban population in the two voivodeships, as was the case in Transylvania.

As I mentioned before, towns sprung up along the main trade routes that crossed our country, from the Danube and Black Sea towards Hungary and Poland, and further on to Central and Western Europe. They also appeared as a result of local trade, as the population grew and the sparsely populated South-Eastern regions of both Danubian voivodeships got more and more inhabitants. Our towns began to prosper and, in the beginning, our

The Bastion of Taylors, part of the fortifications of Cluj, which were maintained by the guilds. This 1890 photograph shows the condition of the structure, built in 1475. Across the mountains, in Moldavia and Wallachia, craftsmen never had a chance to build or even maintain fortifications.

Leeuwendaalder *(Dutch for "lion thaler") minted in the Low Countries in 1576. During the following century, this was the most widely circulated silver coin in our principalities. Because the field bore a lion rampant, Romanians simply called these coins "lions" (Romanian:* lei*) which is what they would continue to call their national currency from 1867 onwards.*

voivodes grew rich – that is, until the Turks took our ports on the Danube and the Black Sea.

At that time, trade routes between Asia and Europe passed through our lands because trading in the Mediterranean had become too hazardous since the Arabs had conquered its entire Southern shore in the 8th century, and especially after the Turks destroyed the Byzantine Empire and occupied half of the Northern shore. Merchants consequently switched to land and river routes, starting from the Black Sea ports and inland into central Europe; some of the main stops on this route were Brașov and Sibiu in Transylvania, and Lwów in Poland.

Direct maritime trade between the Orient and Europe would not be resumed until the 16th century, after the Portuguese discovered a route around the Cape of Good Hope, at the Southern tip of Africa; it was the same daring quest that would eventually lead Columbus to the discovery of America. But what precious goods were they trading over such distances? Westerners were mainly after silk, precious stones and spices, especially pepper, which was in such demand in medieval times that it became as good as hard currency – you could buy this many yards of cloth for this many ounces of pepper and so on. In return, countries like England, Flanders, France, Germany and Italy traded weapons, tools, cloth etc.

The arrival of the Turks – which we will discuss shortly – would drain the treasuries of our voivodeships, as our rulers were no longer in a position to collect taxes from the transit of goods through their territories. Our recently established towns, living off the medieval intercontinental trade routes, began their steady decline.

Thaler of Despot Vodă, minted in 1562. During his short reign (1561-1563) the adventurer-voivode, whose real name was Jacob Heraclides, established a minor monetary system made up of golden ducats, silver thalers and dinars.

Remarks on the feudal system

Now is a good time for me to make a few remarks that I feel are essential. You may have read in Romanian history books about the feudal age and the feudal system. However, we must employ these terms carefully to avoid their political connotations. Lately, when we say "feudal age" we are actually referring to the rule of the boyars, which survived well into the 19th century. This is, quite simply, misuse of language.

Synthetic representation of the feudal system in a 13th century miniature: oratores *(those who pray),* bellatores *(those who fight) and* laboratores *(those who work).*

The feudal system was a political regime that emerged in France around the time of Charlemagne's descendants, the Carolingians, in the 9th and 10th centuries, during the never-ending raids of the Saracens (in the south) and Vikings (in the north) when the authority of the king – powerless to protect his subjects – broke down, and part of his political, military and even some financial and judicial prerogatives were ceded to local rulers, such as the Duke of Brittany, the Duke of Burgundy, the Count of Toulouse etc.

We then see France developing into a pyramid-like structure in which state unity is almost extinct or at best feeble, dependent on the loyalty to one man, anointed by God – the king. The one thing that remained was the oath of the *vassal* to his *suzerain* (n.b. not to his "sovereign" – a distinction that is easier to make in French: *suzerain/souverain*).

This system has never existed in our principalities as such. The great boyars never inherited their titles, or the right to collect taxes, or to dispense justice on their estates – not even the Great Ban of Craiova. Only very rarely did Romanian voivodes temporarily grant their boyars (or some monastery they wished to honour) such privileges, and it was estimated that they never covered more than 20% of the country's territory. The highest-

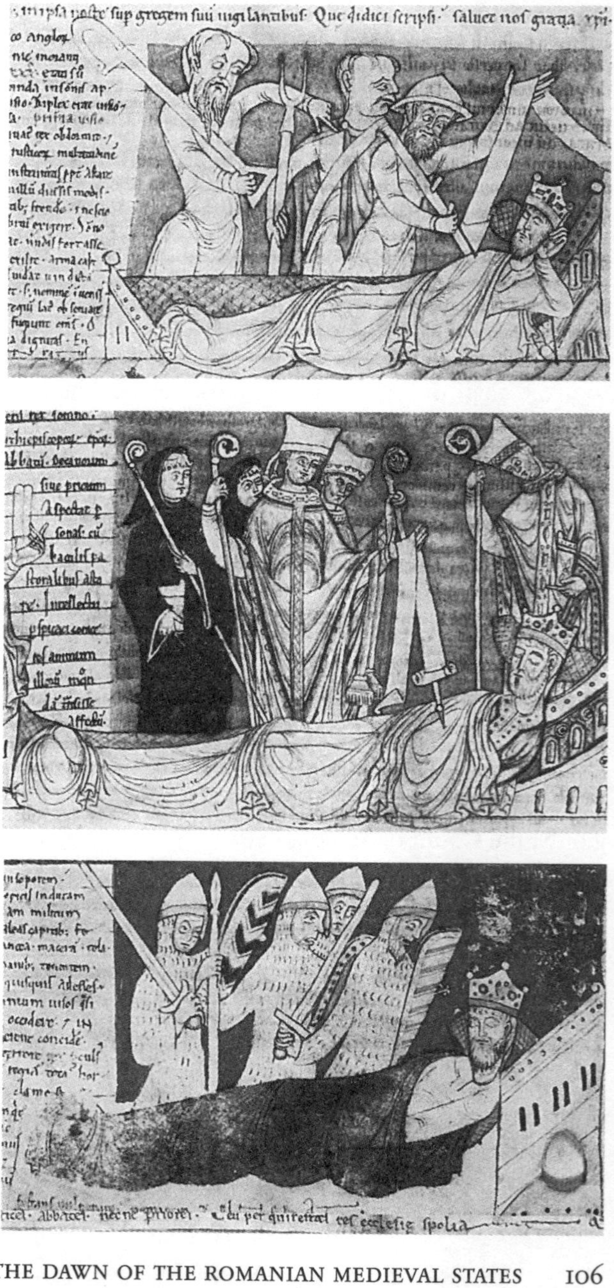

Three sequences making up The Dream of King Henry I of England, which in fact depict the three layers of Western medieval society: those who pray, those who fight and those who work (illustrations from John of Worcester's Chronicon ex chronicis*).*

ranking noble in Wallachia, the Great Ban of Craiova, was never able to pass down his title to his sons – no boyar could do so.

Only at the end of the 15th century and at the beginning of the 16th – but not uninterruptedly – were several generations of the same family appointed Great Ban – subsequently known as the *Craiovești*. It follows that it is incorrect to speak of a feudal system in our past, at least in the sense it had in Western Europe. Our voivodeships made use of a system inherited from the Bulgarians and Byzantium: a powerful nobility (the boyars) which inherited their noble status, but not their titles, and which never formed that pyramid of vassalage through which authority and executive powers were passed down as they were in the West.

If we were ever part of a feudal system, it would be in a wider political context – by virtue of the fact that our voivodes were, intermittently, vassals to the kings of Hungary or the kings of Poland, and thus integrated in a Western-style feudal establishment. But in my opinion, we have never had anything of the kind domestically, so it is better to avoid this term when referring to our country.

Charter of Matei Basarab from 1640, by which he reversed the dedicaton of several monasteries (that is, their submission to Greek monks on Mount Athos). The voivode had risen to the throne from the ranks of the Craiovești boyars, at a time when the office of the Great Ban of Craiova had lost many of the privileges that had previously turned it into the second most important rank in the country, after that of voivode.

Medieval homage ceremony, by which a vassal receives the protection of his suzerain (miniature from the 13th century).

To make matters clear, let us consider the three essential characteristics of Western feudalism and try to identify them in our history:

1. The monarch (whether an emperor, king or duke) had lost some of the prerogatives he had held over his subjects, and was forced by necessity to delegate them to his most important vassals, as he was no longer able to defend the entire country. For example, the king of France was only very rarely in direct contact with his subjects in Brittany, Normandy, Burgundy, Provence or Gascony, who now depended on their respective dukes or counts.

The king was no longer a true sovereign, only a suzerain of his vassals, to which he had ceded almost all his royal prerogatives. A vassal's oath of loyalty was considered sacred, given on one knee, his hands held by those of his master. If the suzerain went to war, his vassals had a duty to provide him with a certain number of knights, servants and provisions that would join the king's private retinue to form the country's army. The authority of the state had thus devolved to a pyramidal structure.

2. The second characteristic (already briefly mentioned) is the surrender of the main royal entitlements, especially the right to raise taxes and administer justice. The suzerain only maintained the right to sit in judgement on appeals and received a relatively low cash allowance. Moreover, his military weakness made the rights

he did keep difficult to enforce, especially the call to arms, which could very well go unpunished.

3. Thirdly, or last but not least, the rule over a domain – large or small – as well as the title that sanctioned it (duke, marquis, count, baron etc.) were hereditary. And as the original reason for the devolution of royal authority had been the inability of the monarch to protect the populace against barbarian raids, each vassal began to build himself one or more castles for that purpose, but not only – he may well have used it to plunder his own subjects or to fight his neighbours in feuds over land or prestige.

Very few traits of the Western feudal system were found in medieval Wallachia and Moldova. Our boyars were very powerful indeed – they owned vast estates, hundreds of serfs and multitudes of servants; they elected the voivode and governed alongside him, they led armies (as *spătari*) and commanded the large border fortresses (as *pârcalabi*) but never did they build castles on their lands, nor passed down titles to their heirs, and so these never became hereditary.

For these reasons I must emphasise again that the term "feudal" should be avoided when talking about Romanian history, as doing so would only amount to politically motivated misuse of language.

Suit of armour of a 15th century knight. The voivodes of Wallachia and Moldavia too would have imported this type of armour at the time, mostly from Transylvania and Italy.

III. ROMANIANS UNDER TURKISH RULE. THE RISE OF OTTOMAN POWER

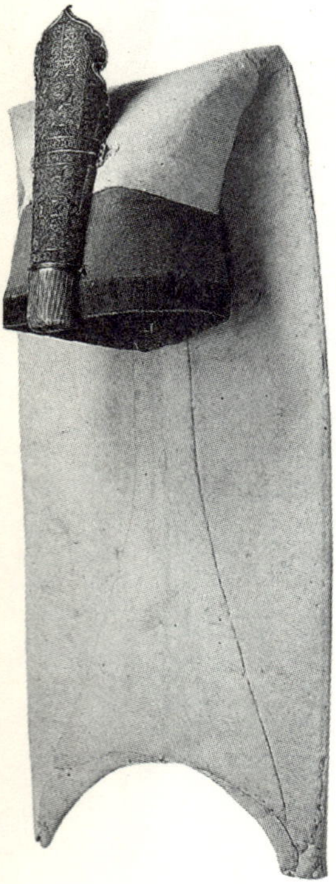

Headgear of a janissary, member of an elite Ottoman infantry corps recruited from war captives and children taken as tribute from Christian peoples, who were then converted to Islam.

The great misfortune that befell our voivodeships was that, precisely at the time when they became sufficiently independent from the Hungarians or the Poles, and began to develop more or less on their own, a new and formidable power arrived on the scene: the Ottoman Turks. A few words about the Ottomans.

I mentioned earlier that the Cumans were a Turkic people, as were the Pechenegs; but between the 11th and the 13th centuries, yet another great Turkic power emerged in Anatolia (present-day Turkey). The Seljuk Turks were close relatives of the Cumans who settled the Northern shores of the Black Sea. When the latter were swept away by the great Mongol wave, to which we have made refeence several times, the state they had founded collapsed, and a new Turkic people, who came to be called the Ottomans (after Osman, one of its founders) appeared in Anatolia, on the territory of the former Byzantine Empire.

But how *did* the Ottoman Turks first arrive in Europe? This is a moment we must remember – for it is a painful one for us, Christians: the first Turks who crossed the Bosphorus were brought over by a Byzantine emperor whose name has an especially pleasant ring to our ears, John VI Cantacuzenus (1341-1355). Internal disputes within the empire – from family feuds to religious unrest – had become so violent that the emperor came to fight his own son-in-law, John Palaeologus, for power. It was for this purpose that he enlisted the help of Ottoman mercenaries from across the Bosphorus. And once they set foot in Europe, the Turks would never leave.

That is how they began to close in on Constantinople, bit by bit, led by sultan Orhan and his descendants.

Such are the consequences of quarrels among Christians. This is a recurring theme in our history – for example, Matthias Corvinus, a great Hungarian king of Romanian ancestry, will be more interested in fighting his European neighbours than to rally his forces against the Turks, while Stephen the Great will never receive the help he was promised by the Poles against the same enemy.

At a time when the Byzantines were fighting each other, powerless before the Ottoman expansion, it was the Serbs who tried to keep the Turks at bay. At the end of the 12th century, the Serbs had created the second largest state in the Balkans, after that of the Bulgarians, under the dynasty of Stefan Nemanja (his son, Saint Sava, later became one of the most revered figures of the Orthodox world). They reached the peak of their power in the 14th century, under Stefan Dušan (1331-1355) a ruler who aspired to the conquest of Constantinople and even crowned himself "emperor" (and so the Serbs too had at least one ruler who called himself by that title). Unfortunately for them, and perhaps for Christendom as well, the Serbian state (which had become quite vast, encompassing present-day Macedonia, Albania and Northern Greece) disintegrated after Dušan's death in 1355 into several principalities, each ruled by a *despot*. The Turkish advance thus found the Serbs divided and weakened.

Ottoman Turk, as depicted in the Nürnberg Chronicle *of 1493*

Battle between crusaders and Seljuk Turks

Marko Kraljević, the legendary son of a Serbian despot. As a vassal of the Ottoman sultan, he fought and died at the battle of Rovine.

One of the great battles of the anti-Ottoman wars took place on 15 June 1389 at Kosovo Polje (a name that means "Blackbird Field"). Despite the fact that a Serb managed to assassinate sultan Murad in his tent, the Turks eventually won the battle and killed Lazar, the Serbian despot. Thus began the Turkish conquest of Serbia.

So impressive was this battle that it spawned into a Serbian *epopee* – a series of epic folk poems of great beauty and one of Europe's most magnificent literary creations: the Kosovo Cycle. But from that point onwards Serbian power was in decline, as some of the despotates which formed Dušan's old Serbia agreed to become Turkish vassals. How baffling the nature of this

Roland, commander of Charlemagne's rearguard and the hero of the Battle of Roncevaux, blowing his horn and trying to break the sword with which he had slain so many Saracens during the Frankish retreat from Spain. The scene is from a 13th century stained glass window of Chartres cathedral.

people: the Serbs were superb warriors, yet once they had sworn allegiance to the Turks, they continued to fight alongside them.

Another famous cycle of folk poems praised the military exploits of Marko Kraljević.

Marko Kraljević – whose surname means "prince" – was the son of a Serbian feudal lord who had fought at Kosovo Polje; nevertheless, Marko swore to obey the sultan and died in the battle of Rovine, fighting the Romanians. Yet he is Serbia's greatest folk hero – which goes to show that people's favour has very little to do with how posterity may judge one's actions and that we cannot always explain why historical figures become folk heroes.

France's great medieval epic poem, the famous *Song of Roland*, tells of heroic deeds during the reign of Charlemagne. We do not know precisely who Roland was – perhaps one of the Frankish emperor's commanders – but the fact is that the great epic focused on him, an unknown quantity, instead of Charlemagne or one of his more famous captains. The same happened in our folk songs from the time of Michael the Brave, which do not sing Michael's praises, but those of *Gruia lui Novac*, a character who left no traces in history, and was probably the son of one of Michael's captains, a Serbian hero named Novak. Let us draw a parallel, however far-fetched, to the popular culture of our time, when people become passionate about a pop star or some actor. It is a question of whom one favours. The great heroes of epic tales are not always those which history deems great captains, kings or emperors, but those who command the love of the people. One such figure is that of Marko Kraljević.

Mircea the Elder

I mentioned earlier that Marko Kraljević was killed at Rovine, but we have not yet talked about what happened there. To do that, I need to leave out the few voivodes who succeeded Basarab and speak about one of his descendents, Mircea the Elder (Romanian: *Mircea cel Bătrân*) – one of the great Wallachian rulers. Why is he called "the Elder"? Because later on there would be other

Our voivodeships after 1389, when Mircea the Elder annexed Dobruja.

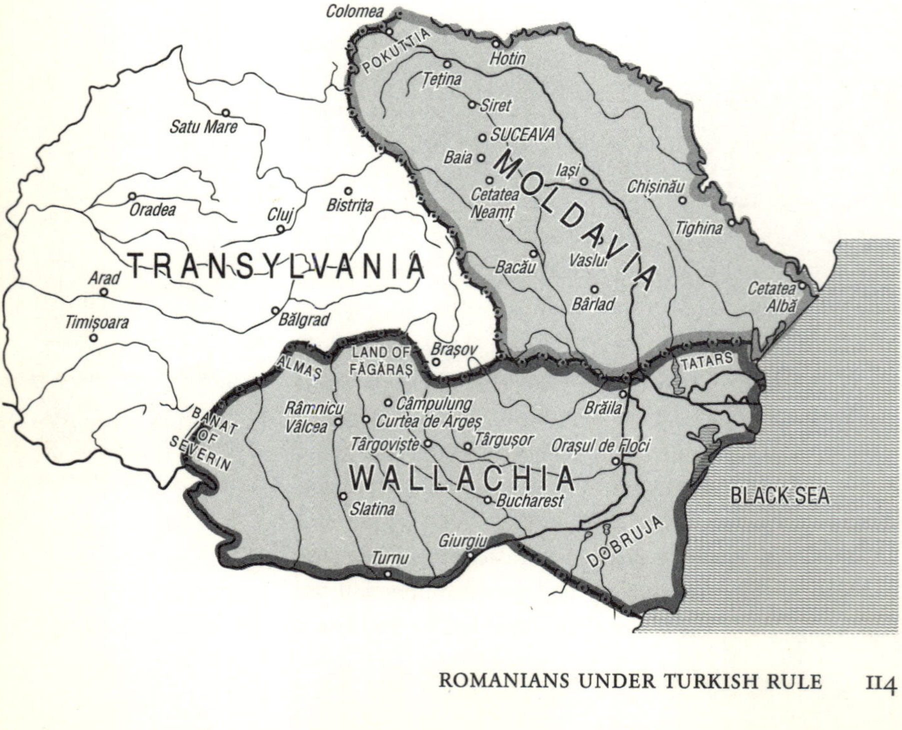

voivodes called Mircea, whom chroniclers wanted to distinguish from the great voivode from the late 14th century. This has mislead even the great Eminescu, who portrayed Mircea as an old man in his poem, when in fact he was still a young voivode at the battle of Rovine. Mircea reigned for 32 years, apart from a hiatus of about 2 years after the great battle, the date of which is controversial: according to a late Serbian source, it took place on 24 October 1394; a more trustworthy contemporary Byzantine source claims it happened on 17 May 1395; one is found at Hilandar Monastery on Mount Athos, the other at Petra Monastery in Constantinople. They mention the deaths of several Serbian magnates, vassals of the sultan, fighting *on the Turkish side* in that battle. Among them were Marko Kraljević and Konstantin Dragaš (father-in-law to the Byzantine emperor Manuel II Palaeologus and maternal grandfather to the last Byzantine emperor, Constantine XI Dragases, who would fall heroically in 1453, during Mehmed II's siege of Constantinople).

Bayezid I, as imagined by a 16th century engraver

In May 1395, Ottoman sultan Bayezid I Yıldırım (the Thunderbolt) who would defeat the Western crusaders the following year at Nicopolis, crossed the Danube and marched against Wallachia. He had come to take revenge on Mircea for having dared to raid his territory south of the Danube the previous spring, in an incursion aimed at destroying a nest of *akıncı* (Turkish brigands that invaded Wallachia periodically) found south of the Balkan Mountains. On 7 March 1395, Mircea had travelled to Brașov to meet with his suzerain, Sigismund of Luxemburg, the king of Hungary and had signed a detailed agreement to support Sigismund's crusade plans, which implied reciprocity in case of an attack on Wallachia. Unfortunately, by May of that year, when Bayezid's great army was pouring over the Danube, the king was forced to remain in Budapest, where his wife Maria was dying after a riding accident. And it was not only concern and heartache that were keeping Sigismund at her side, but also political risks, for it had been her inheritance that brought him the throne. Her demise emboldened those magnates who opposed the king and called for the throne

Sigismund of Luxemburg, king of Hungary (1387-1437) and emperor of the Holy Roman Empire (1433-1437)

Maria, hereditary queen of Hungary. She reigned first as a child (1382-1385) but was then deposed by her kinsman, King Charles II. After his assassination, she ascended to the throne for a second time when she married Sigismund of Luxemburg, who thus became king of Hungary.

to go to Maria's sister, Jadwiga, wife of King Władysław II Jagiełło of Poland. As a result, Sigismund was unable to provide Mircea with any significant support.

Mircea therefore stood alone against Bayezid, and according to a Bulgarian chronicle, the battle that followed was so fierce that "the river [running through the battlefield] turned red with blood". Losses were appalling, but greater on the Turkish side, so Bayezid retreated south of the Danube and rushed to Anatolia, where his realm was facing new threats. The location of the battle has since been known as Rovine, though *no settlement or place bearing that name has ever existed.* It was in fact taken from a Serbian translation of a Byzantine chronicle; the Serbian scribe translated the Greek word *fousato* (Latin: *fossatum*) used in the Byzantine text to describe the location of Mircea's camp as *na rovinah* which meant "among trenches". I believe that Mircea, who was a brilliant strategist, managed to draw the Ottoman army heading towards the capital, Curtea de

Battle of Nicopolis, from a 1540 engraving printed in Nürnberg

Argeș, into a ford of the river Argeș, bordered by thick woodland on either side, where he had dug one or several rows of trenches. These protected several thousand of archers, who wreaked havoc into the ranks of the Turkish host, before the cavalry had even had a chance to join the battle; the enemy was then pursued all the way to the Danube. In effect, it would be more accurate to call it "the battle of the *trenches*".

Bayezid's defeat – acknowledged even by Turkish chronicles as the *Battle of Argeș* – echoed across Europe. Nevertheless, Bayezid had left behind a number of contingents to support the ambitions of one of Mircea's rivals – Vlad, son of Dan, Mircea's older brother. Because of the losses he had suffered, Mircea had to pull back towards the mountains, which led to a bizarre situation, whereby Mircea had to share the rule of Wallachia with Vlad – who appears as voivode in several documents from 1396 – despite his victory against Bayezid. It is unclear how the two rivals divided the country's territory between them (but we do know that Mircea was able to field several thousand cavalry at the Battle of Nicopolis, in September 1396). Then in July 1395, when King Sigismund was finally able to cross the Carpathians and took the fortress of Turnu (also called "Little Nicopolis") aided by Wallachian troops, he was ambushed by Vlad's forces in a pass known as Posada and barely got away. This did not prevent him from taking credit in the West for both the capture of Turnu and for expelling Bayezid across the Danube earlier that year, since that feat had been achieved by his vassal, Mircea. This angered Bayezid, who sent Sigismund an insulting letter – read publicly in Buda on 28 November 1395 – calling the Hungarian king a liar and claiming that he retreated from Wallachia on his own accord, so he could to attend to other matters; finally, he promised he would return and give the king a taste of his power. Which he promptly did in September 1396, when an event of epic proportions took place: the Crusade of Nicopolis. Sigismund of Luxemburg, king of Hungary and future Holy Roman emperor, had lobbied for the support of the powerful Western European nobility, such as those in France and Germany, for many years. Finally, after lengthy negotiations, a great army was assembled in France, led by the son of the duke of Burgundy – the richest and most powerful lord in the West (he was actually referred to as *Le Grand Duc d'Occident*) more powerful than the king of France, because at the time Burgundy controlled much of Flanders (the modern day Low Countries) a technologically advanced country made rich by cloth manufacturing. The Burgundian duke came with thousands of Western knights, and joined the Hungarian army at Nicopolis, on the Danube, in what is today Bulgaria. Mircea was there too, bringing three thousand horsemen to King Sigismund – according to some sources. He was no longer voivode, but still retained the loyalty of his knights. He had fought the Turks before and knew how they could be beaten, and so, before the battle, Mircea advised the war council on how to attack their huge army. Not with a frontal charge, he said – as was the habit of the French knights, who, in their heavy armour, riding heavy war horses, believed they would sweep away everything in their path – but instead using the light cavalry to disperse the levies in the front ranks. Nevertheless, the proud French knights would not listen;

This is what a knight must have looked like in the time of Mircea the Elder (effigy from the tombstone of a German nobleman).

On the left: *Timur Lenk, founder of the Timurid dynasty.* On the right: *Sultan Mehmed I (1413-1421). Both portraits date from the 16th century.*

they arrogantly dismissed Mircea and went on a wild, head-on charge against the Turkish army, which also held the high ground. What followed was a terrible disaster for the Christians: the Turks had placed rows of sharpened stakes in the ground, designed to halt the advance of cavalry; their archers fired volley after volley into the mass of knights, then their infantrymen slid underneath the great horses and cut their hamstrings; finally, wave after wave of horsemen started to pour onto the battlefield. Thousands were taken prisoner. Most were executed that same evening, in revenge for the slaughter of some Turkish captives earlier at Rusciuk, while high-ranking prisoners were kept for ransom. The disastrous failure of this crusade discouraged further attempts by the West to come to the aid of Christian countries in the East – the fault lying solely with the proud French knights.

The only "respite" we got after the tragedy of Nicopolis was due to the rise of another great Turkic conqueror on the Eastern border of the Ottoman Empire (modern Turkestan and Afghanistan): Timur Lenk (or Tamerlane). In the course of a few years, he had become the master of a formidable empire, an unstoppable force resembling that of Genghis Khan, one hundred years before him. Sultan Bayezid, who thought himself invincible, nonetheless decided to wage war on Timur. The great battle

Bayezid I Yıldirim (1389-1402) in an 18th century portrait by a German engraver.

took place near the modern capital of Turkey, Ankara, and it is said to have been a clash of hundreds of thousands; Bayezid was surrounded by his bodyguard unit of Serbian knights, who stood by him until the end, as the battle was eventually lost and Bayezid captured. The sultan was transported to Timur's capital in a cage, where he would perish two years later, in captivity.

Mircea benefited from the demise of Bayezid and the subsequent civil war that broke out between his three sons. It was the first time (and perhaps the last) when a Romanian ruler would intervene on the international political arena and as such, it was quite an exceptional moment. Unfortunately for Mircea, the pretender he backed, Musa Çelebi, reigned for a few years in Adrianople but failed to secure his rule. The victor, Mehmed I, turned against Mircea's son, Michael, whom he defeated and killed in 1420, replacing him with Radu Prasnaglava. The latter was more subdued and surrendered Dobruja and the fortresses on the Danube; it was also during his rule that Wallachia began to pay tribute to the Turks.

However, it is important to note that, at first, the Turks were not as demanding as our former Christian suzerains; they were content with a relatively small tribute and a few dozen stallions (we had beautiful horses back then in Wallachia); at one point, they also wanted to take young boys for the janissary corps, but our voivodes stood their ground, and so we were spared this burden that was imposed for centuries on the Serbs, the Bulgarians, the Greeks and the Albanians.

I also need to mention a little-known, but very interesting aspect: that Mircea and Musa were in fact related. Musa's mother had been the daughter of the Serbian king Lazar, who fell at Kosovo Polje – while Mircea, through his family's kinship with the Bulgarian, Serbian and Bosnian kings (as well as to Hungarian magnate families such as Cillei / Celje) was related to all the neighbouring kings, including Sigismund of Luxemburg, king of Hungary and future emperor. Thus, we find that the bitter rivalry between Christians and Muslims had its limits, and learn that many young prinesses were sacrificed on the altar of state or dynastic interest. Even emperor John Cantacuzenus married one of his daughters to an Ottoman sultan and Tsar Shishman of Bulgaria did the same with his sister. Perhaps some of these princesses, having cried rivers of tears, managed to be happy in their new lives as sultan's wives. There is really no way to know for sure, or else I would be writing novels about it.

Meanwhile, in Moldavia...

As I mentioned earlier, Moldavia was founded about 50 years after Wallachia. Let us again leave out the early rulers to speak of a great voivode and contemporary of Mircea the Elder – Alexander the Good (Romanian: *Alexandru cel Bun*).

Moldavian coat of arms from the bell tower of Saint Demetrius in Suceava, built by Petru Rareș in 1534-1535

Alexander the Good reigned from 1400 to 1432, which was a very long time for that period. He was an able administrator and gradually expanded the country from its original heartland in the north-west, around the capital Suceava and the large town of Baia (in the Middle Ages, *baia* meant "mine", from the Hungarian *bánya*) all the way to the sea. The region was already inhabited by Romanians, but they were not united under one ruler, as they would be in Alexander's Moldavia, which now included the port of Cetatea Albă (literally, the White Citadel; also known in the past by its Turkish name, Akkerman) an ancient Byzantine fortress that had been taken over by Genoese traders. At the time when Moldavia annexed this region, the Genoese still controlled it, but they nevertheless accepted the Moldavian voivode as suzerain. Later on, in the time of Stephen the Great, the Moldavian arms (an auroch's head) would be displayed above one of the gates of the city, where they can still be seen today.

Nevertheless, Alexandru was also a vassal to the king of Poland. We have documents that speak of the circumstances in which he took the oath along with his boyars and not only that, but we have further proof that he fulfilled his duty and took part in two famous battles between the Poles and the Teutonic Order, at Grünwald and Marienburg – both of which the Poles won. After

Alexander the Good, in a 16th century fresco at Sucevița Monastery, celebrating his long and fruitful reign.

their expulsion from Palestine, the Teutonic Knights had settled in the north of Poland and justified their presence there through a religious crusade aiming to convert the Lithuanians (the only remaining pagan people in North-Eastern Europe) to Christianity. Our insult, *liftă păgână* (heathen cur) was originally pronounced *litvă păgână* (literally "heathen Lithuanian") and probably dates from around that time.

The Lithuanians maintained their pagan beliefs until the end of the 14th century; they were excellent soldiers, and under their dukes they had expanded their rule over vast Russian and Ruthenian-speaking territories. Around the year 1350, Lithuania encompassed the modern territories of Lithuania proper, Belarus, central and Eastern Ukraine and huge tracts of Western Russia. It was far bigger than Poland. Through political marriages, the heirless Polish king managed to conclude an alliance with Jogaila (Polish: *Jagiełło*) the newly baptised Grand Duke of Lithuania, who succeeded him to the throne. As a result, around 1390, Poland quadrupled in size through its dynastic union with Lithuania. Over time, however, the Poles (or *leși* as we called them back then, from the name of their ancestors, the Lechite tribes) who had converted earlier and were on a more advanced stage of civilisation, partially assimilated Lithuania and dominated the union.

The common enemy of the Poles and Lithuanians was the Teutonic Order, a religious order of knights who had settled the region known until the Second World

The Battle of Grunwald (15 July 1410) between the Polish-Lithuanian alliance and the Teutonic Knights was one of the largest battles of medieval Europe and the inspiration of countless Polish and Lithuanian legends and patriotic writings.

Ulrich von Jungingen (1360-1410) Grand Master of the Teutonic Knights, was killed in the Battle of Grunwald.

War as East Prussia, cutting Poland off from the Baltic Sea. Alexandru the Good sent a contingent of 400 Moldavian light cavalry to the great battle of Tannenberg (or Grünwald, both names are valid) in 1410 – which may not seem like much, but it was no small feat for the time.

Interestingly, the chronicle says it was those 400 horsemen who decided the fate of the battle by using a military tactic seen in 1205 at Adrianople, where Cuman cavalry in the service of the Asen dynasty defeated an army of French crusaders and captured Baldwin I, the first emperor of the Latin Empire of Constantinople. They charged head on, but just before reaching the enemy they suddenly stopped and feigned retreat, a manoeuvre that the Arabs were using until recently. The armoured knights rushed to pursue them, but as they did so they broke ranks and spread out. Then, just as suddenly as they had fled, our light cavalry turned around again, three or four of them surrounding each knight, slaying them one by one. Thus, 200 years after Adrianople, the same light cavalry tactic tipped the scales of another major battle – yet more evidence that our medieval ancestors had learned the art of war from the Cumans.

Nevertheless, despite supporting the king of Poland again in 1422, Alexander the Good allied himself with Hungary and the Teutonic Order against Poland to gain control of Pokuttia (Romanian: *Pocuția)* a small border territory given by the Polish king to one of Alexander's predecessors in return for a loan of 3,000 silver roubles which had never been paid back. This unfortunate affair will periodically spoil relations between the two states for the next hundred years or so.

But before we speak of Alexander's grandson, Stephen the Great, let us take a look at the other Romanian principality, Transylvania.

The Angevin dynasty in Hungary, the situation of Romanians in Transylvania and Iancu of Hunedoara

First, to get an idea of medieval Transylvania after the Hungarian conquest, you will recall what I mentioned earlier – that the king of Hungary had colonised the new province with Magyars, Székelys and Saxons, since both his own subjects and the Romanians were too spread out and few in number to utilise the land properly.

Over time, the condition of Romanians deteriorated, even more so after the French house of Anjou replaced the Arpadian dynasty. These kings were much too accustomed to the Western feudal system and very loyal to the Pope. From the moment he took power, King Charles Robert, whom Basarab defeated at Posada in 1330, intensified the persecution of Romanians in Transylvania, denying them their noble status unless they converted to Catholicism. This forced many knyaz families to either cross the mountains into Wallachia or Moldavia, or face poverty in their homeland – initially as free peasants, and later on even as serfs. However, some of those who decided to convert did become some of the greatest aristocratic families in Hungary, such as the Drágffy – descended from Voivode Dragoș of Moldavia, whose successors returned to Maramureș after being ousted by the Bogdănești; they remained loyal to the kings of Hungary and even produced a voivode of Transylvania at the end of the 15th century.

Iancu of Hunedoara, Regent-Governor of Hungary, descended from a Romanian family.

There were plenty of other such families, of which I will only mention one illustrious name: the *Corvinești*.

Their story begins with a Romanian knyaz named Voicu, who joined the personal retinue of the king of Hungary and was given the domain of Hunedoara in return for his valour in battle; his son, Iancu of Hunedoara, better known to history by his Hungarian name, János Hunyadi, would become one of the most famous military commanders and anti-Ottoman warriors of his time. A Romanian nobleman by birth, Iancu was appointed voivode of Transylvania, ruling alongside a Croatian magnate called Nicholas of Ilok; after 1444,

Iancu of Hunedoara wearing full battle armour, characteristic of the age (hand painted woodcut from a 1488 edition of János Thuróczi's Chronicle of the Hungarians*)*

following young king Ladislaus' death at the battle of Varna, Iancu rose to the title of Regent-Governor of Hungary.

Iancu was a larger-than-life figure, who led several campaigns against the Ottoman Empire. Unfortunately, he also tasted defeat, as at the battle of Varna. On that occasion, a Christian army had carelessly advanced too deep into Bulgaria, relying on the help of a Venetian fleet, which was supposed to prevent the Turks from crossing the Dardanelles into Europe. But the Venetians were hampered by a counterattack launched by their arch-enemies, the Genoese – yet another example of how internecine conflicts among Christians acted as a principal ally of the Turks in their advance on Europe.

Another ill-fated attempt took place in 1448, when Iancu tried to coordinate his efforts with the struggle of George Kastrioti, known as Skanderbeg, the great hero of Albanian resistance – but was again defeated at the second battle of Kosovo.

Iancu, who built the impressive castle of Hunedoara (later extended by his son, King Matthias Corvinus) was such a powerful lord that he could afford to think of the voivodes of Wallachia and Moldavia as his personal clients or protégés. In fact, it appears that Vlad Dracul (father of Vlad Țepeș) could have been assassinated on his orders, as he feared that the Wallachian voivode and might seek reconciliation the Turks. Iancu, as it turns out, could also be quite a ruthless and authoritarian character.

He quarrelled with the Serbian despot, George Branković, denying himself a precious ally against the Turks, not least because of his pro-Catholic zeal.

In 1439, several years before Iancu set off on his anti-Ottoman campaigns, the Council convened by the Pope in Florence had resulted – after intense negotiations – in reconciliation between Catholics and the Greek Orthodox led by the Patriarch of Constantinople and the Byzantine emperor John VIII Palaeologus. It was effectively a formula for union that would put an end to the Great Schism of 1054 (among the signatories was one metropolitan Damian of Moldavia). The emperor, who by that time held but a thin strip of land around the capital and a vague suzerainty over the despotates of Epirus and the Morea, had very high hopes for the union and was convinced it would signal the rise of a great anti-Ottoman coalition. Nonetheless, upon his return home, he encountered such vigorous resistance from the clergy and even the common people that the Union of Florence was stillborn. Violent protests broke out across Constantinople, among chants of "*Better the sultan's turban than the Pope's tiara!*" Fourteen years later, their wish would come true – tragically so – after the city fell to sultan Mehmed II the Conqueror, who allowed his troops to massacre the entire population of the city.

Iancu too was convinced that the Union of Florence would breathe new life into the idea of a crusade. He became an epic figure, famous even in the West. Novels were written about his exploits in the Balkans – in fact it has recently been proven that he was the inspiration

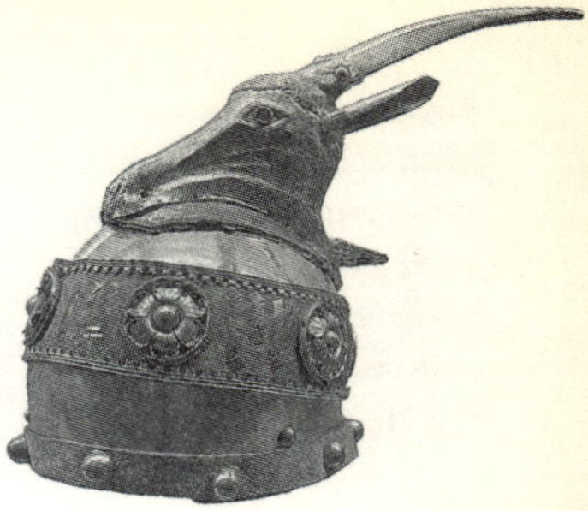

George Kastrioti, known as Skanderbeg (1405-1468) in a 16th century engraving. He is represented without his spectacular helmet seen above.

Matthias Corvinus, son of Iancu of Hunedoara and king of Hungary. To his right is a shield bearing the arms of his family – the raven with a ring in its beak.

De electione dñi comitis mathie in regem.

Cum aūt peregrinis ex relatib⁹fama obit⁹ipsi⁹regis la
dislai in regnū Hūgarie venit:multos ꝯtristauit. maxi
me aūt illos qui eidē rēgi comitis ladislai psuaserāt ne
cē:cū vltores effusi sanguinis ipsi⁹ comitis ladislai eo
audi⁹eo aīosius insurgere : ac inceptā finē ad optatū
pducere vindictā desiderare videbāt. Qđ ꝫ factū fuisset:si,p cō/
ponēdis regni reb⁹:,pq3 eligēdo rege:indicta per totū regnū hū

behind the hero of a very popular 15th century Catalan adventure novel titled Tirant lo Blanch (Tirant the White) which was probably a copying mistake from the original *Blach*, meaning the Vlach.

In 1456, Iancu succeeded in breaking the siege of Belgrade – which was in Hungarian hands at that time – defeating Mehmed II (who had taken Constantinople in 1453) but died of the plague shortly after. Hungary was in turmoil for two years, as the throne remained vacant; finally, owing to Iancu's immense prestige, his second son Matthias was elected king at only 15 years of age. He was to become the great king Matthias Corvinus (Romanian: *Matei Corvin*) who reigned between 1458 and 1490; he got the nickname Corvinus because of the raven on his coat of arms (Latin: *corvus*) linked to a family legend.

We will revisit King Matthias after a brief look at the situation of Transylvania around the time of his ascension to the throne. Transylvania was made an integral part of the Hungarian kingdom, but retained a special status. An interesting thing, from our point of view, was that the highest rank of the land was that of voivode, which was not a Hungarian title, but a Slavic term that was only applied to the ruler of a country by the Romanians.

The situation of the three privileged social categories (the nobility, the Saxons and the Székelys) had not changed from the previous century; however, that of the peasants had become deplorable because of the endless wars that had ruined the economy.

Peasants, whether Romanian or Hungarian, became serfs (Romanian: *iobagi*, from the Hungarian word for "serf") on the lands of Hungarian nobles or the Church. Together they rebelled against the aristocracy in 1437 and held out at Bobâlna for several months in a fortified camp organised in the manner of the Hussite rebellion in Bohemia; they were eventually defeated, and their situation only worsened.

Before long, Hungarian nobles, Saxon burghers and Székelys would set up a formal alliance named *Unio Trium Natiorum* (Latin for "Union of Three Nations") that lasted for centuries. Yet the word "nation" carried a different meaning than it does today. *Natio* in those days meant a kind of privileged social category; in Transylvania, the "nations" meant the Saxon towns and their surrounding villages, the Székely counties in the Carpathians and all the lands of the Hungarian nobility.

Meanwhile, Romanians were treated as a politically insignificant entity, despite making up the majority of the population. A notable exception was Iancu of Hunedoara, a Romanian who did accede to the highest possible ranks and whose son became king of Hungary – but one must not forget he was already a Catholic, and that his wife was a Hungarian noblewoman.

We will speak of King Matthias again, once we have mentioned some of his contemporary voivodes.

Sultan Mehmed II and Patriarch Gennadius II, shepherd of all Christians in the Ottoman Empire, shown on a mosaic inside the Ecumenical Patriarchy of Constantinople. The two seem to display a gracious, conciliatory manner.

Vlad Dracul and Vlad Țepeș

Coat of arms on a commemorative plaque from 1483, confirmed to be that of the Order of the Dragon

As I stated from the outset, the purpose of this book is not to list all the voivodes squabbling for the throne throughout our history. We will only look at the most significant rulers.

Mircea the Elder (also rightfully called "the Great") had many sons, of whom I will only mention Vlad II Dracul, father of Vlad Țepeș. But why was he called "Dracul" (meaning "the Devil" in modern Romanian)? It was not to compare him to Satan or because he was unpopular with his subjects. He was called "Dracul" because Sigismund of Luxembourg, king of Hungary, took a liking to this son of Mircea and made him a knight of an order he had founded – the Order of the Dragon. The reign of King Sigismund had been relatively favourable to us Romanians, not least because he did not persecute the Orthodox in Transylvania – a liberal ruler for his time, we could say, although it was the Council that he assembled at Constance that condemned the Czech reformer Jan Hus and burned him at the stake.

It was a time when many such "orders" sprang up all over Europe: first, the Order of the Garter, created by the king of England and still in existence today; this was soon copied by the king of France – after all, we are in the middle of the Hundred Years' War. They were a kind of exclusive club, a guard of honour made up of great lords whom the king trusted and who swore loyalty to him until death. King Sigismund created the Order of the Dragon at a time when his hold on the throne was weak and he was still uncertain of victory over other pretenders. It was made up almost entirely of Hungarian magnates* loyal to Sigismund and only three foreigners: the despot of Serbia, a prince of Ruthenia and Vlad.

Vlad was so proud of this knighthood that when he became voivode of Wallachia he had the Order's

* The Late Latin word *magnate* was used for the great nobility of Hungary and Poland, who enjoyed enormous wealth and privileges. Their counterparts in Wallachia and Moldavia were the great boyars.

Three portraits of Vlad Țepeș, which we owe to his terrible reputation among the Saxons: the one on the left is from a 1488 engraving; the middle one, from a 1491 German engraving; the third dates from the early 16th century.

emblem – a dragon – minted onto coins and used as his personal seal. The people therefore called him "Dracul", which meant "the Dragon" at the time. That is the origin of the name Dracula or Drăculea given to him and his sons, and that is how Vlad Țepeș became known to foreigners as Dracula.

I will not dwell on Vlad II too much, even though he too was an interesting character. He reigned twice and made war on the Turks, but bent the knee before them when it was in the country's best interest – leading to his assassination at the orders of Iancu of Hunedoara.

A more important historical figure – and unfortunately, also one of myth – was his son Vlad III, nicknamed "Țepeș" (the Impaler) because of his habit of impaling his enemies and anyone who disobeyed him. It is said that shortly after he came to the throne in 1456, he ordered that all cripples, thieves and beggars in Târgoviște be assembled in a great hall, where he threw them a big feast, only to have the place boarded up and set alight with everyone still inside. He simply impaled rebellious or disobeying boyars.

Impalement was a truly horrifying ordeal: first, a long sharpened stake would be driven into the ground, or a young tree would be stripped of its branches, sharpened and then greased; next came the most terrible part: the condemned would very slowly be lowered into the stake, which penetrated the anus and exited close to the head, missing the heart and the vital organs to avoid instant death; the victim took days to die, their eyes

Forest of stakes at Târgoviște (German engraving from 1500, printed in Strasbourg)

gouged out by ravens. It was a barbaric execution method that made Vlad infamous across Europe, and rumour went that he had impaled thousands upon thousands of people.

Having said that, we must remember that the 15th century had been marked by cruelty and atrocities all over Europe; for example, in 1415, the English and the French fought at the battle of Agincourt (well, let us say it was more of a feudal clash between two French royal dynasties rather than one between two nations; incidentally, if you ever get a chance to see the 1944 film *Henry V* starring Sir Laurence Olivier, which depicts this battle, I advise you not to miss it – to me, it is the most magnificent cinematic rendering of a medieval battle ever made). The English were winning and took around

6,000 prisoners whom they intended to ransom, as was the medieval chivalric custom of the time, but rumours came that the French were regrouping and about to counterattack. King Henry V, fearing that the prisoners would join in and strike at his lines from the rear, gave the order for them to be slaughtered, and thus 6,000 heads duly rolled onto that field. This is why the horrors attributed to Vlad Țepeș must be seen in the wider historical context.

As soon as Vlad became voivode in 1456, he decided to get rid of the Ottoman yoke. He had spent many years in Turkey, where he served as a hostage to ensure his father's loyalty. He was well-versed in the language and vices of the Turks, and counted on the help of Matthias Corvinus, king of Hungary, to whom he was also related through his wife (a cousin of Matthias; it is unclear whether she was a Corvinus or a Szilágy). Vlad stopped paying the annual tribute (Turkish: *haraç*) crossed the Danube and launched a terrible raid through Bulgaria; in 1462, the conqueror of Constantinople himself, sultan Mehmed II, led a punitive campaign against Vlad and Wallachia. Vlad Țepeș and his small army faced the Turks alone, as in the end he received no assistance from King Matthias. One night Vlad personally commanded a daring raid into the Ottoman camp, but failed to find the sultan's tent and kill him. He then retreated to the mountains, using scorched earth tactics as he went. The sultan was horrified by the macabre spectacle that lay before him on the way to the capital Târgoviște: a forest of stakes onto which thousands of Turks captured in battle the year before had been impaled. A Turkish chronicler speaks of the sultan's horror, but also mentions his sense of admiration for a ruler capable of such acts.

With his great army beset by starvation, Mehmed abandoned the idea of taking the capital, retreated towards Brăila and temporarily relinquished Wallachia. However, he left behind an army corps led by Vlad's brother, Radu the Fair, who within three months was able to persuade the majority of the boyars that Vlad's policies were disastrous for the country, that help from

Siege engines used by the Saxons in the 15th century

The most famous portrait of Vlad Țepeș, displayed at Ambras Castle in Austria

our Christian neighbours was not forthcoming – neither from the Hungarians, nor the Poles, not even from Stephen of Moldavia – and that it was wiser to bend the knee, as his illustrious grandfather, Mircea the Elder, had eventually done. The Turks, he said, would not turn Wallachia into a *pashalık* (an Ottoman province) nor absorb it into the empire, as they had done with all the neighbouring countries to the south, but would be content with an oath of loyalty and the payment of the *haraç*.

Deserted by the boyars, Vlad Țepeș looked for support and sanctuary in Transylvania. But as he had impaled a great many Saxon merchants for disobeying his ban on their "retail trade" in Wallachia, and had actually made terrible incursions towards Brașov and its surroundings, even impaling women and children (which could be the source of the "snake" legend) the Saxons had made him so infamous that King Matthias, instead of providing support, actually imprisoned him in his castles for 12 years. His most famous portrait – a very lifelike depiction found at Ambras castle in Innsbruck, Austria, which to a physiognomist could denote a character of unspeakable cruelty – dates from that period.

In 1476, when King Matthias Corvinus finally chose to wage war on the Turks, he decided he needed the Impaler and put him on the throne in Târgoviște once more. Despite his reinstatement, Vlad was murdered

Vlad Țepeș regained his throne after the Battle of Târgoviște (autumn of 1476) but was later assassinated, probably by Laiotă Basarab's men.

after several weeks in unknown circumstances, probably by boyars who feared retribution.

Thus ended the reign of Vlad Țepeș, a remarkable historical character, infamous throughout the world because of his atrocities. Over time, his negative image became almost a caricature – such as his representation in the late 19th century novel of Irish writer Bram Stoker, *Dracula* (the origin of a string of horror films bearing this name). This caricature is now commercially (and irresponsibly) exploited by modern Romanian regimes.

Laiotă Basarab, also known as Basarab III, portrayed as a Christian voivode at Horezu Monastery. Nevertheless, his religious beliefs did not stop him from allying himself with the Turks to seize the throne.

Vlad's notoriety was built upon three main sources: Turkish chronicles; then a Slavonic tale of unknown origin called *The Tale of Dracula the Warlord* – which in fact portrays him in a positive light – rumoured to have been the favourite book of Russian tsar Ivan the Terrible; but mostly through Saxon manuscripts, apparently spread on purpose throughout Germany by Matthias Corvinus to justify his failure to set out on the crusade for which the Pope had already paid him large sums of money – at least this is the hypothesis proposed by historian Șerban Papacostea, and it is an interesting one. It basically means we could be looking at one of the first cases of "state propaganda" or even a "smear campaign" using the newly invented printing press, which enabled the Saxon scare stories about Vlad to spread wider and faster than ever before.

Other authors, however, use various documents to attribute the first commissioned piece of writing against Vlad Țepeș to a Saxon nobleman with whom he had had a legal dispute – all of which makes it very difficult to tell fact from fiction in the stories about him.

He certainly used impaling on a scale never before seen, which in itself is sufficient to make anyone infamous; but it is also possible that his reputation could mostly be derived from certain eccentricities attributed to him in these stories, such as nailing the turban of a Turkish envoy to his head for failing to remove it before the voivode. Which of these should we believe?

Matthias Corvinus

Matthias Corvinus, king of Hungary (from a 16th century engraving)

Let us now return to Matthias Corvinus. He was one of the greatest kings of Hungary and a true Renaissance ruler, very able and cultivated, who brought scholars and artists from Italy to his court. Domestically, he relied on the lesser nobility against the magnates, who were hostile to him (including his own uncle, Szilágy) and was quite protective of the peasantry.

An ambitious and power-hungry man, Matthias fought for the throne of Bohemia, which would have opened the way to the title of Holy Roman emperor. He made war on the German emperor three times and even occupied Vienna in 1485.

Here I must digress: it is in fact an error to speak of a "German emperor" because until the 19th century the realm was officially named the "Holy Roman Empire of the German Nation". We cannot speak of an "Austrian emperor" – not even under the Habsburgs – before 1807, when Napoleon brought an end to the old European

Battle between the Turks and the Black Army of Matthias Corvinus (from a 16th century engraving)

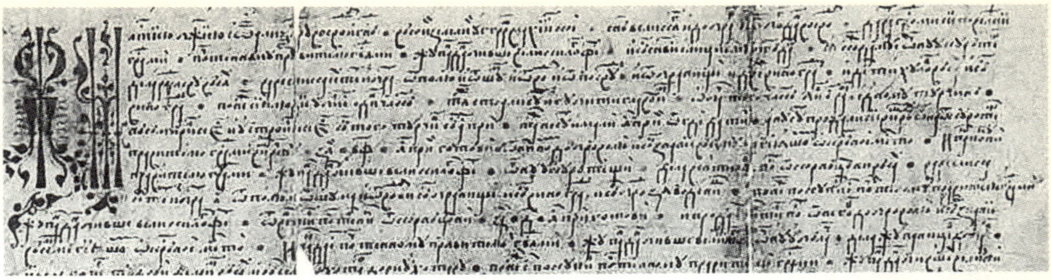

Charter of confirmation issued to the Monastery of Tânganu, built by Radu the Fair. He was the brother of Vlad Țepeș, and ruled twice, between 1462-1473 and 1474-1475.

medieval order, in which there was only *one* emperor in Europe, who, according to protocol, preceded all other European rulers – even at times when the king of France was a more powerful ruler.

Matthias Corvinus wasted his energies in sterile wars against his Western neighbours instead of fighting the Turks. The result was that 36 years after his death, the Hungarian kingdom for which he had such high ambitions crumbled before a single Ottoman attack. The weakness of Hungary after his reign could also be explained through socio-economic causes: following the 1437 Bobâlna uprising, not only had Hungarian feudal society not improved the condition of the peasants, but it had actually made it worse, partly through a constant state of warfare – "modern" warfare, using expensive firearms and trained mercenaries, who cost vast amounts of money – and partly through oppression.

In 1514, a new peasant revolt spread through Transylvania and Hungary, under the leadership of a Székely mercenary called Dózsa György (Romanian: *Gheorghe Doja*). As with previous such revolts, it united peasants of all ethnicities and like previous revolts, it was drowned in blood. The kingdom emerged from the turmoil severely weakened, which resulted in the nobility facing the Turkish attack of 1526 on its own.

Again, note that it can be unwise to pass judgement on history, for in the beginning of Ottoman domination of the Balkans and Central Europe peasants were often less oppressed by taxes and labour duties under the new "pagan" masters than they had been under their Christian feudal lords.

Stephen the Great

Pommel of the sword of Stephen the Great, which bears the title of the voivode: "I, Stephen, voivode of Moldavia".

Let us now look to Moldavia, which in the 15th century produced its greatest historical figure: Stephen the Great (Romanian: *Ștefan cel Mare*).

Stephen III the Great was one of Alexandru the Good's many grandsons. According to the aforementioned custom of the land, the great boyars elected the new voivode from among the sons and grandsons of the previous ruler. Stephen's anointment ended a period of internal struggles for the throne, despite being an illegitimate son of Bogdan II – which made him a more difficult choice. Nevertheless, Stephen had exceptional qualities, demonstrating not only bravery in battle, but also strategic and organisational abilities and, to the benefit of Moldavia and Romanians in general, enjoyed 47 years of rule. It was the longest reign of any ruler before that of King Carol I in modern times; he became voivode in 1457 (a year after Vlad Țepeș in Wallachia) and reigned uninterrupted until 1504. He inherited a nascent country, developing as a result of the trade between central Europe, Poland and the Black Sea ports. Moldavia controlled two such ports – Chilia and Cetatea Albă – whose customs brought in substantial revenues.

Stephen the Great and his third wife, Maria Voichița, dedicating the church of Voroneț Monastery to Christ

Mehmed II the Conqueror (1451-1481) depicted in a 15th century Ottoman miniature

Chilia had belonged to the voivodes of Wallachia, with the consent of Hungary, but Stephen took it from them, attracting the wrath of Matthias Corvinus. Trade revenue made him a rich voivode for such a small country. Yet towards the end of his reign, the loss of the two important fortresses would spell disaster for Moldavia.

It is said that Stephen the Great always fought the Turks, but this is not quite true. He fought all those who sought to rob him of his relative independence. Thus, he fought Matthias Corvinus, who wanted to force him back into vassalage after he took Chilia from the Wallachians; Stephen beat the king of Hungary at Baia and drove him back across the Carpathians.

Later on he would also fight against the Poles. However, it was his battles against the Turks that were forever ingrained in the memory of the people, especially the

gnam inierunt. Fuit aūt auxilium dn̄i cum hungaris: a quorū fa-
cie dux ſcepedictus ſe in fugam conuertit: perſecuti ſuntq; eum
hungari vſq; ad danubium: & ibi pre timore in danubium ſe ia-
ctauit: in quo pre aquaru; vehementia ſuffocatur. Retradit aūt

dn̄s hungaris pannoniam: ſicut tradiderat filijs iſrahel tempo-
re moyſi terram ſeon regis ammorreorū & omnia regna chanaan
in hereditatem. Dum ergo capitancus iſte arpad vtereť ſpecia-
li quadā dignitate in ſcythia: & hanc haberet ipſa generatio con-

Battle of Baia (December 1467). The army of Stephen the Great torched the city and put the invaders to flight. Scene from the Chronicle of the Hungarians (1488), *by János Thuróczi.*

one fought in 1475, when Moldavia was invaded by a great Ottoman army led by Suleiman Pasha, the most prominent Turkish general of the time. Remember, this was happening during the reign of Mehmed II, conqueror of Constantinople, almost the height of power for the Ottomans. Yet Stephen's small army inflicted a crushing defeat upon them at the great battle of Vaslui. His fame spread far and wide: Polish chronicler Jan Długosz called him "the worthiest ruler in all of Europe", while Pope Sixtus IV proclaimed him *Athleta Christi* (Champion of Christ). Sadly, enraged at this defeat, the Turks returned a year later, this time under Mehmed II himself. Moreover, they ordered the Tatars of Crimea and modern Ukraine to attack Moldavia from the east. This resulted in most of Stephen's Bessarabian free peasant troops (the *răzeși*) leaving his army in order to defend their homesteads against the marauding Tatars. Stephen the Great was left with an even smaller army, now only made up of the boyars, their retainers and several burgher contingents. He was defeated at Războieni in 1476 but managed to retreat north, while Mehmed II failed to take his two strongholds at Suceava and Cetatea Neamț (the ruins of which are still visible to this day). After laying waste to the countryside to prevent the Ottomans from re-supplying, Stephen the Great held on to the throne voivode of Moldavia and Mehmed II was forced to retreat.

Following this venture – so to speak – Stephen recognised the need for a settlement with the Turks, but things took a turn for the worse just a few years later, in 1484, when sultan Bayezid II embarked on a new campaign aimed at conquering the two ports I mentioned above, Chilia and Cetatea Albă. Both citadels fell into Turkish hands, probably through betrayal on the part of their Genoese inhabitants, who must have realised they were vulnerable under the protection of a minor Christian voivode and decided it was futile to try and resist the Ottoman Empire. The loss of the two Black Sea ports would be a severe blow to Moldavia. Its large towns began to decline, preventing the country from developing in the same way Transylvania did, with castles, a rich merchant class, trade etc. Thus, the year 1484 was a key turning point in the economic and political evolution of the Romanian principalities.

Stephen the Great ruled into old age. Toward the end of his reign, he defeated King Jan I Olbracht of Poland at the battle of Cosmin Forest. Legend says that so many nobles of the Polish *szlachta** were slaughtered there that blood covered the entire field, which the prisoners were then made to plough (it appears this is what actually happened). And so it becomes evident why – even in the days of Stephen the Great – the voivode and his council of ministers were coming to a bitter realisation: that they would never get any real help from Christian kings; that the Turks were far away and promised protection against other enemies; that they did not come to our country to build mosques; that they allowed us to keep our autonomy, our system of government, our boyars and our churches; and that we should submit to the Turks and pay them an annual tribute. At first the tribute was symbolic, both in Wallachia and Moldavia, but it began to increase soon enough, as the Turkish advance into Europe came to a halt, lucrative conquests dwindled and the empire needed more and more money.

Bayezid II (1481-1512)

* Generic name given to the Polish nobility; in this context, the army corps made up by the nobles and their retinues.

Lithurgic standard of Stephen the Great, a very fine Byzantine embroidery depicting Saint George, military saint and patron of the Moldavian army

The Ottoman Empire grew with astonishing speed, reaching its greatest extent during the first half of the 16th century: by 1517 the Ottomans had conquered Syria and Egypt, then Arabia, North Africa up to the Moroccan border and even Hungary, under Suleiman the Magnificent (1520-1566). Over time, however, these overexploited conquests stopped being "profitable" and became a burden. That is why the Romanian principalities, with their fertile land and numerous herds of sheep and cattle, became indispensable to the imperial treasury, and especially to the food supply of the capital Constantinople.

Another myth about Stephen the Great is that he built a church every year, or after each victory – because we have 47 churches left from him. Most of the beautiful monasteries of Bukovina (Romanian: *Bucovina*) were built under his patronage, but what makes them special are the exterior paintings, dating from the reign of one of his sons, Petru Rareș.

Stephen was succeeded by his legitimate son, Bogdan III, whom he had imposed on the boyars from his deathbed, beheading a few who opposed it in the process. Bogdan III was nicknamed "the One-Eyed" (Romanian: *Chiorul*) after losing an eye in a battle against the Tatars. He was not an outstanding voivode, but not a bad one either; he ruled for 17 years and accepted Turkish suzerainty.

It is from his time that we have the anecdote about chancellor Tăutu in Constantinople. Contrary to a Turkish legend seeking to explain the origin of the old Turkish name of Moldavia (which is *Bo dan*) the voivode did not make the journey himself, but sent chancellor Tăutu, his foremost boyar, to represent him paying the tribute, as a sign of submission. The anecdote tells of Tăutu burning his throat with hot coffee after drinking it quickly, like a shot of *țuică* (a strong Romanian spirit prepared from plums). Nevertheless, the legend is somewhat inaccurate – since we know coffee had not yet reached Europe until later that century – but our boyar may have had some other hot drink similar to it.

Tombstone of Stephen the Great from Putna Monastery. The inscription says: "I, most worshipful Stephen, by the grace of God voivode of Moldavia, son of Voivode Bogdan and builder of this holy place, have moved to my eternal resting place in the month of … of year 7…, having reigned for … years". The date of his death is not legible, but we have it from a tombstone cover commissioned by his son Bogdan III: "… moved to this eternal resting place on the fourth hour of the second day of the month of July, year 7012 [1504]".

Petru Rareș

Bogdan III's reign was followed by the brief rule of his son, and then, in 1527, the boyars elected Petru IV Rareș, one of Bogdan's stepbrothers and an illegitimate son of Stephen the Great. To the history of Moldavia, he represents one of the last surges of ambition and aspiration for independence. He was an extremely interesting character, but alas, not a sensible one. He fought both the Poles and the Turks, and, as we are about to learn, was actively involved in the conflicts in Transylvania, siding against the faction that favoured the Habsburgs (at that time, the voivode of Moldavia held two powerful strongholds in Transylvania, at Ciceu and Cetatea de Baltă, as well as other domains).

Eventually, in 1538, the illustrious Ottoman sultan Suleiman the Magnificent (or the Lawgiver) himself would come to depose Petru, while using the opportunity to gnaw away at the territory of Moldavia: the Turks occupied all of Budjak (the southeast of the country) and the fortress of Tighina on the river Dniester (which

Stephen III the Great's heirs: Bogdan III the One-Eyed (1504-1517), Stephen IV (1517-1527) and Petru Rareș (1527-1528; 1541-1546) on a fresco from the Church of Saint Nicholas in Dorohoi

Turkish army during a march (16th century woodcut)

they renamed Bender) with its surroundings, and turned them into two new *raya* (directly administered territories of the empire) right in the side of Moldavia. Its voivodes thus came under close and permanent Turkish supervision, as those of Wallachia had been since the establishment of three similar "beach-heads" at Brăila, Giurgiu and Turnu (the future Turnu Măgurele).

Three years later, the restless Petru made peace with the sultan and became voivode for a second time, but it was only five years before he fell victim to a plot of the boyars.

The end of his rule seems to be the end of an era in our history during which, for over 200 years Romanians thoroughly organised themselves internally and stood out internationally. Rulers such as Mircea the Elder, Iancu of Hunedoara, Vlad Țepeș and Stephen the Great were personalities as important as any other in Europe at the time, combining bravery in war with the political ability needed to face three great powers simultaneously. However, during the second half of the 16th century, circumstances became extremely hostile: once the Hungarian kingdom had fallen and the Tatars submitted to the Turks, our principalities were effectively surrounded and paralysed militarily – notwithstanding the short but epic burst that was the reign of Michael the Brave. The effects of these events were compounded by a technical revolution in warfare and the development of firearms, which required resources far beyond those available to smaller countries, as well as the use of professional soldiers, more difficult to recruit in exclusively agricultural regions.

The 14th and 15th centuries remain the greatest period in Romanian history. Eminescu's poetic instinct did not fail him when he chose the battle of Rovine for a splendid depiction in the poem *Epistle III.*

It was Petru Rareș who had the Moldavian monasteries adorned with their wonderful exterior frescoes, of which only about a tenth survive to this day. It was said that they carry a hidden meaning, of resistance against the Turks: let Christians far and wide see what our faith is all about, on the outside of our churches.And on almost all of them we see a particular fresco – the city of Constantinople besieged by the Persians in the year 600,

Somewhat anachronistic depiction of the Siege of Constantinople, dating from 1537, in an exterior mural of Moldovița Monastery

but which actually illustrates the fall of the imperial city to the Ottomans less than a hundred years earlier (the attackers are depicted wearing turbans and shooting cannons). Yet art historians vary in their interpretation of the siege: some believe it is symbolic: Byzantium is the celestial city, which can never fall to the pagans. Others believe it represents the actual fall of Constantinople, by which Rareş intended to remind all Christians how God had punished them for failing to stand united.

Either way, the fact is that some 50 years after it had started, the painting of frescoes ceased completely (possibly as a result of an Ottoman interdiction).

I have not yet mentioned why the Turkish central government was called the "Sublime Porte" (or simply the "Porte"): it was because of a large, artistically decorated gate (*porte* is French for "gate") found at the entrance of the sultan's palace of Topkapı in Constantinople, which no one, not even foreign ambassadors, could pass through without special permission and an accompanying procession; it came to represent the sultan's power in the same way that the "White House" is now regularly used as a metonym for the United States administration, "Downing Street" for the British cabinet, or "Quay d'Orsay" for the French foreign ministry.

A turbulent century for Moldavia

Following the rule of Petru Rareş, Moldavia went through a tumultuous second half of the 16th century, marked by endless fighting between various claimants to the throne and frequent interference by the Porte in the election of voivodes. Worse still, the throne fell into the hands of foreign adventurers who were not "of the blood" of voivodes, such as Jacob Heraclides (better known as Despot Vodă) a character straight out of romantic novels, whose Greek origin is still inconclusive; he studied medicine in Montpellier, in the south of France, and was even granted an audience at the French court; he travelled through Germany, where he became a Protestant, and then Poland; eventually, through foreign intrigue (and

Dinar issued during the reign of Alexandru Lăpuşneanu, voivode of Moldavia

Alexandru Lăpușneanu, twice voivode of Moldavia (1552-1561 and 1564-1568) as depicted in a fresco from Dochiariou Monastery on Mount Athos

mostly Habsburg support) he managed to rule for two years in Moldavia, where he favoured the introduction of Protestantism. In the end, he was overthrown by the Moldavian boyars and accidentally killed during his arrest.

I should also mention Alexander Lăpușneanu, the legitimate son of Bogdan the One-Eyed, who married Ruxandra, a daughter of Petru Rareș, and was the inspiration behind Costache Negruzzi's short novel *Alexandru Lăpușneanu*, the first masterpiece of modern

Romanian prose. He is best known to history for the large number of boyars he put to death to secure his throne, though recent historiography has somewhat tempered the fearsome reputation of Negruzzi's hero, describing him as a pious voivode, a builder of churches and benefactor of monasteries on the Holy Mountain (Mount Athos).

Another name I should mention is that of John III the Terrible (Romanian: *Ioan Vodă cel Cumplit*) who made a heroic but rather unwise attempt to hold off Turkish domination during his short time on the throne (1572-1574) as his resistance was not coordinated with any other similar attempts or anti-Ottoman coalitions. He was an illegitimate child of Ștefăniță, son of Bogdan III the One-Eyed, and his Armenian mistress. Chroniclers (who came mostly from boyar families) called him "the Terrible" because he too had many boyars executed. His last clash with the Turks, somewhere in Southern Moldavia, ended in defeat and capture after some of his boyars betrayed him; John III was put to a horrible death – his limbs tied to camels, which tore his body to pieces.

Copper coin with the effigy of voivode John III the Terrible

At the end of the 16th century, a family of great boyars descended from the Bogdănești on a maternal line came to the throne – the Movilești. They would give no less than seven voivodes to Moldavia (and Wallachia) and represent an interesting moment in our history, both politically and culturally, because of the Western influence they brought with them through their close ties with the great Polish aristocracy.

Thus, a daughter of Ieremia Vodă Movilă (Polish: *Jeremi Mohyła*) married a Polish magnate and later became the grandmother of Polish king Michał Wiśniowiecki; another of his daughters married a Potocki (yet another illustrious name in Poland) and was an ancestor of King Stanisław I Leszczyński, whose daughter Maria became the wife of French king Louis XV – therefore, a drop of Movilă blood flowed through the veins of King Louis XVI, beheaded by French revolutionaries in 1792. Most notably, however, Peter Movilă, son of Simion (voivode of Wallachia in 1601 and brother of Ieremia) became a key personality in the development of modern

Below: Simion Movilă, brother of Ieremia Movilă, twice voivode of Wallachia (1600-1601; 1601-1603) and then of Moldavia (1606-1607). We know what he looked like from a tombstone cover. To the right is Ieremia Movilă, who ruled twice in Moldavia (1595-1600; 1600-1606) and was considered to be the man of the Poles (also depicted on a tombstone cover).

Ukraine. Peter was raised in Jesuit schools in Poland but remained true to the Orthodox faith and went on to become the metropolitan of Kiev (under Polish rule at that time); he would play a pivotal role in the reformation of the Ukrainian Church – not without stiff resistance – as well as the grounding of Orthodox doctrine through his *Catechesis*.

So revered was his name after death, that three cities in modern day Ukraine and Belarus are called Mogilev (the name Movilă would sometimes be pronounced "Moghilă").

Wallachia, from Neagoe Basarab to Peter II Cercel

I briefly mentioned earlier that medieval Wallachia was made up of three regions, each with somewhat different traditions and interests, each with its own boyar factions and their antagonistic policies: 1. The central part, around Argeș, where the power of the Basarab dynasty originated. 2. Oltenia, in the west, which maintained a distinct character throughout our history (could it be the consequence of a more intense Roman colonisation?) 3. Finally, the Eastern counties. At the end of the 15th century, it would be a boyar family from Oltenia who rose to the most prominent positions in the land and held the title of Great Ban of Craiova for three generations – the Craiovești. In 1512, after a few years of internal fighting, two Craiovești brothers contrived to put one of their half-brothers on the throne, Neagoe, thought to be the legitimate son of a Basarab – and as such, is known to history as Neagoe Basarab (do not pronounce his name Neagóe, as if he were I. L. Caragiale's hero in *Domnul Góe!* but Neágoe, the Slavonic form of an authentic Romanian name, Neágu).

Neagoe Basarab, shown as an apprentice of the Patriarch of Constantinople, Nephon II

Votive painting of voivode Neagoe Basarab and his family at Curtea de Argeș Monastery

Neagoe Basarab was a major historical figure – an energetic and highly cultured man, married to Despina Milița (*despina* means "lady" in Greek) a princess descended from the old Branković family of Serbian despots and half-sister of Elena Branković, consort of Petru Rareș of Moldavia. It is fair to mention here that medieval Serbia – which had come into being a few centuries before Wallachia and had received its core of Byzantine culture earlier, as well as a certain Italian influence through its Adriatic coast and proximity to

Venice – had undoubtedly made a significant contribution to the cultural development of Wallachia during its first two centuries of statehood. When Serbia was turned into a pashalık, our relatively wealthy voivodes "repaid" this debt through their eagerness to preserve the Orthodox faith and, for centuries to come, became great builders and patrons of Christian monastic establishments throughout the Balkans and the Holy Land.

Neagoe Basarab is celebrated for two major achievements: 1. The beautiful monastery at Curtea de Argeș, which displays strong Oriental decorative influences, consecrated in the presence of several high-ranking clerics of the Orthodox churches and considered one of the wonders of the East in its heyday. The monastery was overzealously restored during the reign of King Carol I, which somewhat dampened its charm, especially since the old monk cells and surrounding structures were replaced by new buildings of a different style than that of the church; finally, the old murals from the time of Neagoe Basarab were replaced with modern portraits of King Carol and Queen Elisabeta). 2. The book he wrote for his son Teodosie, known as *The Teachings of Neagoe Basarab*, a priceless document on the morals, vices and institutions of the time, containing advice written in a hesychastic* style.

There is evidence that Neagoe would have liked to take up the struggle against the Turks with help from the West. However, he died a young man, too young to even begin realising his plans, as did his son, Teodosie, whose succession he failed to secure.

Neagoe's son-in-law, Radu Vodă of Afumați, led another daring attempt at resistance against the Ottomans. His grave can be seen inside the Princely Church at Curtea de Argeș, where all his battles and victories are listed – though they were ultimately in vain, for Radu too fell victim to a faction of boyars who believed that, under the circumstances, resisting the Turks would ultimately

Tombstone of Radu V of Afumați, who reigned four times between 1522 and 1529, when he fell victim to a boyar plot. The inscription makes mention of his battles against the Turks and ends with the words: "God has granted me a realm and a sceptre, I was clad in purple and girded with a studded belt, crowned with honour, riches and glory, surrounded by my host. I have come to the help of many and spread mercy to all, and now I lie in a small grave, waiting to hear the voice of the Archangel, the last of all clarions, resurrection of the world, redeeming of souls, and I pray that those to whom God shall grant my succession shall keep this eternal resting place and abode of my bones untouched."

* Hesychasm is a tradition of prayer in the Eastern Orthodox Church which preaches introspection and ignoring the senses.

Petru Cercel, on a fresco in Căluiu Monastery

spell disaster for the country. He was murdered in a church by two boyars who also happened to be his kinsmen.

The following period coincided with the collapse of the Hungarian kingdom and the peak of Ottoman power. It goes without saying that any hopes of independence our voivodeships may have nurtured were entirely unrealistic; apart from the Moldavia's short border with Poland, our lands were surrounded on all sides by Ottoman territories: Hungary was reduced to a pashalık, as were Serbia, Bulgaria and the Banat; to the north, Transylvania was a Turkish dependency, while to the east, the Tatars of the Budjak and Crimea were Turkish vassals.

This context enabled the Turks to interfere more and more often in the succession of our voivodes, making Wallachia's internal wrangling appear trivial. Nevertheless, let us recall the names of some rulers: Mihnea I the Wicked, Mihnea II Turcitul*, Mircea V the Shepherd and his wife Lady Chiajna – who, between themselves, put so many boyars to death (as Alexander Lăpușneanu had done in Moldavia) that for a while our historians believed that the medieval boyar class of both principalities had been virtually exterminated by the 17th century, and that those who came after were an entirely new set of people. That, however, is an exaggerated view – as in fact there was some continuity among the class of great boyars.

A voivode who made a better impression was Pătrașcu the Good, who ruled several times and is known to history as the alleged father of two interesting voivodes – each in his own way – Peter II Cercel and Michael the Brave.

Peter II was nicknamed "Cercel" (which means "earring" in Romanian) because of his taste for earrings, a look he picked up while in exile at the highly refined and luxurious court of French king Henry III, where he was seeking support for his ambitions of gaining the Wallachian throne. The king of France – who was an ally of Turkey against the house of Austria since the time of

* Literally meaning "the one who turned Turk".

Francis I and sultan Suleiman the Magnificent – intervened with the sultan in Peter's favour. Even so, Peter II had only been on the throne for two years, when he was deposed by the same man he had replaced – Mihnea II – in 1585. It is said he was planning to build a beautiful palace at Târgoviște (where he had moved the capital) and introduce Western customs to the country (apparently influenced by the Italian secretary who accompanied him). Peter II Cercel was a fascinating character and a true romantic hero; he died in a shipwreck in the Aegean Sea.

Peter's half-brother was none other than Michael the Brave, but before we speak of him, let us take a brief look at Transylvania during the 16th century, where major changes had occurred.

16th century Transylvania in the aftermath of the Mohács disaster

Two unrelated events that happened in the first half of the 16th century would have highly significant consequences on the situation in Transylvania: the first was the collapse of the Hungarian kingdom after the battle of Mohács, in 1526; the second was the emergence, in 1520, of a religious movement initiated by a German monk named Martin Luther, and which rebelled against Papal authority and the corruption that had taken root in Rome, soon to become known as Protestantism. Spreading at an amazing rate through Christendom, Protestantism would soon spawn a multitude of denominations and doctrines, all of which were considered to be not just schismatic (separated) but downright heretical by both the Catholic and the Orthodox Churches, since it had done away with some of the tenets laid down by the Church Fathers, which are considered essential and untouchable.

Ducat minted in 1539 during the time of John Zápolya, prince of Transylvania. After the disaster at Mohács, the province had a political and diplomatic status similar to those of Moldavia and Wallachia

One of the causes behind the Mohács defeat had been the hesitation (though perhaps we should call it betrayal) of both the ban of Croatia and the voivode of Transylvania, John Zápolya (or Szapolyai, also of Croatian

First Battle of Mohács (1526) shown here in a Turkish miniature, meant the collapse of the Hungarian kingdom. In 1687, at the Second Battle of Mohács, the Turks would be defeated by a coalition of Habsburg and Bavarian troops.

descent) who did not come to the aid of the royal army in time. Hungarian nobles widely opposed the idea of a Habsburg being offered the Hungarian crown, as had been previously agreed between King Louis II of Hungary and Ferdinand of Habsburg, brother of Emperor Charles V (Louis II's brother-in-law). The death of King Louis II on the battlefield immediately sparked the internal struggle for Hungarian succession, undeterred by the fact that the Turks were advancing into the country's heartland; one faction supported Ferdinand, the other John Zápolya – even at the price of Turkish support, which at the time meant vassaldom. A long struggle thus ensued between the partisans of Ferdinand and Zápolya (whom Petru Rareş also joined, as previously mentioned, but only for a while, for he switched sides

John Sigismund Zápolya, king of Hungary and prince of Transylvania, appropriately depicted prostrating before sultan Suleiman I the Magnificent after the Battle of Mohács

and backed Ferdinand, provoking the sultan's punitive campaign of 1538). Eventually, the Turks intervened again in force, in 1541, occupied Buda and turned central Hungary into an Ottoman province. For the next 150 years, Hungary would be divided in three parts: the territory west of Buda, as well as most of Croatia and all of Slovakia down to Satu Mare in Maramureș would come under Habsburg rule; central Hungary and the Banat fell under direct Turkish administration; while Transylvania, Maramureș and Crișana (temporarily called by its Latin name, *Partium*) were to be John Zápolya's fiefdom, and then pass to his son, John II Sigismund – not with the title of king, but as prince of Transylvania, a vassal of the sultan and subjected to tribute, like the voivodes of Wallachia and Moldavia. During the 16th and 17th centuries, the richer, more populous and less exposed Transylvania enjoyed a far better fate than the countries to the south and east of the Carpathians – indeed, as we are about to discover, the international context in fact favoured what we might call moments of political affirmation and cultural blossoming (at least for the three privileged "nations").

Protestantism brings great changes in Europe

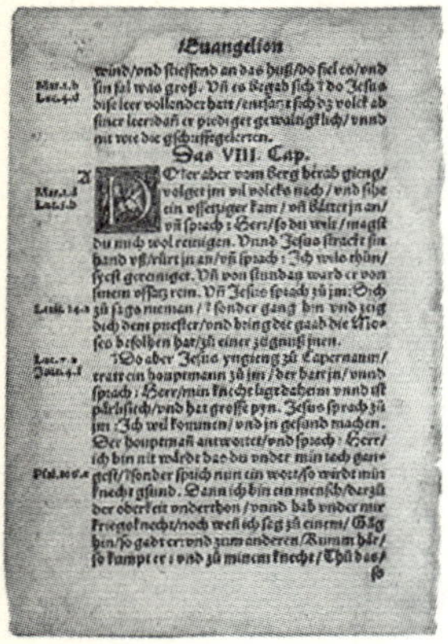
Euangelion

Das VIII. Cap.

Page from the German translation of the Bible, published by Martin Luther in 1529

The second element – the spread of Protestantism – was a pan-European (and later global) phenomenon which, along with Martin Luther's demand for the reformation of the Catholic Church, brought about a new chapter in the history of Western civilisation.

The first effects of the movement initiated by Luther were political; however, as Protestantism began to spread, it caused profound changes in mentality, culture and even the economy, for historians are now able to bring convincing arguments in support of the claim that Protestant mentality has played a crucial part in the rise of capitalism.

From a political standpoint, Protestantism brought more than a hundred years of conflict between Catholics (who still formed the majority) and an ever-growing number of Protestants rebelling against the Papacy's failures across all Western nations – chiefly in Germany and France.

Interestingly (from a historical philosophy perspective) as Western nations became gradually split between Catholicism and Protestantism, it became obvious that most Protestant countries were of Germanic heritage, while the majority of countries that remained Catholic were of Latin heritage. So we could note that ethnicity does carry a certain weight, and makes a definite impact on the cultural and religious choices we make. There were exceptions, of course: in Switzerland, for example, a part of the Francophone population became Protestant, while some regions in Germany, such as Bavaria and the Rhine Valley, remained Catholic; nevertheless, the division between Catholics and Protestants had a predominantly ethnic basis.

Uppercase letters used by Gáspár Heltai (German: Kaspar Helth) at his printing press in Cluj

What happened when Protestantism reached Eastern Europe? At one point, the Poles nearly became Protestants; Bohemia (modern day Czech Republic, where a century earlier the great reformer Jan Hus had been declared a heretic by the council of Konstanz and burned at the stake in 1415, leading to a long civil war with consequences reverberating to our principalities) was the setting for a great struggle between Catholics and Protestants. In Transylvania, the ethnic element would play a vital role. Thus, Lutheranism would prevail amongst the Germans; Calvinism (which emerged in Francophone Switzerland, led by a Frenchman named Jean Calvin) became predominant amid the Székelys, while many of the Hungarian magnates remained Catholic; of course, the great mass of the population were Romanian Orthodox, which means that around the mid-16th century we find four religions (or rather branches of Christianity) in Transylvania. And yet a fifth one began to spread, persecuted in other countries as heretical – *Antitrinitarianism* (or Unitarianism) which rejected the Holy Trinity doctrine. Intriguingly, the state of political confusion led to a lack of constraint, which, at first glance, could pass for an oasis of religious tolerance, where Catholics, Lutherans, Calvinists and Unitarians could live side by side without being forced to change their creed. These four denominations were officially protected, while Orthodox Romanians were merely tolerated in a tacit fashion.

Destruction of icons in Zürich (1524) during a violent anti-Catholic riot. The city was under the sway of Huldrych Zwingli, who, alongside Jean Calvin, was one of the most important leaders of the Reformation in Switzerland.

Chronika az magyarok viselt dolgairól *or* the Chronicle of the Past Deeds of the Hungarians, *a translation and adaptation of Antonio Bonfini's* Rerum Hungaricum Decades. *Heltai was a Saxon, but his work as an editor, writer, typographer and paper manufacturer was mostly in the service of the Hungarians.*

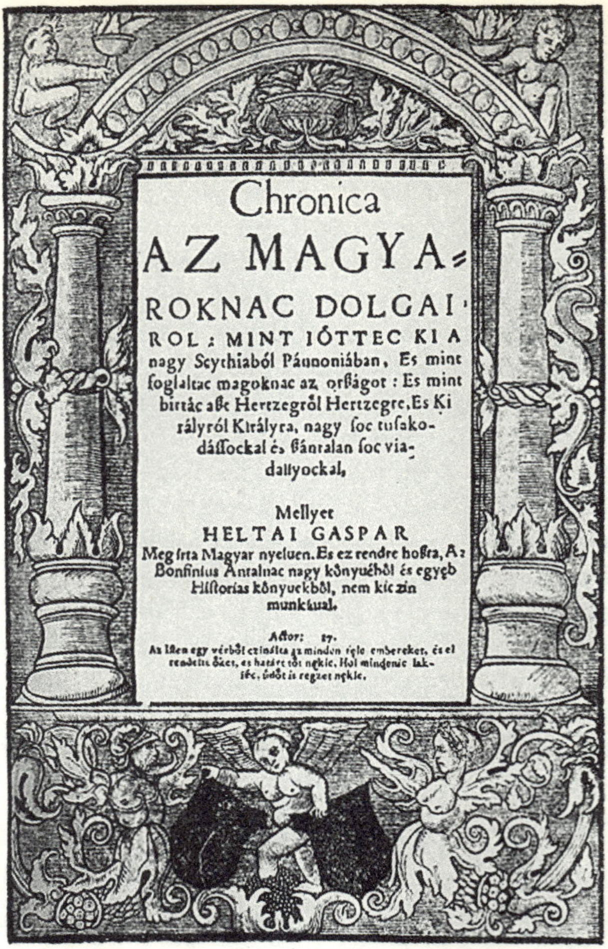
Chronica
AZ MAGYA=
ROKNAC DOLGAI-
ROL: MINT IÓTTEC KI A
nagy Scythiaból Páunoniában, Es mint
ſoglaltac magoknac az orßágot: Es mint
birtác aßt Hertzegről Hertzegre, Es Ki
rályról Királyra, nagy ſoc tuſako-
dáſſockal és ßántalan ſoc via-
dallyockal,

Mellyet
HELTAI GASPAR
Meg írta Magyar nyeluen. Es ez rendre hoßta, Az
Bonfinius Antalnac nagy kőnyuéből és egyéb
Hiſtorias kőnyuekből, nem kic zin
munkáual.

Actor: 17.
Az Iſten egy vérből czinálta az minden féle embereket, és el
rendelte őket, es határt tőt nekic, Hol mindenic lak-
ſéc, üdőt is regzet nekic.

No one paid much attention to them until both the Papacy and the Habsburgs realised that the Romanian Orthodox masses could be used as an ally against Protestantism.

Culture and politics

Together with the introduction of the printing press, the political and religious effervescence that followed the Italian Renaissance so favoured by Matthias Corvinus had a profound effect on cultural life, especially within the German community.One name worthy of mention is that of Johannes Honterus (whose Latinised surname reflects a popular trend in Germany at the time) a very influential German scholar who introduced the Lutheran reformation to Braşov in 1541. The cultural awakening he initiated then spread among the Hungarians, especially in Cluj (Gáspár Heltai).

It was inevitable that such a vast movement would also affect the Romanians, especially as Protestant proselytism became increasingly active. Its influence was indirectly exerted through the printing press, which produced the first translations of religious texts into Romanian. One of the most important reforms brought about by Protestantism was the use of local languages instead of Latin during religious services. That is why German printing houses in Transylvania encouraged Romanians to translate their religious texts from Old Church Slavonic to Romanian. Deacon Coresi (who had begun his printing work in Wallachia) moved to Transylvania, where he enjoyed the support of the German elite and had access to better technology. Soon after, however, Orthodox Church authorities in both Wallachia and Transylvania became alarmed by the subtle heretical interpretations (clearly influenced by Protestant ideas) creeping into Romanian texts as they were being translated. Their fears temporarily slowed the pace of these translations, coinciding with the reign of Lăpuşneanu in Moldavia and its violent reaction to that of the Protestant Jacob Heraclides; this hit not only the Protestants, who were forcibly brought back into the "true faith", but also the important Armenian minority – the motivation here was not only religious (as the Armenian Church is seen as heretical by the Orthodox) but also economic, since the Armenians were very successful merchants.

Nevertheless, it must be said that despite the strong resistance of the Orthodox Church to Protestant ideas appearing in Romanian religious texts, the move towards religious literature in our language continued, and led to magnificent cultural achievements both in Wallachia and Moldavia during the following century.

Page from a Slavonic Gospel Book printed by Coresi in 1562: "At the behest of Hans Berger, I, Deacon Coresi, servant of Christ, and Tudor Diac have laboured to print this book."

Stephen Báthory, prince of Transylvania and king of Hungary

Politically, the liberal thinking influencing Transylvania was (strangely) accompanied by a worsening situation for the peasantry. I have briefly mentioned the great peasant revolt of 1514, led by Gheorghe Doja, who was executed in the most horrendous manner (sat naked on a red-hot iron throne, crowned with a red-hot iron crown) after his defeat. John Zápolya's subsequent repression saw the peasants crushed under even heavier dues in money and labour – even the Székelys – and bound to the land, meaning they were not allowed to move from one master to another. The domination of Hungarian nobility in the provinces became overbearing, as the weakening (and then disintegration) of royal authority removed the last counterweight to its power.

The new assembly of estates was controlled by Hungarian nobles, without the assent of which a new Transylvanian prince was practically unable to govern. The Diet, as it was called, could elect him, but after Hungary had submitted to the suzerainty of the Porte, Transylvanian princes had to be confirmed by the sultan, as in Wallachia and Moldavia.

In fact, we know that, in 1571, Stephen Báthory had been nominated by the Porte even before he was elected by the Diet. He was the third Báthory to come to the throne of Transylvania, with no less than four more to follow.

Let us remember his reign as an attempt to stave off the decline of Catholicism (he brought in the Jesuits, among others) but also for his exceptional election to the throne of Poland in 1576, where he reigned as king until his death in 1586 – leading to a measure of neglect towards the principality.

Suleiman I the Magnificent (1520-1566)

Following the death of Suleiman the Magnificent in 1566, the Ottoman throne was taken up by a succession of mediocre sultans, who, in addition, faced great difficulties on the Eastern border of the empire, in the form of wars with the Persians, who were going through a golden age under Shah Abbas.

With support from the Pope, the new Habsburg emperor Rudolf II (crowned in 1576) decided to take advantage of the situation and formed a new coalition together with Spain, Venice, several Italian duchies and eventually Poland in yet another attempt to expel the Turks from Europe; thus, Transylvania, Moldavia and Wallachia would find themselves on the front lines of the new alliance.

This was the international context that saw the meteoric rise of Michael the Brave (Romanian: *Mihai Viteazu* or *Mihai Bravul*).

Michael and his braves

Wheellock carbine from the late 16th century

Much has been said and is still being said about Michael the Brave, whose legend has grown over the centuries to a point where it can no longer be completely separated from historical truth. That he was a brilliant general and a political genius is undeniable. His victories over the Turks echoed far and wide – King Henry IV of France wrote to his ambassador in Constantinople asking for information on "the Wallachian", while his exploits became the basis of folk ballads across the Balkans, among the Greeks, Bulgarians and Serbs. Yet, paradoxically, Michael was not well loved by the people of his own country. How could this be? Firstly, because his military efforts severely worsened the condition of the peasants. Michael needed a powerful army, and by his time (the end of the 16th century) it was no longer possible to deploy peasant armies – not after cannons and firearms had appeared on the battlefield. You needed mercenaries, professional soldiers who knew how to handle firearms – a phenomenon that also occurred across Western Europe.

Here is just one example: in 1525, Francis I of France fought Charles V, king of Spain (and Holy Roman emperor) at the battle of Pavia. Technically, the battle was a clash between Spain – which, by that time, possessed colonies in the Americas, its fleets of ships returning laden with gold and silver every year – and the kingdom of France, the most populous and united country in

Soldiers from the 16th century, armed with harquebuses. At the time, firearms were the height of military technology for any army.

One of the most famous portraits of Michael the Brave, made in Prague in 1601. Due to its obvious aesthetic values, it became the "canonical" representation of the voivode in Romanian historical iconography.

Europe. Francis I, who was captured during the battle, fielded 25,000 men and faced a Spanish army of equal size. But it is interesting to know who the actual combatants were: as it turns out, the French army consisted of only 5,000 French knights supported by 20,000 Swiss mercenaries, while on the other side, 20,000 German mercenaries made up the bulk of a Spanish army, which included just 5,000 Spanish knights. In a way, one could say that the battle of Pavia was a showdown of sorts between German and Swiss soldiers of fortune.

Michael the Brave waged his wars using the boyars around him, their household troops, as well as some *răzeși* (free peasants) but mostly with mercenaries, unfortunately – and they did not come cheap. We still have all the payrolls, so we know exactly how many Serbian, Albanian, Hungarian or Székely mercenaries he used, and who they were.

As I have already mentioned, Michael was thought to be an illegitimate son of Pătraşcu the Good. Yet, interestingly enough – as several historians have recently proven – his mother, Teodora, was a Cantacuzenus, and as such, a descendant of one of the most illustrious Byzantine families, which produced two emperors in the 14th century. Ruined after the fall of Constantinople, the Cantacuzenes went into hiding for two or three generations after that and reappeared at the beginning of the 16th century in Constantinople; one member in particular stood out: the infamous Michael Cantacuzenus, nicknamed *Şeytanoğlu* (Turkish for "son of Satan") whose sister Teodora is said to have been. Either way, recently discovered documents prove beyond a doubt that she was indeed a Cantacuzenus who had come to Wallachia as a wealthy merchant, and that it was her family's money and influence with the Grand Vizier that secured Michael the Brave's election as voivode.

The coalition of Emperor Rudolf II

Rudolf II (1576-1612) the Holy Roman Emperor in the hands of whom Michael the Brave placed his fate.

By the end of the 16th century, our voivodes were no longer elected by the boyars. The Ottoman sultan could intervene if he so wished, which meant that Michael the Brave was, originally, *his* man, and that of the Greeks in Constantinople; but Michael was an ambitious man and a great strategist, and almost immediately turned against his former protectors. Here I must again refer to the international context: a time of crisis in Constantinople, with border wars in Asia and unpredictable successions to the throne; at the same time, in the Christian world, an emperor in Prague (which was the imperial seat at the time) who decided to take up arms against the Turks and was sending envoys to the prince of Transylvania – yet another Báthory, Sigismund – and to the voivodes of Wallachia (Michael the Brave) and Moldavia (Aaron the Tyrant; Romanian: *Aron Tiranul*) trying to persuade them to join his coalition. Thus, Michael the Brave's incredible story begins at a time when the emperor was setting out on an anti-Ottoman crusade, with support from the Pope.

Sigismund Báthory, prince of Transylvania, and, according to the legend around this portrait, voivode of Wallachia and Moldavia as well

Therefore, the campaigns of Michael and his boyars were not just a reckless attempt to shed the Turkish yoke, which had become heavier and heavier. The empire of the Ottomans had reached is greatest territorial extent and we now know it entered an era of economic decline. For example, inflation caused the Ottoman silver asper (Turkish: *akçe*) to lose its value, or to become devalued, in modern terms. As a result of this, the sultan demanded ever more in tribute from Wallachia and Moldavia – at first, ten times more; then a hundred times more. The social impact was devastating: peasants had to pay such high taxes that there was hardly anything left of the harvest for them to survive on. Extreme poverty led many free peasants – *moșneni* and *răzeși* – to enter serfdom on a boyar's estate to avoid paying the haraç and have someone to protect them, and so the 16th century

Turks building a bridge at Giurgiu before the Battle of Călugăreni, in an engraving by a master of the technique, Theodorus de Bry.

marks the beginning of a very painful historical phenomenon in our principalities, whereby more and more people of the free peasantry became serfs to the great nobility. In the meantime, the great boyars, who were responsible for collecting the tribute, grew poorer themselves and were eager to get rid of the Turks. Michael the Brave's wars cannot be separated from the international context and the severe economical hardships of the time, to which liberation from Ottoman tyranny was the only alternative.

But before he could fight the Turks, Michael had to accommodate the emperor and enter a treaty with the prince of Transylvania. The treaty of 1595 may seem humiliating to us today, in that the prince of Transylvania – the megalomaniac Sigismund Báthory, a young nephew of King Stephen Báthory who called himself *crai*, or king, and had ambitions to reign over the three Romanian voivodeships – effectively became the suzerain of both Wallachia and Moldavia after their boyars signed it. And thus one prince, Sigismund, came to rule in Transylvania, in Moldavia and in Wallachia. People then asked: how could it be that Michael's boyars had signed such a thing? It was treason… either that or they did not know what they were signing. Not at all. They signed the treaty because it was in their interest to do so. The Wallachian delegation consisted of 12 great boyars, the metropolitan and two bishops. The clergymen were interested in Sigismund extending their jurisdiction over the Orthodox in Transylvania, while the boyars used the treaty to request that their voivode could no longer put them to death without permission from the prince of Transylvania – precisely what the *majores terrae* had requested back in 1247, before the dismounting, from the king of Hungary, that is, to be able to appeal to the royal court before his vassal's death sentences were carried out. The treaty also stipulated that "executive" powers, as they are called nowadays, would be shared between the voivode and the 12 ministers of the Sfat.

Therefore, both the clergy and the boyars had a clear vested interest in the treaty, and Michael the Brave had no choice but to accept it, because he needed financial and military support from Báthory. War broke out immediately after the treaty was signed, and the Turks crossed the Danube led by their most famous general, Sinan Pasha. This was when the famous battle of Călugăreni

Battle of Călugăreni, in a contemporary engraving. The medallion, however, shows Sigismund Báthory, who took credit for this victory in the West, as Michael the Brave was, theoretically, his vassal.

Another portrait of Michael the Brave, made by the same engraver who depicted the unfortunate Cardinal Andrew Báthory

Andrew Báthory, beheaded by the Székelys

took place, on 13/23 August 1595*, halfway between Giurgiu and Bucharest. The Romanians found themselves facing the enemy on their own. It was a victory, but, like that of Rovine, it did not expel the enemy from the land. The Turkish army was not completely destroyed and did not retreat across the Danube, which forced Michael the Brave to retreat to the mountains and wait for Sigismund. Báthory arrived with reinforcements and their combined armies, almost equal in size, defeated the Turks three times and threw them across Danube. Naturally, Sigismund took full credit for the victory in the West and returned to Transylvania, not before accepting some changes to the treaty with Wallachia, which Michael had requested – such as relinquishing control of Wallachia's treasury.

The following year, however, the Turks were on the offensive again, this time aiming at central Hungary, where they defeated the imperial armies in the autumn of 1596, forcing the Austrians to temporarily sue for peace. Michael succeeded in doing the same, and was again confirmed as voivode of Wallachia by the sultan, in exchange for paying the tribute. In the meantime, he also signed a new treaty directly with the emperor in 1598, without involving Sigismund Báthory. A fickle and power-hungry character, Sigismund had abdicated because of conflicts with the magnates of Transylvania; he was replaced by one of his cousins, Cardinal Andrew Báthory, who broke with Sigismund's policy and refused to ally himself with Rudolf, Wallachia and Moldavia. He was a friend of the Poles, and they wanted peace with

* Starting from 1582, Pope Gregory XIII introduced a new calendar to replace the Julian calendar (named after Julius Caesar) which, over the course of time, had accumulated a delay of 10 days behind astronomic time. The new calendar, called Gregorian in his honour, added 10 days to the Julian calendar, then 11 days after the year 1700, 12 days after 1800 and 13 days after 1900. Some of the Eastern churches did not accept his reform, even to this day (e.g. the Russian or Serbian churches) while we only adopted it in 1924 (he who is writing these lines is old enough to have lived through the event as a child).

Michael the Brave, in a contemporary engraving by Ioan Orlando

the Turks at the time, so they could fight their wars elsewhere, against the Germans or the Russians. Thus, the Poles made peace with the Turks, ousted Michael's ally, Stephen VIII Răzvan (yet another bastard, the son of a Gypsy man, who was probably responsible for introducing the Iranian name Rezvan, the equivalent of the Archangel Gabriel, to our country) and placed Ieremia Movilă, a client of the Polish king, on the throne of Moldavia. For this reason, Michael crossed the mountains in October 1599 and defeated Prince Andrew Báthory at Şelimbăr, near Sibiu. It is interesting to note that it was Székely mercenaries who captured and beheaded the cardinal. Here I will digress and emphasise that it is a mistake to look at the past from a modern perspective. If conflicts nowadays are largely ethnicity-related, back in the 16th century they were more likely to have a social cause (serfs against nobles etc.) or a religious one. As we have already seen, Reformation had effectively transformed the whole of Catholic Europe into a vast battleground between Catholics and Protestants – in our case, the Székelys had almost entirely converted to Calvinism, whereas their new prince was a Catholic, and a high-ranking one at that: a cardinal. But above all, the foremost reason for their hatred towards Andrew Báthory was the fact that, shortly after coming to the throne, he had reinstated some of the heavy taxes that his predecessor had waived.

That is why those Székely peasants sided with Michael against Báthory, whose slaying had not been ordered by the Wallachian voivode. According to a chronicle, as the triumphant Székelys were presenting Michael with Báthory's bloodied head, Michael was said to have exclaimed "*Poor priest...*"

Michael, ruler of Transylvania and Moldavia

Widely known seal of Michael the Brave, from the year 1600. For the first time, the heraldic emblem of a Romanian voivode incorporated the coat of arms of Moldavia, Wallachia and Transylvania.

After his conquest of Transylvania, Michael the Brave favoured the Orthodox Romanians, and especially their clergy, but it was not long before this had to change. To govern the province, he needed the support of the Diet, which was dominated by the Hungarian nobility. He even had to punish the peasants who had revolted. Consequently, when he entered Alba Iulia in a triumph, the Diet recognised him as the emperor's representative (Latin: *locum tenens*) though Michael called himself "Voivode of Wallachia and Transylvania" in his Romanian (or rather, Slavonic) official documents. It is difficult to imagine how things would have evolved had Michael's rule lasted. The fact is that he was influenced by the Wallachian boyars, who were probably feeling more secure in Transylvania and had started to covet the fortunes and privileges enjoyed by the local magnates (Hungarian: *gróf*) which would later attract the hostility of the Hungarian nobility. During his short reign over Transylvania, Michael tried to achieve a subtle balance between the various forces and tendencies in the province, which included a rapprochement towards the Catholic clerical courts and a preference for Lutherans of all Protestants.

In the meantime, the situation was changing fast. Concerned about news he had received of a Polish plan to overthrow him in his own country, Wallachia, and put Simion Movilă (brother of the Moldavian voivode) on the throne, Michael swiftly crossed the mountains into Moldavia (in May 1600) and drove away Voivode Ieremia Movilă. And thus, for a few months, Michael the Brave ruled that province too; the coins he minted during that time proclaimed him voivode of Wallachia, Transylvania and Moldavia. It was the first time that all Romanians were united under the same ruler.

This was but an ephemeral achievement. In Transylvania, the Hungarian magnates began to revolt, Polish forces invaded Moldavia (led by one of the illustrious figures in their history, Grand Hetman Jan Zamoyski) and put the garrison Michael had left there to flight; therefore, Moldavia was lost after a mere few months.

Michael the Brave's ephemeral union of the three Romanian principalities in the year 1600

At the same time, Michael was defeated at the unfortunate battle of Mirăslău (in September 1600) which cost him Transylvania. By late autumn of that year, he was no longer voivode of Wallachia either, where the Poles had managed to impose Simion Movilă upon the throne. At that point, Michael travelled to Prague himself, in a desperate attempt to persuade the emperor that he was the more capable ally.

It is from that time that we have the image of Michael the Brave – found in an allegorical painting by Francken the Younger, a renowned Flemish painter who happened to be working in Rudolph II's palace at the time. Francken wanted to depict the emperor as King Croesus of ancient Greek legends, showing his riches to Solon; close by is a character clad in armour, of whom we know is Michael the Brave, alongside his beautiful daughter Florica, who had accompanied her father to Prague. The emperor again pledged his support and ordered General Giorgio Basta, an Albanian who commanded the imperial army, to ally himself with Michael and take back Transylvania from the Hungarians, who

Battle of Gorăslău (3 August 1601) won by Michael the Brave. The voivode did not have a chance to take advantage of this victory, as he was assassinated by his Walloon mercenaries shortly after the battle.

King Croesus Showing His Riches to Solon *(painting by Francken the Younger, of the Flemish school)*

had asked Sigismund Báthory to return. Basta and Michael the Brave were victorious in a new battle, at Gorăslău (August 3, 1601) but Basta decided to assassinate Michael under the pretext that the Wallachian did not agree with his future military plans. Basta probably

Assassination of Michael the Brave at Câmpia Turzii (engraving from 1703)

wanted the voivodeship of Transylvania for himself. Either way, a few days after the battle (August 19, 1601) he summoned Michael to his tent, behind which several Walloon mercenaries were lying in wait. They killed Michael the Brave, who defended himself with his sword (he was left-handed) but eventually fell, speared by several men and then beheaded. Could the emperor have ordered his demise, thinking he was too ambitious or fearing he would ruin the Habsburg plan to annex Transylvania? This is still unclear.

The head of Michael the Brave was smuggled back to Wallachia by one of his boyars, Radu Florescu, who was apparently his half-brother. It was a tragic end to the story of Michael the Brave. In the meantime, the Buzești brothers, who were the most valiant of Wallachia's great boyars, had ousted Simion Movilă.

But the struggle against the Ottomans was not yet over. The new voivode of Wallachia, Radu Șerban (1602-1610) who called himself "Basarab" because he was descended from a sister of Neagoe Basarab, fought the Turks alongside the Habsburgs for several years, with some success. It was from around this time that we have an episode which seems cut right out of legend, about the chamberlain Stroe Buzescu, who was sent at the head of an army corps to stop a Tatar invasion. Buzescu challenged the Tatar khan to single combat and, after an incredible duel, slew him as his horde fled. Yet our boyar too was seriously injured and taken to Brașov – we can only imagine the difficult conditions, through woods and mountain paths, most likely through the Neajlov Valley – where he died of his infected wounds, which doctors were powerless to do anything about in those days.

Here is something which may seem rather surprising at first: for a long time, Radu Șerban was far more present in the memory of the people than Michael the Brave. Again, we must look at this within the historical context. Michael the Brave was not a popular voivode. As I mentioned before, he had passed a law called "the bondage of Michael the Brave", which forbade peasants to run away from one estate to another, and effectively tied peasants to the land; it also cancelled a ban on boyars hunting down runaway serfs on other estates in order to get them back. The measure served an exclusively economic and fiscal purpose. I should also add that Michael favoured the expansion of the boyars' great estates, at the cost of the free peasantry – having bought dozens of villages for himself, before as well as after becoming voivode. It was because of these reasons that Michael was not well loved and why there was little mention of him during the 17th and 18th centuries. It was not until the 19th century that our brilliant historian Nicolae Bălcescu rediscovered the story of Michael the Brave.

Radu Șerban, a resolute anti-Ottoman fighter. He was a dregător *under Michael the Brave and then ruled Wallachia twice (1602-1610 and June 1611 – September 1611). Below is a detail from one of his charters, issued in 1605, in which he made a donation of 15,000 aspers to Iviron Monastery on Mount Athos.*

IV. A PROLONGED MEDIEVAL AGE IN THE ROMANIAN PRINCIPALITIES

A look at Transylvania in the 17th century

Gabriel Bethlen, a devout Calvinist, ruled as prince of Transylvania (1613-1629) with the blessing of the Turks

After Michael the Brave's brief rule, fighting continued not only between the Turks and the Habsburgs, but also between the various Hungarian factions, some supported by the Austrians and some seeking the help of the Porte. Nevertheless, at a time when the Turks were less present in Europe, some Transylvanian princes managed to hold on to power for longer and even played a part in the politics of central and Western Europe. Of the Hungarian magnate families who gave princes to Transylvania during that time, at least three are worthy of mention: Báthory (whom we have already come across) Bethlen and Rákóczi. The Thirty Years' War, which began in Bohemia in 1618 as a war between Catholics (supported by the emperor) and the Protestant princes, only ended in 1648 after the intervention of Catholic France on the side of the Protestants, in order to curtail Habsburg supremacy in Germany. Prince Gabriel Bethlen, who would rule Transylvania for 16 years, played an important part in the conflict, so that, for a while, his principality appeared as a somewhat significant political entity to Westerners. In the meantime, however, Romanians remained in the shadow of the "Three Nations", even when they served as soldiers; they were allowed to hold

George I Rákóczi, prince of Transylvania (1630-1648). To the right, his son George II Rákóczi, who succeeded him to the throne (1648-1660).

on to their Orthodox faith, but were excluded from political life, apart from the few who had become integrated in the Hungarian nobility.

Of the Rákóczi family, George I and George II ruled one after the other between 1630 and 1660, and both of them maintained very close ties with the voivodes of Wallachia and Moldavia; there was even a short-lived resistance against the Turks under George II Rákóczi, in 1659, joined by Mihnea III of Wallachia and Constantin Șerban of Moldavia. The Turks swiftly restored control by deposing all three voivodes.

The siege of Vienna in 1683 and its aftermath, the Peace of Karlowitz (1699)

Jan Sobieski, king of Poland (1674-1696) and Saviour of Vienna in 1683

An event which happened at end of the 17th century had unexpected consequences for the Balkans: in one of their last bouts of aggression, under a Grand Vizier of the Albanian Köprülü family, the Turks launched a great offensive against the Habsburgs and besieged Vienna in 1683 (the voivodes of Wallachia and Moldavia, Șerban Cantacuzino and George Ducas, were forced to join the Turkish army). But after Polish forces under King Jan Sobieski joined the battle, the Turks were defeated and withdrew. Gradually, the Austrians and their allies – the Poles, the Venetians, and later the Russians – set out on a long but successful counter-offensive (the war lasted

Turkish camp outside the walls of Vienna, in 1683. The battle took place on 12 September 1683 and ended in disaster for the Turks, largely because of the intervention of Jan Sobieski's fearsome Polish cavalry. The commander of the Ottoman forces, Kara Mustafa Pasha, was strangled several months afterwards at the orders of Sultan Mehmed IV.

for 16 years) which ended in 1699 with the Treaty of Karlowitz.

The principal negotiator of this peace treaty was Alexander Mavrocordatos, dragoman of the Porte, a position similar to a foreign affairs minister. He became a prominent character in European politics through his close ties with foreign ambassadors in Constantinople and even corresponded directly with the emperor (who actually made him a count of the Holy Empire, a highly coveted title across Europe). Mavrocordatos managed to persuade each side that the other wanted peace and both eventually agreed to the Treaty of Karlowitz, which was, in fact, disastrous for the Turks: Venice was to keep Morea (the Peloponnese) and part of the Dalmatian coast; Poland got Pokuttia and part of Ukraine; Russia got the Azov; while the Austrians got all of Hungary, Slovenia, part of Croatia and Serbia, as well as Transylvania – after lengthy negotiations with the "estates" in the principality.

For several years now, the dramatic events of the former Yugoslavia have been the centre of attention and the tragedy of Kosovo has led to the intervention of Western Europe and the United States via NATO. In light of this,

I want to emphasise an event of paramount importance which took place 300 years ago during that war: at one point, the imperial armies, having advanced too far into the Balkans, were beaten back several dozen kilometres by a Turkish counter-offensive. In the year 1690, the Serbs, who had dared to help the imperial forces, feared Turkish reprisals; thus, led by Patriarch Arsenije III, they left their ancestral homes by the hundreds of thousands and took refuge behind the Austrian border. This massive displacement became known to the Serbs as the "Great Migration" (estimates range between 200,000 and 500,000

Map of South-Eastern Europe in 1690. The cartographer only completed seven of the sixteen coats of arms on the border, but three of those belong to our principalities: Transylvania, Moldavia and Wallachia (here represented by the lion of Oltenia instead of the eagle).

people; the most accurate record speaks of 37,000 families; but as a Serbian *zadruga*, including the children and grandparents, was more likely to number 10-15 members in those days, not just 5-6 such as a modern day family would, I feel more inclined towards the 500,000 estimate, roughly the same as the population of Wallachia). That was how most of Kosovo and medieval Serbia were left empty. The Austrians colonised some of these refugees in the Banat, to the detriment of Romanians, some in Vojvodina, to the detriment of Hungarians, and some in Croatia, in a region later called Krajina – a move that lies at the origin of many modern conflicts in that part of the Balkans.

The "Union" with Rome

Leopold I (1658-1705) emperor of the Holy Roman Empire

Starting with the 1690's, a major change occurred in Transylvania: the "master" was now in Vienna. The goal of Emperor Rudolf II, set at the time of Michael the Brave, was reached almost 100 years later – that is how long it can take for history to take its course.

Of course, the Austrians could not impose radical changes in their new province. They had to contend with the Diet, dominated by the Hungarian nobility, and they could hardly have hoped to touch the centuries-old privileges enjoyed by the Germans and Székelys. But emperor Leopold, a staunch and militant Catholic, was convinced that the only way to re-establish a Catholic majority in Transylvania (where Protestant Calvinists, Lutherans and Unitarians now dominated) was to bring the Romanian Orthodox under the rule of the Pope. After three years of arduous negotiations in which the Jesuits had played a crucial part, Metropolitan Atanasie, leader of the Romanian Orthodox Church in Transylvania, accepted the 1439 Union of Florence in exchange for a promise of privileges for the Orthodox clergy, equal to those of Catholic priests. That is when the Uniates appeared in Transylvania.

In the beginning, the entire Orthodox Church in the principality converted to Uniatism. However, as years went by, it became clear that the new Austrian rulers were not intending to keep to their commitments, as they still did not dare take on the determined opposition of the "Three Nations". Indeed, all Habsburg policies – not just the union with the Orthodox – met with violent resistance from the now mostly Protestant Hungarian aristocracy, and not just. It all came to a head with the widespread uprising led by prince Francis II Rákóczi, supported by King Louis XIV of France, who, at the time, was fighting the House of Austria in the War of Spanish Succession (the war concluded with the ascension of the French Bourbon dynasty to the throne of Spain, where it is still reigning today). Rákóczi's uprising lasted from 1703 until 1711 and enjoyed widespread support, especially among the Székelys, inspiring poems and a famous march (used by the French composer Berlioz in one of his operas). That year, the majority of Hungarian nobles made peace with the Habsburgs, while Rákóczi himself, accompanied by a group of faithful supporters, chose exile – where he also died.

Atanase Anghel, Romanian Uniate bishop of Alba Iulia until 1713

Inochentie Micu-Klein (1692-1768)

There were some Romanians among prince Rákóczi's partisans, in particular those who opposed the "union" with Rome. To this day, we find Transylvanian families who bear the surname *Curuț* (the nickname given to Rákóczi's partisans, from the Hungarian *kuruc*).

As the Romanians realised that the promises made at the time of the Union were not being fulfilled, a part of the clergy, and eventually, over half of the Uniate Church – encouraged by their brothers in Wallachia and Moldavia, and by the persistent missions of the Russian Church – returned to Orthodoxy, despite the incredibly brutal measures taken by imperial authorities to put and end to this process (however, the fact that the Austrian army then demolished churches and shot its cannons at defenceless villages does not justify the oppression of the Uniates, two centuries later, by Romanian Communists, who forced them to renounce their faith and convert to Orthodoxy; the endless application of the ancient principle of "an eye for an eye" will never lead to progress towards civilisation).

Thus, from that time onwards, there would be two near-equal Romanian Churches in Transylvania: the Uniate Church (also known as the United or Greek

Holy Trinity Cathedral in Blaj, in a postcard from the inter-war period. The Uniate cathedral was commissioned by Inochentie Micu-Klein and completed in 1748 (the two baroque towers were added in 1838).

Catholic Church) and the Orthodox Church. The latter, however, no longer had its own leader (instead being dependent on a Serbian metropolitan) while the Uniates found themselves in a somewhat more favourable situation than the Orthodox. Nevertheless, we must remain objective and admit that, despite the immense pressures exerted upon the Orthodox Church to convert, the effects of the Union on Romanians were ultimately beneficial. Because several decades later, a Uniate bishop called Inochentie Micu-Klein, who had pressed for the rights promised to Romanians and had been exiled to Rome for it, was granted the right to send young priests to study in Rome and Vienna in compensation. And it was these young Uniates who returned enthused by their discoveries, and primarily by the *pride* of being Romanian. Indeed, they were the first to introduce Western elements to the Romanian principalities – the first scholars to write about our history, to compile grammar and produce works of literature and science in the Romanian language. They were all former Uniate students in Rome and other great Western centres of learning. The likes of Petru Maior, Gheorghe Şincai and Samuil Micu-Klein – to mention but a few names, whom you probably know from the history books, which, nonetheless, never make any mention of the fact that they were Greek Catholic – spread the idea of our Latin heritage, of the noble origin of our people, which would become the pivotal idea behind the awakening of our national conscience.

Nowadays, we might point out a flaw in their passion: for a long time, the desire to assert the Latin origin of our language led to excesses of "Latinisation", both in orthography and vocabulary, which created an almost caricatural gap between the spoken language of the people and those trained to produce an artificial language, unfit for authentic literary creation. Fortunately, common sense prevailed in time, and the excesses of the "Latinist School" were all but undone.

The great peasant uprising of 1784

Meanwhile, the situation of Romanian peasants, both Orthodox and Uniates, continued to be deplorable, which led to a great peasant revolt against the ruling Hungarian elite in 1784. Its leaders were three prominent peasants, nicknamed Horia, Cloşca and Crişan. Horia, the more audacious of the three, had repeatedly travelled to Vienna to plead before the emperor Joseph II (the eldest son of empress Maria Theresa, widely regarded as an "enlightened" ruler – a recent notion at that time) and trusted the assurances he had been given regarding the fate of Transylvanian serfs. Yet shortly after, realising they were only empty promises, Horia raised high the banner of rebellion and started a large-scale peasant uprising, attacking manors of the Hungarian magnates. The Austrian army drowned the rebellion in blood.

Joseph II, the emperor who, Transylvanian Romanians hoped, would end the oppression of the Hungarian nobility.

Of the three leaders, Crişan killed himself in his prison cell, while the other two were executed by the breaking wheel – a horrific punishment, which consisted of breaking every bone in one's body using a cartwheel, or just iron rods – in front of thousands of peasants,

Horia and Crișan (to his left, in military uniform)

who were forced to watch what would happen to those who dared rise against the established order. All of this happened during the tenure of baron Samuel von Brukenthal, who, as governor of Transylvania, was charged with keeping the peace (to this day, his priceless art collection can be admired in his beautiful palace in Sibiu).

The public execution of Horia and Cloșca in Alba Iulia, on 28 February 1785

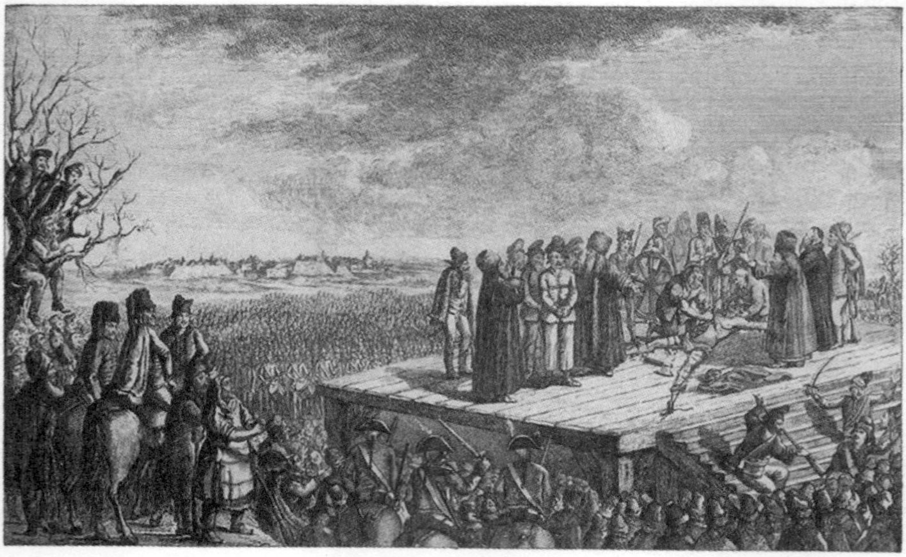

It was on the eve of the French Revolution, when there existed in Europe a liberal movement and a free press – which meant that, for the first time, the "Wallachian revolt" had resounding echoes in the West.

Therefore, at the end of the 18th century, the Romanian peasantry continued to be oppressed – but by that time, a new intellectual class had risen, made up of both Uniates and Orthodox (who had been stimulated by Uniate activity); these Romanian intellectuals began to send protests and demands of greater freedom and equality for Romanians to Vienna. In 1791, they sent emperor Leopold II a petition known as the *Supplex Libellus Valachorum Transsilvaniae*, that is, the "Petition of the Romanians in Transylvania", which presented very clear demands, supported by historical, legal and demographic arguments, most likely influenced by the ideas of the French Revolution. The outcome of the petition was

Samuel von Brukenthal, governor of Transylvania and founder of the homonymous museum in Sibiu

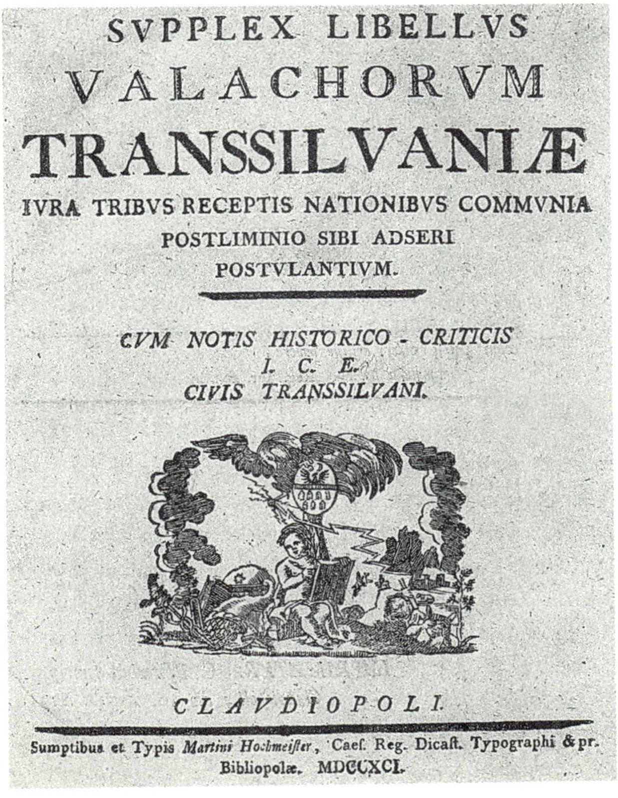

SVPPLEX LIBELLVS
VALACHORVM
TRANSSILVANIÆ
IVRA TRIBVS RECEPTIS NATIONIBVS COMMVNIA
POSTLIMINIO SIBI ADSERI
POSTVLANTIVM.

CVM NOTIS HISTORICO - CRITICIS
I. C. E.
CIVIS TRANSSILVANI.

CLAVDIOPOLI.

Sumptibus et Typis *Martini Hochmeister*, Caes. Reg. Dicast. Typographi & pr. Bibliopolæ. MDCCXCI.

Title page of the Supplex Libellus Valachorum, *printed in Cluj*

not favourable, and the situation of Romanians was very slow to improve. For instance, Greek Catholic priests were (gradually) granted equal rights to the Protestant or Catholic clergy. More and more schools were opened, sending an increasing number of students to the West. So it cannot be said there was no progress over time.

Let us now go back in time nearly two hundred years, to the principalities across the Carpathians, which evolved very differently under the considerably more oppressive rule of the Ottoman Empire.

The 17th century in Wallachia and Moldavia

Mihnea III, voivode of Wallachia (1658-1659)

During the 17th century, Wallachia and Moldavia had no illustrious military leaders. After Radu Şerban, only one voivode, Radu Mihnea III of Wallachia, would dare ally himself to George II Rákóczi, prince of Transylvania, and wage war against the Turks – to no avail. From that point on, our voivodes knew they had to obey; they no longer had a local army, employing only mercenaries. Nevertheless, both countries produced several important cultural figures: Matei Basarab, Şerban Cantacuzino and Constantin Brâncoveanu in Wallachia; and Vasile Lupu in Moldavia.

Matei styled himself "Basarab" because he was descended from the Craioveşti boyars on a maternal line. In fact, he was of house Brâncoveanu, nicknamed Aga Matei of Brâncoveni before becoming a voivode. He was a good soldier, who ruled for a relatively peaceful 21 years, built many new churches and restored older ones. To the misfortune of his country, he spent much of his reign fighting his neighbour to the north, Voivode Vasile Lupu of Moldavia. Descended from an Albanian father who had been made a boyar in Moldavia, he called himself Lupu (Romanian: *the Wolf*) and took the first name Vasile (Romanian for *Basil*) as *Vasileios* meant "royal" in Greek. Thus, his (rather foolish) ambition was to revive the Byzantine Empire. His court was lavish and somewhat arriviste, but his reign conferred a bit of glamour on Moldavia – foreigners were amazed at the Western-style luxuries, jewellery and silverware of its voivode. Unfortunately, his ambition led him to covet the throne of Wallachia for his son, so he could be *de facto* ruler of both principalities; and so, instead of forming an alliance, the two already impoverished countries ended up fighting each other. Vasile Lupu invaded Wallachia several times, but Matei Basarab (aged 70) was victorious at the battle of Finta (1653) the last clash between the two princes; both armies made heavy use of mercenaries, as well as foreign allies – Poles on the Wallachian side, Cossacks on that of Vasile Lupu, who had even wed his daughter Ruxandra to the son of Bogdan Khmelnitsky, Hetman of Ukraine.

Vasile Lupu (1634-1653; 1653)

Matei Basarab's mercenaries – most of whom were Serbs – rebelled over pay during the last year of his reign, killing several high-ranking *dregători* (among them, treasurer Ghinea and Preda Brâncoveanu, commander of the army and grandfather of the future voivode, Constantin Brâncoveanu) and wreaking havoc across the country, proof that the people themselves harboured deep resentment against the regime of the boyars. It took many months and help from George II Rákóczi of Transylvania to put down the rebellion.

Matei Basarab (1632-1654)

What the two voivodes lacked in political clout and military prowess, they made up in cultural development. Their successors followed in their paths, which is why

Cossack troops from the late 17th century, as envisaged by an engraver of the time

the 17th century appears, in retrospect, to be a century of great cultural transformation and remarkable artistic accomplishments.

The cultural advances of the 16th and 17th centuries

The Apostle and Holy God, *from an edition printed in 1683*

Time now to take a break from the flow of events and evoke some aspects of the cultural life in the three principalities.

From the outset, our culture clearly displays two distinct, and sometimes intertwining strands: a folk art with deep ancient roots, and a parallel, more recent element, of Byzantine origin, passed down to us through Slavic intermediaries – mostly Bulgarian and Serbian, but not always so.

When looking at our material culture (clothing, pottery, architecture, songs, legends, poems etc.) specialists find it difficult to establish what the local origins, influences and innovations are – what is part of the local, pre-Roman heritage (for instance, it has been noted that the cut of the *ie*, a traditional women's garment, is the same as that of Dacian women shown on Trajan's Column in Rome); what comes from the Mediterranean culture of the Roman colonists (such as the surprising case of an incantation rhyme, word by word an almost identical version of that quoted by a late Gallo-Roman author); and what the Slavs have given us (as well as what we have given them) – for when it comes to music and national dress, it is most difficult to distinguish precisely how much one gave to the other.

Alongside this local "stock", we get Byzantine and Slavic influences in architecture and religious painting, which make us a part of the late Byzantine civilisation – but not before the 13th century. We would soon put our own stamp on culture, either through pure creation or Gothic additions from the West, and even fleeting Turco-Arabic or Armenian influences (such as can be seen at Curtea de Argeş monastery and Trei Ierarhi Church in Iaşi, respectively). In Wallachia, the predilection towards the classic Byzantine style is more evident – a style which had already emerged by the time of emperor Justinian and the building of his monumental church of Hagia Sofia in Constantinople (turned into a mosque by the Ottomans, now a museum) and which broke completely with the ancient Greek model, whose immortal exponent, to this day, is the Parthenon in Athens, while the new Christian art had its roots in Syria and Iran.

However, in Moldavia, Gothic influences merged beautifully with the Byzantine style from south of the Danube. The same Gothic elements are even more obvious in the little wooden churches of Maramureș, the shingle spires of which soar boldly towards the heavens.

Zodiac from the Gospel Book of Matei Basarab

Church of the Three Hierarchs, built during the reign of Vasile Lupu, seen here in a lithograph from 1845, before the restoration work by French architect André Lecomte du Noüy, nowadays considered to have been unsuccessful.

In literature, local ballads and legends remained oral until the end of the 16th century, while all the written literature was exclusively in Old Slavonic, which, in my view, also had social implications. The printing press brought with it something new – the first religious translations in Romanian. Printing had first been introduced in Wallachia by an illustrious Montenegrin refugee, hieromonk Makarije. But the true pioneer of printing in the Romanian language was deacon Coresi. He and those who came after him were fully aware that they were writing for the Romanian people, for all those who spoke the language – from the Banat in the west, to the Dniester River in the east – and stated it explicitly. Their statements were among the first pieces of evidence that Wallachians, Transylvanians and Moldavians – because they spoke the same language – felt that they were one people, descended from Rome (Old Romanian: *Râm*).

Note this particularity, because it has not been emphasised enough: we are the only large country in Europe whose unity is exclusively based on *language* (in fact, the Romanian word for "language" itself used to be a synonym for "people"). Most other European states were built on the basis of a common historical background, mostly made up of populations speaking different languages and dialects (e.g. France, Spain, Italy, Switzerland, Britain etc.).

Little by little, writings in Romanian began to emerge – at first religious, then historical in nature. The work of Moldavian chroniclers such as Grigore Ureche, Miron and Nicolae Costin, and Ion Neculce, was richer and of superior quality to that in Wallachia, where chronicles remained largely anonymous, known only by their title (e.g. *The Cantacuzene Chronicle* or *The History of Wallachia*). We know very few names, beginning with Goran of Olănești, and later on Radu Popescu and the Greceanu brothers, commissioned to translate the Gospels by Șerban Cantacuzino.

Romanian Book of Learnings *or The Homily of Varlaam, printed in Iași in 1643*

The effects of the Renaissance, a spiritual and artistic movement which was manifested simultaneously in several Western European countries, but primarily in Italy (Tuscany, to be more precise) and the Low Countries during the 14th and 15th centuries – were eventually felt in our principalities too. The initial drive behind the movement had been the enthusiastic rediscovery of classical Greek and Roman culture, spurred on by the multitude of Greek scholars fleeing to the West after the fall of Constantinople in the 15th century.

Its influences came through Matthias Corvinus' Hungary and through Poland, brought over by the Movilești and the young boyars who got to study at Polish universities. A certain Italian influence got through from the Greeks of the islands, who had had centuries of contact with Italy, and even from those of Constantinople, where some of the elite dared send their offspring to study at the University of Padua (a Venetian possession at the time) which was famous for its liberal teachings and popular with Protestants and Orthodox alike – that was also where Alexander Mavrocordatos, the future dragoman, had studied. It was also, for a short while, attended by the future seneschal Constantin Cantacuzino, brother of Voivode Șerban Cantacuzino.

Another traveller, whose journeys took him even further – both west and east – was Nicolae Spătarul (we call him Milescu because that was the name his brother and his descendants took for themselves, while he called himself Spătarul because he had briefly been the army commander, or *spătar*, in Wallachia). Having been suspected of ambitions to rule, he had been marked by the partial cutting of his nose (he was nicknamed *Cârnul*, the snub-nosed) as tradition dictated that severely scarred individuals could not accede to the throne. He took shelter in Russia, where he used his knowledge of languages to build himself a surprising career at the Greco-Slavo-Latin academy founded by Petru Movilă and earned the trust of tsar Michael I to such an extent that he made him ambassador to China, where he was sent along with a great procession. The journey took him years. Nicolae Spătarul returned without having seen the Chinese emperor, because he adamantly refused to comply with the imperial protocol that required him – the envoy of a ruler who thought of himself as equal to that of China – to prostrate himself until his forehead

touched the ground. He did bring back an account of his journey through Siberia and Mongolia, containing an account of Chinese customs, which, to the present day, is one of the most valuable documents we have on China at that time; he is known to Russian historiography only as "Nikolai Spatar", which makes no mention of him being Romanian (or rather, to be completely honest, half Romanian, since his father was Greek, as was that of Constantin Cantacuzino).

The Renaissance left few visible traces in Wallachia and Moldavia: some ornamental elements in architecture, next to nothing in religious painting (as artistic, lay painting did not even exist) and somewhat more profound musical influences (as was the case in Russia). There was no question of influence on literature, since Romanian writings were limited to religious writings or translations of oriental legends, such as *Alexandria* or

Map of Wallachia from 1700, printed in Italy and attributed to Constantin Cantacuzino, the seneschal who studied in Constantinople and Padua

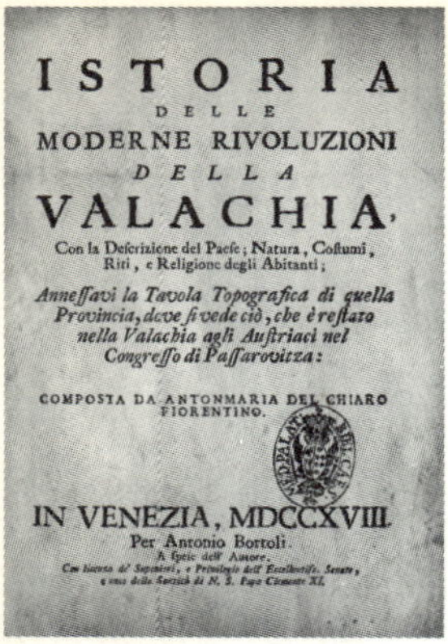
ISTORIA
DELLE
MODERNE RIVOLUZIONI
DELLA
VALACHIA,
Con la Descrizione del Paese; Natura, Costumi, Riti, e Religione degli Abitanti;
Annessavi la Tavola Topografica di quella Provincia, dove si vede ciò, che è restato nella Valachia agli Austriaci nel Congresso di Passarovitza:
COMPOSTA DA ANTONMARIA DEL CHIARO FIORENTINO.
IN VENEZIA, MDCCXVIII.
Per Antonio Bortoli.
A spese dell' Autore.
Con licenza de' Superiori, e Privilegio dell' Eccellentiss. Senato, e [illegible] della Santità di N. S. Papa Clemente XI.

Title page of Antonio-Maria Del Chiaro's Istoria delle moderne rivoluzioni della Valachia, *printed in Venice in 1718. The former Italian secretary of voivode Constantin Brâncoveanu explained what his book was about in the subtitle: "A description of the country and its nature, and of the costumes, traditions and religion of its inhabitants".*

Barlaam and Josaphat. Yet such writings did slowly begin to spread, to the extent that Wallachian and Moldavian voivodes felt the need to establish centres of learning, precursors of the famed late 17th century and early 18th century Princely Schools (in Bucharest and Iași, respectively) which we will mention later on.

In Transylvania, the Renaissance and its late embodiment, the Baroque style, would be considerably more visible both in religious and civil architecture, and not only in Saxon and Hungarian spheres – which was only natural, given the Catholic and Protestant links to the West – but also, over time, in Romanian ones, especially in the new Greek Catholic churches.

However, there was one important obstacle to the spread of Western ideas and art to the east and south of the Carpathians: the ever-increasing intervention of the Ottoman Porte into the daily lives of Romanians, as the threat of the Austrian advance became more evident.

The presence of Westerners at our courts was not well-regarded, and it was virtually forbidden for voivodes and boyars to send their sons to be educated abroad. An account by Antonio del Chiaro, the Italian secretary of Constantin Brâncoveanu, mentioned that as soon as a Westerner arrived to work at the court in Bucharest, he would receive a gift of several yards of cloth to make himself new clothes in the local fashion, so as not to be seen wandering outside in "German dress".

And when a boyar named Colțea, who had been an officer in the army of Charles XII of Sweden, built a fire lookout tower in the middle of Bucharest (close to present day University Square, in front of the hospital which still bears his name) the Turks demanded that the exterior frescoes be erased because they depicted soldiers in Swedish uniforms.

Paradoxically, dress and customs in the Principalities were more influenced by Constantinople from the late 17th century onwards than in the Middle Ages.

The Turks impose foreign rulers on our principalities

Grigore I Ghica (1660-1664; 1672-1673).

As I have mentioned before, as early as the 16th century, Ottoman suzerains had begun to appoint princes in our principalities without the consent of the boyars – that is, without them being "chosen by the country". In the 17th century, this became the norm, and it was how several foreign dynasties ascended to the throne, one of which was assimilated very quickly: the Ghiculești. In 1658, Gheorghe Ghica, an Albanian who had become a boyar in Moldavia under Vasile Lupu (himself of Albanian descent) was imposed on the boyars as their new voivode by Grand Vizier Mehmed Köprülü (himself an Albanian, but a Muslim, while Ghica was a Christian). He ruled for a short time, both in Moldavia and Wallachia, and was succeeded by his son, Grigore I (nicknamed Grigorașcu Vodă); over the next hundred years, more members of this family would rule during the so-called "Phanariote era", of which we will speak shortly, and three more during the 19th century, by which time they had become so assimilated through marriages with Romanian women of the old boyar class, and displayed such patriotic attitudes that they would be considered "native" voivodes, as opposed to the Phanariote rulers.

There were also two voivodes of the Duca family in the 17th century, of obscure Greek origins, and during the 17th and 18th centuries, two of the Rosetti family, descendants of another great house from Constantinople (although, for a while, they were called *Ruset* or *Rusăt* in our principalities, as in *Antonie Vodă Ruset*). I will not burden your memory with more names, but remember that during the 17th century, the Porte could generally afford to appoint voivodes in the Principalities without the agreement of the boyars, so that the beginning of the Phanariote period did not feel like a change of regime.

Antonie Ruset (1675-1678)

But before we speak of that age, we should mention two illustrious native voivodes of Wallachia – Șerban Cantacuzino and Constantin Brâncoveanu – and one of Moldavia – Dimitrie Cantemir.

Şerban Vodă Cantacuzino

Şerban Cantacuzino in a fresco from the Princely Church in Târgovişte

I intentionally called Şerban Cantacuzino a "native" voivode, because his famous Byzantine family had become so well assimilated in our country that it was actually at the head of the boyar faction fighting to contain the influence of "recently arrived" Greek families – while the pro-Greek party was led by the great boyar Gheorghe Băleanu, of actual Romanian origin. It is, however, true that Şerban's father, foreign minister Constantin Cantacuzino (grandson of *Şeytano lu*) had married a daughter of Radu Şerban Basarab, and so his sons felt they were, to some extent, heirs to our voivodes of old.

Constantin Cantacuzino had been a well-respected figure – a minister of great wisdom, held in high esteem by the voivodes he served, especially by Matei Basarab. Unfortunately, having just ascended the throne in 1663, Voivode Grigore I Ghica paid heed to a number of malicious rumours according to which the minister's sons coveted the throne and had the old man strangled. This sparked a bitter, vendetta-style feud between the Cantacuzino and Ghica families. So when he became voivode in 1678, Şerban Cantacuzino took a terrible revenge on the boyars of the Ghica faction (even one of my mother's ancestors, Vâlcu Grădişteanu, was impaled near Snagov monastery at the orders of Şerban Cantacuzino, despite being related to the voivode). Thus, even an enlightened ruler such as him, builder of churches and monasteries, could be terrifying in his wrath (to think that impalement was still in use at the end of the 17th century). Nevertheless, it is fair to say that such horrific practices had survived across Europe: brilliant monarchs like Louis XIV of France employed savage methods both abroad, during his wars in Germany, as well as domestically, against the Protestants.

It was said that Şerban Vodă nurtured hopes of resuming the struggle against the Turks, but it was precisely during his reign (1678-1688) that the Ottoman Empire launched one of its last expansionist efforts and besieged Vienna in 1683 – as we have already mentioned. Şerban

Vodă, along with the voivode of Moldavia and prince Michael I Apafi of Transylvania, had been forced to join the Turkish forces with his small army. Legend says he had his cannonballs filled with straw, so as not to cause too much damage to the besieged Christians; he also raised a stone cross to the Christian dead of the Turkish army. But this was far from open resistance against the Turks. In October 1688, Şerban Cantacuzino died suddenly, and with various rumours surrounding his death.

Battle flag left by Şerban Cantacuzino alongside his stone cross, after the Siege of Vienna in 1683

Of his brothers, seneschal Constantin Cantacuzino became a great scholar (he had studied at Padua) while commander Michael Cantacuzino, after a pilgrimage to Saint Catherine's monastery on Mount Sinai, built the monastery at Sinaia, the construction of which – midway through a heavily wooded, seldom used mountain pass, at an altitude of 1,000m – we might today consider a genuine accomplishment. He also built the Colțea hospital and the church in front of it, where his statue was erected in the 19th century.

Also during the time of Şerban Cantacuzino, a different kind of revolution would take place – this time, in food and agriculture – through the introduction of corn, a cereal discovered by the Spanish in Mexico over a century and a half beforehand. Romanians realised that cornmeal was very similar to millet flour, which they had used to make their *mămăligă* (a traditional porridge, similar to polenta) since the time of the Romans (according to documentary evidence) and probably long before that. For centuries, millet had been a staple crop for Romanians, perhaps because of its very short germination – if you sow it on 1 May, you can harvest it by 15 June; in a land plagued by savage raids and wars, if you were lucky enough to have peace during those six weeks, you would basically be able to put away the next year's worth of food. If the Turks or Tatars invaded, you piled up your sacks and your children into the cart and made for the mountains. Corn brought with it a series of new advantages: it gives a higher yield per hectare, its flour tastes better, its grains are better suited for horse and bird feed – but most importantly, corn cobs can be burned for fuel, and if dried, they can

The old church of Sinaia Monastery, built by Mihai Cantacuzino between 1690 and 1695

feed the oxen through the winter. Which is why it slowly spread throughout the country during the 18th century, until it became the main crop both in Transylvania, as well as across the Carpathians, year after year (as people's culinary traditions are very enduring). It would be called *porumb* in Wallachia (because of the cob's resemblance to a pidgeon – Romanian: *porumbel*); *păpușoi* in Moldavia (meaning "big doll") and *cucuruz* in Transylvania, after its German name.

Some authors believe that the introduction of corn could be one of the causes of the population increase in the Principalities during the 18th century, despite the hard times.

Constantin Brâncoveanu – Able statesman, patron and martyr

After the death of Șerban Cantacuzino, the great boyars assembled to elect the new voivode – the Porte did not intervene on that occasion – and as Șerban's son was still a child, they chose instead the nephew of the late voivode, Constantin Brâncoveanu, a mature and experienced boyar who had held several offices. At first, he wanted to call himself Cantacuzino-Brâncoveanu (by adding his mother's name) but the overly proud Cantacuzino family strongly opposed it, saying the voivode wanted to "become a stallion when he was only a mule". So he went one generation further and took the name of his grandmother (Elina, daughter of Radu Șerban Basarab) and styled himself Basarab-Brâncoveanu.

I will not dwell on his reign much, but we know he was a wise, yet shrewd ruler, who concealed his intentions from the Turks, the Austrians and the Russians, and also sought to impose his own candidates to the Moldavian throne; he was an ambitious and able man, who ruled for 25 years – the last voivode of the Principalities to hold on to the throne for so long. After him came the long line of Phanariote rulers, whom the Turks rarely allowed on the throne for more than 2-3 years in a row.

Brâncoveanu restored many of the buildings and churches his family had built long before him, commissioned new monuments and even "invented" a new architectural style (known to us by his name – Romanian: *brâncovenesc*) which, alongside the old local or Balkan tradition, included certain Italian influences, possibly

The veranda of Brâncoveanu's palace at Potlogi, Dâmbovița County, built in the architectural style that would bear his name

Constantin Brâncoveanu and his four sons, who were executed before his eyes: Constantin, Ștefan, Radu and Matei. The portraits are from Del Chiaro's book, published in 1718.

brought over by his uncle, seneschal Constantin Cantacuzino. Horezu monastery in Oltenia, or Mogoșoaia Palace near Bucharest (beautifully restored by Princess Marta Bibescu in the 20th century and the only presentable old monument in the area around the capital) are representative of this style.

Therefore, culturally, his was a reign of the greatest importance, continuing and encouraging the development of local means of artistic expression – already, during his uncle's rule, the Bible had been translated into Romanian and the Princely School had been founded in Bucharest.

However, it was how Brâncoveanu's reign ended that still touches us to this day. The Turks suspected he was conspiring against them, secretly attempting to ally himself to the Austrians and Russians (we will see, further on, what happened in 1710-1711, when Prince Dimitrie Cantemir of Moldavia openly entered an alliance with Peter the Great of Russia). A more prudent man, Brâncoveanu refused to join the alliance, but the cloud of suspicion continued to hang over him after two of his Cantacuzino cousins joined the Russians (later creating a Russian branch of Cantacuzino princes). The Turks became convinced that Brâncoveanu sided with the Westerners, especially after the Austrian emperor conferred on him the title of "Prince of the Holy Empire". In fact, we now know that he repeatedly held secret talks with both the Russian tsar and the emperor, but stopped short of taking the decisive step as long as he believed the Turks to be too strong. He even crossed the mountains into Transylvania in 1690, alongside its pro-Turkish prince Imre Thököly, defeating the Austrians at Zărnești, while Șerban Cantacuzino's son-in-law, Constantin Bălăceanu, died in that battle as a general in the Austrian army.

Constantin Brâncoveanu, founder of Horezu Monastery, depicted with his sons on a fresco inside the monastery church, dedicated to the Holy Emperors Constantine and Helen.

It was even rumoured that his Cantacuzino uncles, Michael (the army commander) and Constantin (the seneschal) concerned that Brâncoveanu was no longer taking their counsel, betrayed him to Constantinople. In the spring of 1714, the Porte duly sent an envoy (Turkish: *kapıcı**) to Bucharest, to bring the voivode and his entire family to Constantinople. So weak was Wallachia by that time – only a century after the deeds of Michael the Brave and Radu Șerban Basarab – that it was enough for a Turkish *kapıcı*, accompanied by only a handful of soldiers, to come to Brâncoveanu's palace and place a black ribbon on his shoulder (a sign that he had been deposed) for everyone to freeze where they stood and for his whole family to be loaded onto carriages and taken to Constantinople – with not a single gesture of opposition from the courtiers and all those around them. This speaks volumes about the degree of military and political decay of the Principalities.

---

* The *kapıcı* (or usher of the sultan's palace in Constantinople) was often used by the Ottoman ruler as an envoy to the Principalities, whose mission was to depose or even execute our voivodes.

Brâncoveanu was taken to Constantinople, locked up in the Fortress of the Seven Towers (Turkish: *Yedikule*) and tortured until he revealed where he was hiding his treasures (he was famously rich). On 15 August (the day of the great Orthodox celebration of the Dormition) Constantin Brâncoveanu, his four sons and his closest advisor, Ianache Văcărescu, all of them in long white shirts, were brought before the sultan and his court; the executioner was waiting, axe in hand, by the chopping block. Văcărescu was beheaded first, then the voivode's oldest son, then the second and then the third. Each of them was offered their life if they converted to Islam, or "turned Turk" as it was called back then. The fourth son, a child of 12 or 13, replied that he would do it and be spared. His father chastised him by saying: "*Better to die a thousand times than renounce your faith.*" The boy retracted his words, saying that he too would die a Christian, and placed his head on the block. The young head rolled onto the sand, as did that of the old voivode, shortly after. Their terrible deaths shocked the whole of Europe, and inspired the creator of an anonymous folk ballad, sung over the centuries: "*Brâncoveanu, boyar of old / Voivode and Christian lord...*"

Dimitrie Cantemir – Scholar of European renown, unrealistic prince

Dimitrie Cantemir in Oriental attire

To fully understand why Phanariote rule was imposed on the Principalities later on, we must talk about a brief, but very significant period in the history of Moldavia – the reign of Dimitrie Cantemir (1710-1711).

Dimitrie Cantemir was the son of an elected voivode, Constantin Cantemir, who had been a simple soldier from a Moldavian free peasant family of Tigheci (bordering the Budjak, in the southeast). A brave and capable man, he had served as a mercenary in the Polish army, where he attained the highest rank, then returned to his country and was made a boyar. In 1685, Moldavian boyars elected him voivode almost by accident, as they could not agree on any of the candidates descended from previous voivodes or the great boyar class. He

Portrait of Dimitrie Cantemir from the first German edition of Descriptio Moldaviae *(1771)*

ruled until 1693, and despite having served Poland for such a long time, he fought King John III Sobieski when he attempted to conquer Moldavia (it is from this period that we have the legend of Sobieski and the garrison of Neamț Castle).

Constantin Cantemir had two sons, who ruled one after the other – Antioh and Dimitrie. The latter was exceptionally intelligent – one chronicler speaks of how the old voivode, who could not read, liked to have the child read out old manuscripts to him. However, an old practice dictated that the voivode had to send young Dimitrie as a hostage in Constantinople, as a guarantee of his loyalty – just as Vlad Țepeș and his brother, Radu the Fair, had been sent as hostages as early as the mid-15th century. Dimitrie spent no less than 20 years as

Antioh Cantemir, voivode of Moldavia (1695-1700; 1705-1707) and brother of Dimitrie Cantemir

a hostage in Constantinople. He learned all the languages spoken there at the time: Arabic, Persian and, of course, Turkish; the ancient languages – Greek and Latin; the modern Greek language; of the Western European languages – Italian, German and some French; add to that Romanian and Russian (which he learned while in exile, in Russia) and we can safely say he was a veritable polyglot. He was well acquainted with the Byzantine and Islamic cultures, as he was surrounded by both; he actually devised a method of transcribing Turkish music, known to this day as the invention of "Kantemiro lu" (meaning "son of Cantemir"). He had thorough knowledge of the Greek and Roman classics from books, and was also familiar with Western culture through his readings and his frequent contacts with foreign ambassadors (Dutch, English, French and German). Because he was highly regarded at the Ottoman court, the Grand Vizier believed he was the right man for the throne of Moldavia, as it was rumoured that Tsar Peter I Romanov (who would later be called "the Great") was making preparations for a war against the Turks after defeating the Swedish king, Charles XII, a brilliant general.

But no sooner had he taken up the throne in Iași than he tried to enter into contact with the tsar, hoping to start a war of liberation from Turkish domination. In 1697, at the age of 24, he had witnessed the great Turkish defeat at Zenta, at the hands of the Austrians; watching the battle from the ranks of the Ottomans, who were routed, Cantemir hastily concluded that the Ottoman power had reached its nadir. Finally, in the spring of 1711, using emissaries chosen from amongst the lesser boyars (who were more loyal to him) he signed a treaty with Peter the Great, placing Moldavia under the protection of the tsar – in effect, turning the country into a vassal state of Russia. We, who know what followed during the next three hundred years, know what a catastrophic mistake he was making: had the Russians won on that occasion, all of Moldavia would, in time, have suffered the same fate as Ukraine, Georgia or Bessarabia, which were simply turned into provinces (or gubernias) of the Russian Empire.

Incredibly, even at *that* time there were a few great boyars, such as Iordache Rosetti or Lupu Costache, who understood that Cantemir's policies were disastrous, and that full-fledged Russian power was an even greater threat to the country's independence than Turkish domination was, and did everything they could to sabotage the voivode's plans and the entire campaign. Tsar Peter I duly arrived with his army in Iași, where Cantemir had hastily assembled 20,000 (rather poorly trained) men, but their supply train – under minister Lupu Costache – did not arrive (gathering supplies was difficult anyway, in a country regularly affected by droughts). The Russian army and its Moldavian contingent, advancing south along the Prut River valley, was surrounded by the Turks at Stănilești and surrendered after two days – defeated not by arms, but by hunger. The tsar sued for peace and got off relatively easy – Russia had to surrender the Black Sea port of Azov, which it had only recently conquered. It was said that the tsar paid a hefty sum of money to buy off the Turkish vizier, while the tsarina, who had accompanied her husband, gave up all her jewellery to add to their ransom. More importantly for us, Dimitrie Cantemir – a traitor in the eyes of the Turks – was allowed to retreat to Russia, along with his family and around 5,000 of his boyars, courtiers and soldiers. Many of them became unhappy and returned to Moldavia a few years later – among them, a boyar called Ion Neculce, the future chronicler, from whom we know a lot about this great adventure.

Peter the Great, tsar of Russia (1682-1725) as a young man, wearing traditional Russian attire

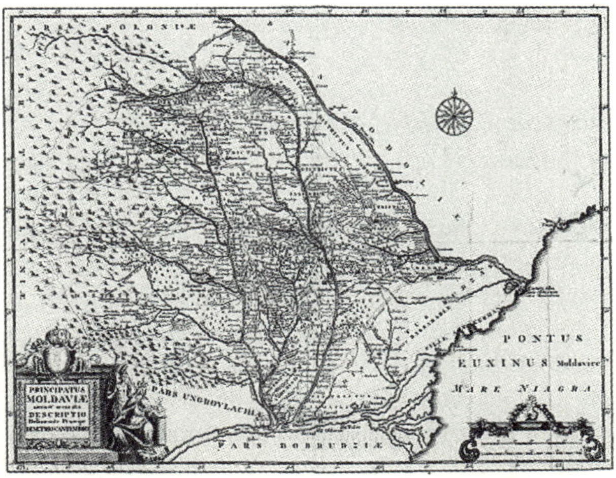

Map of Moldavia, prepared by Cantemir for his Descriptio Moldaviae

Antiokh Kantemir, son of Dimitrie Cantemir

Cantemir remained in Russia until his death, in 1723, all the while hoping that the tsar would resume the war against the Ottomans, which did not happen. The tsar held Cantemir in the highest esteem, making him a prince of Russia, his confidant and a member of his "Senate". It is from that period that we have his famous portrait, found in all the history books, showing him clean-shaven, in Western dress – in armour, donning a French wig and a marshal's baton – as Peter the Great had already begun his authoritarian campaign to westernize Russia. Before his exile, in Moldavia, we see him bearded, wearing a kaftan and a tall fur hat, like all our other voivodes. However, without that fateful battle on the Prut, and the twelve years of exile in Russia, Cantemir would probably never have left behind the works that made him famous across Europe, such as *The History of the Ottoman Empire* and *The Description of Moldavia*, both of them in Latin – the latter written for the Royal Academy of Berlin, whose member he had become in 1714. Thus, in hindsight, we recognise that Cantemir's exile had positive consequences for posterity. His fame was enhanced by that of his son, Antioh, a precocious genius, who was the first Western-style poet in Russian literature, and served as ambassador in Paris and then London while still a young man. Antioh did a lot for the reputation of his father, encouraging the publication of *The History of the Ottoman Empire* in English and French, and establishing contacts with famous scholars in Paris, such as Voltaire.

Were our Principalities pashalıks or protectorates?

These two crucial moments in the evolution of our relations with the Porte – the betrayal of Dimitrie Cantemir in 1711 and the execution of Brâncoveanu in 1714 – resulted in an increased degree of Ottoman control over the Principalities. The Turks no longer trusted the local voivodes elected by our boyars and decided to appoint them by themselves, from among that aristocratic oligarchy of money and birth – the Greek dignitary

Turks in Europe, an English 18th century map showing territories under Ottoman domination. It is not the most precise of maps, since the author mixed up the names of Moldavia and Wallachia.

families of the Phanar district (Turkish: *Fener*) in Constantinople. It was the start of what we call the "Phanariote era" – from 1711 in Moldavia and 1716 in Wallachia, after the Turks also executed Brâncoveanu's successor, his cousin Ștefan Cantacuzino, along with his father, the learned seneschal Constantin Cantacuzino, and his uncle, commander Mihai Cantacuzino. If the rumours were true and they had indeed plotted Brâncoveanu's downfall, they paid for it.

To better appreciate the situation of the Principalities and the dilemma in the above title, we should briefly explain the difference between a *pashalık* and a protectorate of the Ottoman Empire. We have seen how Christian countries around us fell to the Turks, one after the other – two Bulgarian tsardoms, the Serbian kingdom (following the famous battle of Kosovo Polje) the remnants of the Byzantine Empire, and finally, the Hungarian kingdom – all of them turned into provinces of the Ottoman Empire, each governed by a *pasha* – a Turkish general and governor – hence the name *pashalık* given to the main administrative division (the Turks

Sultan Ahmed III (1703-1730) during whose reign local voivodes were replaced with Phanariote Greeks.

themselves called it *vilayet*). In these provinces – that is, in Greece, Albania, Bulgaria, Macedonia, Serbia and Bosnia – the Turks could settle Turkish colonists, build mosques and spread Islam (through various methods) which had lasting effects on several regions of the Balkans, felt to the present day: two thirds of Albania, half of Bosnia, parts of Bulgaria and Macedonia became Muslim, contributing to recent conflicts in Bosnia, Kosovo etc.

So why did Wallachia and Moldavia, and then Transylvania, remain autonomous, and not turned into pashalıks, directly administered by Turkish governors? Historians disagree on this and there is no single, satisfactory explanation. Some say it was caused by the stiff resistance of voivodes like Mircea the Elder, Vlad Țepeș, Stephen the Great or Petru Rareș. Other believe that the Turks understood that it was in their interest to maintain a "buffer zone" between them and the Hungarian and Polish kingdoms, but which, as vassals of the Porte, no longer represented a threat the Ottoman Empire. A third and original explanation was suggested during the interwar period by historian Petre P. Panaitescu, according to which the Turks would have noticed that the lands they administered directly had quickly become impoverished and were no longer able to provide vital supplies to the empire – and especially its capital, Constantinople. Meanwhile, the semi-independent Romanian principalities, under local voivodes, had remained the granary of Constantinople for centuries; the Porte had long imposed a monopoly on exports such as grain, cattle, honey and wax, at prices it alone dictated.

It is likely that every explanation has a grain of truth, but I believe that, for the Ottomans, the need to maintain a relatively neutral territory to the north – at first between them and Hungary, then Poland, and finally, Russia and Austria – must have been the main determinant. Nevertheless, there was an additional, less obvious (and certainly unofficial) reason, which mattered greatly to the Turks during the Phanariote era: the fact that Phanariotes sent to rule in Bucharest and Iași had been used as informers, reporting on events happening in the West, in Poland and in Russia. For generations, their knowledge of languages, their reading and translating of Western newspapers, and their merchants and agents enabled Phanariote rulers to act as a sort of official spies for the Porte. And when you become an informer, the temptation of turning into a double agent is great indeed.

The Phanariote century (1711-1821)

The so-called "Phanariote era" received plenty of bad press during both the 19th and the 20th centuries. But it has to be said that Phanariote rule was the lesser of two evils, at a time when the Turks feared we would take the side of Austria or Russia, and the chances of regaining our independence were non-existent. We could either be a pashalık or be ruled by what were, in effect, Greek governors appointed by Constantinople. The second option was thus preferable, all the more so since the first Phanariote rulers were not half bad. Nicolae Mavrocordat had a grandmother of the Mușatini and thought of himself as being "of the blood" of voivodes. His father, the famous dragoman Alexander Mavrocordatos, had been an extremely capable and intelligent man; nicknamed *Exaporitos* (Greek for "keeper of secrets") due to his position as a secretary of state, he was not allowed to hold the rank of minister, but was second only to the Turkish Grand Dragoman. It was he who had drafted the treaty of Karlowitz in 1699, which saw the Turks relinquish all of Hungary and Transylvania, as well as parts of Serbia and Croatia. Interestingly, the Turks beheaded the minister, but allowed Mavrocordatos to keep his head. His sons, Nicolae and Ion, went on to become voivodes of Wallachia and Moldavia. His wife, Soultana Christoskoleos, was the daughter of Princess Cassandra of Moldavia and, as such, a descendant of Stephen the Great. This branch of the Mavrocordatos family were thus considered to be "of the blood" of voivodes, and were never seen as foreigners in the Principalities. It is also intriguing that all Phanariote families that succeeded them to the throne – apart from a madman

The only known portrait of Alexander "Exaporitos" Mavrocordatos, dating from 1854

Contemporary engraving of the peace talks at Karlowitz, where the Exaporitos (father of Nicolae and Ioan Mavrocordat) gave the measure of his skill.

named Nicholas Mavrogenes (1786-1790) – were related to the Mavrocordatos family, as if they too were "of the blood", but as it were, of the second degree – even the Ghiculeşti, who had already ruled during the 17th century, and the two families of Romanian origin, houses Racoviţă and Callimachi (originally *Călmaşul*). Therefore, the Phanariote era did not start off as a complete break with the past, and neither our boyars, nor the people felt it was a change of regime. But over time, things took a turn for the worse, as all these Phanariote grandees, who paid the Porte and bribed the viziers to become voivode, brought their retinues with them – relatives or creditors from Phanar.

The Phanar was a neighbourhood of Constantinople, located outside the city walls, halfway up the Golden Horn gulf. Apparently, its name comes from the French word *fanal*, after a beacon found in the area in the time of the short-lived Latin Empire of Constantinople, created after the crusade of 1204. A few decades after they conquered the city, the Turks began to repopulate Constantinople and allowed the Greeks to return and settle this quarter. At first, they allowed the peasants who lived around the city to sell their produce and supply the new Turkish population of administrators, soldiers, craftsmen and merchants. Before the city gates, when the taxman asked where they were going,

Constantinople in the late 18th century. In the centre stands Validé Sultan Mosque; not far from it, to the right, is the Phanar, the Greek quarter of Constantinople.

the peasants would reply "*is tin polin*", meaning "*to the city*" in Greek – which is the origin of its current name: *Istanbul.* In time, the Ottomans permitted those Greeks who had proven themselves useful for the running of their capital and empire to put down roots in the slum of Phanar, which became a sort of Greek "ghetto" in Constantinople. And this was how some of the prominent families of old Byzantium – the Cantacuzenes, the Notaras or the Rallis – came to live there. Most Phanariote Greek families, however, were rich merchant families from amongst which the Porte – that is, the sultan and his viziers – began to choose the administrators of their empire. Why did the Turks do that? It was because a literal interpretation of their religion forbade them to learn Christian languages, which were considered

Procession of Prince Konstantinos Ypsilantis heading towards the Sublime Porte on the day of his appointment by the sultan

Nicolae Mavrocordat, voivode of Moldavia and Wallachia, as shown by the two coats of arms underneath the medallion

"unclean". So they needed these Greeks, who had learned Western languages such as Italian, French, as well as Latin, and used them as interpreters and "clerks", as we would call them today. During the mid-17th century, the Ottomans created the office of "Grand Dragoman", or interpreter to the sultan and the Grand Vizier; almost from the outset, the office became highly influential, because the man who held it was privy to the secrets of government and to the dealings with foreign envoys (let us not call all of them "ambassadors", since at that time, the title was reserved to the emissaries of only two or three great powers).

The first two Mavrocordatos voivodes had first been Grand Dragomans before their appointment by the Porte to Wallachia or Moldavia – which became almost an unwritten rule: ambitious Phanariotes who wanted a throne knew they had to become Grand Dragoman first.

During the 18th century – from 1711 in Moldavia and 1716 in Wallachia – times got a lot harder for the Principalities, hence the idea that Phanariote rulers were the cause of it all, which is unfair, at least in part. *They* were not the "root of all evil", but the harsh, corrupt Turkish regime, characteristic of the Ottoman Empire's period of decadence. Its need to make money through any means possible meant that the thrones in Iași and Bucharest were being sold for hard cash. To the "official" price, the buyers added lavish gifts and bribes for the Grand Vizier and other dignitaries who had made the "deal" possible. The debt-laden voivode then brought his creditors to the Principalities and made them boyars, so they could recover their investment.

This made things far worse for the peasant masses, which grew even poorer than they had been a hundred years before, and caused great discontent among the local boyars. In the defence of Phanariote rulers, we should mention some of the positive aspects, first brought to light by the historian Nicolae Iorga. Firstly, some of these Phanariotes were men of culture – such as Grigore II Ghica and his cousin, Constantin Mavrocordat – who showed interest in introducing some administrative reforms to the Principalities. The latter, a highly cultivated and undoubtedly honourable man, reigned no less than ten times (in both countries) and was concerned about the fate of the people. He was the voivode who abolished serfdom – first in Wallachia, in 1746, and then in Moldavia, in 1749 – after prolonged debates in the assemblies of estates; he decreed that peasants working on someone else's lands were no longer tied to them, and limited the number of days of corvée (unpaid, forced labour) to 6 per year in Wallachia and 12 in Moldavia – whereas, in neighbouring countries such as Transylvania, Poland and Russia, these often amounted to several days per week. Moreover, serfdom lasted another hundred years in these countries. However, the relaxation of state control (bypassing the boyars) and the concurrent rise in Turkish financial expectations were interpreted by Mavrocordat's enemies as a harsher fiscal policy; peasants must have seen it the same way, since they often fled from the census, which made the population of the Principalities appear to have decreased by half under Constantin Mavrocordat. In fact, it had only been peasants running away from the count.

Constantin Mavrocordat also reformed the boyar class: according to the new order, only those who held a public office of a certain rank, whether at court or around the country, could be considered boyars; if no public officials (*dregători*) were chosen from a family for two generations in a row, that family would be demoted

Grigore III Ghica, several times voivode of Moldavia and Wallachia, shown with his consort, Lady Ruxandra, in a votive painting from Frumoasa Monastery in Iași

Constantin Mavrocordat, son of Nicolae Mavrocordat, several times voivode of Wallachia and Moldavia

to the rank of *mazili*, a lesser social status, ranked between boyars and free peasants – making boyars more dependent on the voivode.

Be that as it may, Mavrocordat did not grow rich during his ten terms as voivode. The last time he was appointed voivode, in 1769 – when a new war had broken out with Russia and the Porte needed an experienced administrator in Moldavia – he was so poor that the sultan gave him several bags of gold to pay for the journey. Mavrocordat arrived in Moldavia with a Turkish army, but failed in his attempt to defend the border; he fell prisoner and was killed by a Russian soldier who hit him in the head with the butt of his rifle. The embarrassed Russian commander did, however, provide him with a princely funeral.

A generation later, we had two more voivodes from the Mavrocordat family, both of them named Alexander. The second of them fled to Russia in 1786, during the time of Catherine the Great, and with him ended the Mavrocordat dynasty. Phanariotes were beginning to betray the Porte.

The Phanariote regime lasted for another 35 years after the "betrayal" of house Mavrocordat, featuring rulers from many other families: Mourousis – *Moruzi*, Ypsilantis – *Ipsilanti*, Hantzeris – *Hangerliu*, Soutzos – *Șuțu*, Karatzas – *Caragea* and Callimachi (the hellenised name of the Moldavian *Călmașul* family). Oppression, corruption and injustice became more and more blatant and difficult for the population to cope with. It is the memory of that time that we have preserved, and the idea that all of our country's misfortunes stem from the Phanariote regime.

Alexandru Moruzi, who ruled both principalities between 1792 and 1801.

During the following century, local boyars would seek to entrench that version of events, in an attempt to justify their submission to that regime – and at times, their taking advantage of it.

Nevertheless, it is worth mentioning a more enlightened rule from this period – that of Alexander Ypsilantis, in Wallachia (1774-1782). Together with his advisor, Ienăchiță Văcărescu, great boyar and scholar, he governed the country efficiently during a reign that was relatively long reign for that time. In fact, the Phanariotes brought with them a tradition of charitable work, whereby donors (Romanian: *evergeţi*) did things for the public good, especially caring for the sick; several hospitals were founded during their time, managed by public institutions (Greek: *eforía*) endowed with large estates – which was greatly admired by a number of Western travellers.

Also, during two of the last Phanariote reigns – that of Ioan Caragea in Wallachia (1812-1818) remembered for the bubonic plague epidemic which occurred during his time, and that of Scarlat Callimachi in Moldavia (1812-1819) – the first two relatively modern codes of law in the Principalities were compiled; the former closely followed Byzantine tradition, while the latter was more influenced by Austrian law.

Another aspect we must emphasise is the advances in culture. For instance, it has recently come to light that, during the Phanariote era, more books were printed in Romanian than in Greek. Additionally, the two Princely Schools founded in Bucharest and Iaşi had become higher education institutions attracting students from all over South-Eastern Europe. The majority of lecturers were Greek scholars who had studied in Western universities, with some of the courses taught in Italian or French. In particular, the introduction of French language studies was an accomplishment with far-reaching consequences (French had become the *lingua franca*, or working language, in Western Europe).

From the mid-18th century, another channel for the spread of French influence was the "institution" of the French secretaries employed by our voivodes. Under the pretext that they required a decent French clerk in their chancelleries, Phanariote rulers began to use secretaries recommended by the French ambassador in Constantinople – some of whom were highly cultured individuals, who kept the West informed about the Principalities. Others put down roots and married within the boyar class.

Perhaps they also introduced freemasonry – a phenomenon we shall discuss later on.

Above: The Callimachi Code of Moldavia, *adopted in 1817, was only translated into Romanian in 1833. Below: The Caragea Statute of Wallachia, a compendium of civil law norms adopted in 1818, and valid until 1864. Both codes were replaced by the 1864 Civil Code of Cuza, applied in the United Principalities (and then Romania) until very recently.*

The Austro-Russo-Turkish wars

Prince Eugene of Savoy (1663–1736) whose brilliant victories against the Turks resulted in the Peace of Passarowitz

To fully appreciate the prolonged tragedy that was the Phanariote century, we must not forget one important aspect: the Porte saw the Phanariote regime as a necessary countermeasure to the sudden belligerence of the Christian powers, namely Austria and Russia, and the threat they represented to the Ottoman Empire. Keep in mind the huge progress the Austrians had made between the siege of Vienna in 1683, when the capital itself was in danger, and the peace of Karlowitz in 1699, when they annexed Hungary and Transylvania; and remember Peter the Great's attempt of 1711, which Dimitrie Cantemir had supported. Because during the entire Phanariote era, wars between the three powers raged one after the other, mostly on our territory, leaving a trail of misery behind them – not to mention repeated Turkish requisitioning.

Here are but a few of the Austro-Russian-Turkish wars that followed the Peace of Karlowitz and Peter I's misadventure of 1711:

– The Austro-Turkish war of 1716-1718 ended with the Treaty of Passarowitz (Serbian: *Požarevac*). The Turks ceded control of the Banat of Temeswar (Romanian: *Banatul Timișoarei*) and Oltenia. Like all former Turkish possessions, the Banat was largely depopulated, so the Austrians proceeded to colonise it with Germans from Swabia and German-speaking settlers from Lorraine (a duchy which the Austrians had been forced to hand over

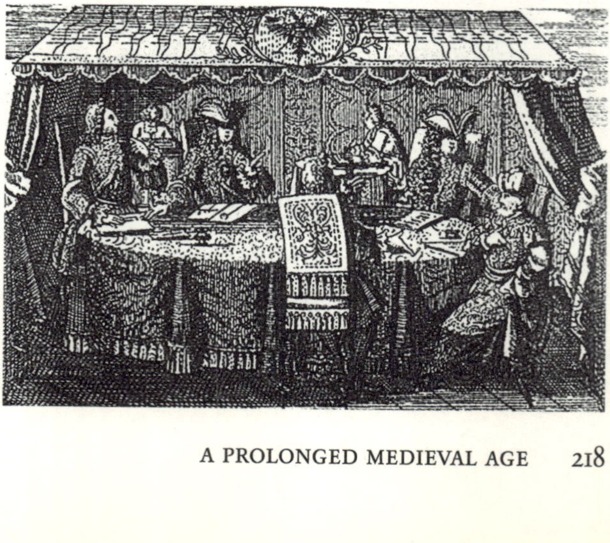

Contemporary engraving of the Treaty of Passarowitz, when the Turks ceded Oltenia and the Banat of Temeswar to the Austrians

to France, namely to Stanisław Leszczyński, former king of Poland and father-in-law to the French king, in 1738). In the Banat, these German-speaking Catholic colonists came to be called Swabians (Romanian: *şvabi*).

– The Austro-Russian-Turkish war of 1735-1739 saw the Russians press south through the Ukraine, towards the Black Sea; the Austrians were less fortunate, and were bound by the Treaty of Belgrade to return Oltenia to Wallachia. During 20 years of occupation, the Austrians had introduced a series of administrative reforms and left us some valuable census information, the kind of which we lack completely from the time of the Turkish rule. However, Romanians did not thrive under Austrian domination – with the exception of a few "collaborationist" boyars. There were concerns about being separated from their brothers across the river Olt and about religious pressure from Catholicism, so that the Peace of Belgrade – negotiated by Voivode Ioan Mavrocordat on the Ottoman side – was well received.

– Finally, the Russo-Turkish war of 1768-1774 (mentioned above in connection to the death of Constantin Mavrocordat) which ended with the Treaty of Küçük-Kaynarca. Russia extended its territory to the river Bug and acquired navigation rights in the Black Sea, as well as a the right to intervene in matters concerning the

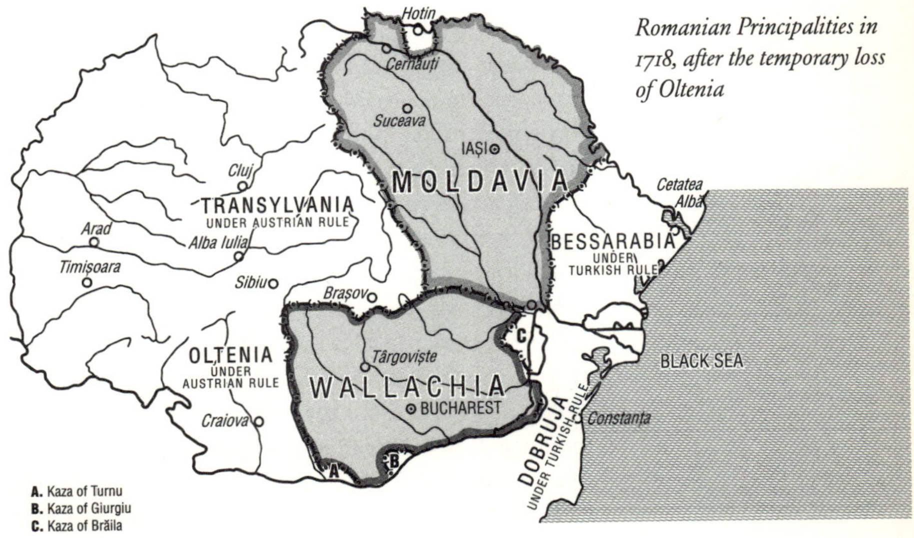

Romanian Principalities in 1718, after the temporary loss of Oltenia

Romanian Principalities. Our boyars used the opportunity to submit political reports to Saint Petersburg, making a series of demands which would form part of the political manifesto of Romanian patriots a century later: the return to the countries' old ways, with local rulers etc.

The loss of Bucovina (1775) and the first annexation of Bessarabia (1812)

Coat of arms inspired by Moldavian heraldry, awarded to Bukovina in 1862 (the province had become a dukedom in 1848).

Unfortunately, the Treaty of Küçük-Kaynarca had an unforeseen and dramatic consequence: in 1775, as a reward for its diplomatic intervention, Austria obtained a portion of Northern Moldavia, under the pretext that it would ease its access to Southern Poland, which it had acquired after the first partition of that country in 1771; the territory would henceforth be called by the Slavic name Bukovina (Romanian: *Bucovina*) meaning "beech forest". Grigore III Ghica, voivode of Moldavia at the time, protested against the Porte's dismemberment of the country, which went against the traditional agreement between a suzerain power and a "protected state" – to no avail. In actual fact, his protest was not entirely without effect, since the Grand Vizier sent a *kapıcı* who strangled the voivode in his own palace (1777).

The province of Bukovina was well administered – as were all the other lands governed by the Austrians – but because it too was scarcely populated, the imperial administration favoured the immigration of Ruthenians (who were already present, but in small numbers) so that, over time, the percentage represented by Romanians decreased dramatically – even more so after 1830, when Bukovina was on the route of the great Jewish migration south from Galicia and Russia.

After yet another Austro-Russian-Turkish war (1787-1792) the Austrians, who had advanced deep into our territory, suddenly retreated and sued for peace (Treaty of Sistova, 1791) because the outbreak the French Revolution demanded their urgent attention in the west. The Russians made peace at Iași (January 1792) and for the first time, their borders reached the river Dniester. Note that we have not always been their neighbours; at first, we bordered the Ruthenians, and further east, across the deserted steppes, there lived the Cossacks. Muscovite Russians only began to expand towards the Black Sea after the reign of Peter the Great, advancing further south after each war, occupying territories once dependent from the Crimean Tatars or even the Turks themselves (Western Ukraine). First, they reached the river Dnieper, then the river Bug, and in 1792, the Dniester. Their next step was the annexation of the "Danubian Principalities", as we had started to be called in the chancelleries of Europe. Up to that point, Russia's ambitions did not extend to Wallachia because of Austria's rival intentions. But in the aftermath of the French Revolution, wars against the French Republic and then Napoleon had kept Austria pinned down in the west. Russia took advantage of this situation and unleashed a new war on the Turks, occupying the Principalities for six years (1806-1812). Peace negotiations dragged on for months on end, finally taking place in Bucharest, in an inn that had recently been built by an Armenian adventurer named Manuc Bey (Romanian: *Hanul lui Manuc*). By that time, the Russians were in a hurry, as it had become obvious that Napoleon was preparing an attack on Russia. Great Britain,

Catherine II the Great (1762-1796) during whose reign the expansionist policy of Russia became even more evident

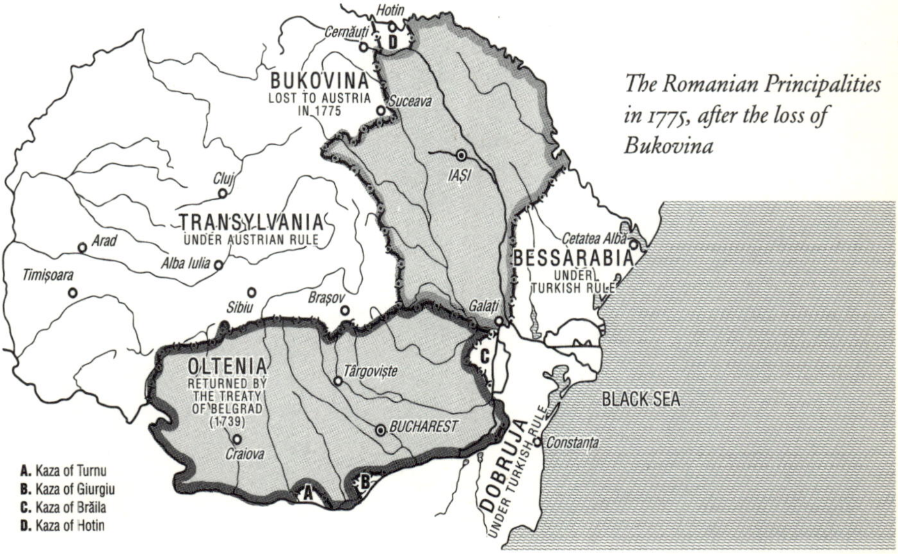

The Romanian Principalities in 1775, after the loss of Bukovina

the linchpin of the anti-Napoleonic coalition, made huge efforts to get Russians and the Turks to the negotiating table. Meanwhile, Napoleon's diplomacy made an incredible blunder: the position of French ambassador to Constantinople had become vacant, and by the time the newly appointed ambassador arrived (travelling like a prince) the treaty had already been signed (16/28 May 1812). Russia gave up Wallachia and even the Western half of Moldavia, but annexed the Moldavian territory between the rivers Prut and Dniester, which they would call Bessarabia (a name given only to the southernmost part of the country during the Middle Ages). Six weeks later, Napoleon's *Grande Armée* invaded Russia, so the Russian divisions that had faced the Turks along the Danube were already on their way home, where they would take part in the annihilation of the retreating Napoleonic army at the battle of Berezina.

For almost 200 years, historians, diplomats and politicians have asked themselves how it had been possible for the Turks to agree to such a detrimental peace just weeks before Napoleon's attack on Russia. Naturally, the question was immediately asked in Constantinople, and a scapegoat quickly found in Dimitrie Moruzi –

The Romanian Principalities in 1812, after the loss of Bessarabia

Great Dragoman, son of a Phanariote ruler and candidate for a throne in the Principalities – who had supposedly advised to sue for peace. This may well have been true. However, we now know that the Turkish government had indeed had knowledge of all the elements it needed to weigh the alternatives, because the French chargé d'affaires had handed the Turkish foreign affairs minister a note on behalf of Napoleon's government, urging the Porte not to make peace before its imminent attack on Russia. As it turns out, the note was hotly debated in the Divan – in the presence of the sultan, the Grand Vizier and all officials concerned – and after careful consideration, the decision was made to sign the peace at once, as the prospect of a Napoleonic victory appeared to be a bigger threat to the Ottoman Empire than Russia's proximity (and perhaps rightly so).

Seal of Ion Gheorghe Caragea, voivode of Wallachia between 1812 and 1818

Thus began the tragedy of Bessarabia, nearly 200 years ago. Should we place the blame squarely on the Phanariotes?

To this day, there are historians who claim that the group of Phanariote families which had schemed behind the scenes of Ottoman diplomacy for hundreds of years – often paying with their heads for their ambition and audacity – had devised a secret "long term" plot aimed at gradually weakening Ottoman power, until they would be capable of building a Christian empire (under their rule) made up of all the Orthodox peoples in the region. The fact is that all Greeks (not just the Phanariotes) overly proud of their ancient and Byzantine past, have always had a superiority complex towards neighbouring peoples, including the Romanians, so they believed it was natural not to heed local and regional interests, since it was their "calling" to rule all Orthodox nations. This mentality was perpetuated by the fact that, shortly after the fall of Constantinople in 1453, sultan Mehmet II had appointed a new patriarch, Gennadius II (who had opposed the Union of Florence) and charged him with shepherding all Christians in the former Byzantine Empire and the Balkans – so that, paradoxically, the Patriarchate of Constantinople had more political influence under the Turks than ever before.

Christian peoples rebel against the Turks – Etería *and Tudor Vladimirescu (1821)*

The sword of Tudor Vladimirescu, of Oriental type, which carries an inscription in Latin characters, one in Arabic characters and Tudor's name in Greek characters.

The beginning of the 19th century was marked by large-scale revolts that began to erupt among the Christian peoples of the Balkans. The spark came partly from the French Revolution, which had awakened the peoples of Europe to the ideas of liberty and social equality.

The first to rebel were the Serbs, led by two men descended from well-to-do peasant families of swineherds, for the country had neither a feudal aristocracy, which had perished along with the Serbian medieval state (apart from those who had "turned Turk" or fled into exile, many of them to the Principalities) nor a bourgeoisie, which would emerge later, largely as a result of an Aromanian immigration. The first of these two men, George Petrović, nicknamed "Black George" (Serbian: *Karađorđe*) proclaimed himself Great Leader of Serbia in 1808, but was ultimately defeated and assassinated at the orders of a rival, Miloš Obrenović, a shrewder and more diplomatic man, who managed to obtain autonomy from the Turks, with himself ruling as a sort of pasha; the country remained under Ottoman suzerainty and paid tribute, with no significant changes apart from the removal of Turkish troops from its territory. Obrenović received the title of prince before the great powers, but the Serbia he ruled was far from encompassing all Serbians. He led the life of a nouveau-riche, and, in reality, much like the pashas he replaced, it seems he often confused the state treasury with his own coffers, buying large estates for himself in Wallachia. His descendants would include several princes, then kings of Serbia, who chose their queens from Romanian boyar families (such as Keșcu or Catargi) and took turns at ruling the country with the descendants of Karađorđe. By 1903, the Karađorđević family were the only ones left standing after butchering all of house Obrenović.

However, in terms of the consequences for our country, a more important uprising was that of the Greeks, which broke out simultaneously in Greece proper and in the Principalities, in 1821. But why would a Greek uprising take place the Principalities? Because Phanariote rulers and even some Romanian boyars believed that by joining forces with the Greeks, they would gain more freedom in Wallachia and Moldavia. Thus, the Greek anti-Ottoman rebellion began as a two-pronged attack: one in Greece itself (led by Alexander Mavrocordatos, a descendant of Phanariote voivodes, famous for his success during the first siege of Missolonghi) and one in the Romanian Principalities (where another son of a Phanariote ruler, Alexander Ypsilantis, had come from Russia to lead the rebels).

It was not only Romanian boyars who had joined the *Philiki Etería* (Greek for "Society of Friends") but also free peasants such as Tudor Vladimirescu, who was an exceptional character. As a young man, he had enrolled as a volunteer in the Russian army. Together with thousands of Romanians from all social classes, he had fought in the war of 1806-1812 (which took place on the territory the Principalities) alongside the Russians and even advanced to the rank of *poruchik* or lieutenant as we say today. He had good knowledge of battle tactics and how to use modern weapons and artillery.

After the 1812 Treaty of Bucharest – a catastrophe for the Principalities – unrest began to spread among Romanians and Greeks alike, as we pondered how to shake off the Turkish yoke. Tudor Vladimirescu was among those who dreamed of fighting the Ottomans, so that when the Greeks rebelled in 1821, he joined them with about 8,000 militiamen (Romanian: *panduri*) free peasants from Oltenia, who had either fought alongside the Russians in the war, like he had, or joined them while in our country. For the first time in many generations, men were enlisting to protect their lands against the raids of a ruthless Bosnian adventurer named Osman Pazvantoğlu, pasha of Vidin, who had repeatedly wreaked havoc in Oltenia and had even crossed the river Olt, causing panic in Bucharest (that is the origin of the Romanian expression *'from the time of Pazvante'*, which originally meant "a time of trouble" and now means "a time long past").

George Petrović (1804-1813) founder of House Karađorđević and leader of the 1804 uprising, was murdered at the orders of Miloš Obrenović.

Miloš Obrenović, founder of House Obrenović, the rivals of House Karađorđević. He reigned twice as prince of Serbia. One of his nephews, also called Miloš, married Maria Catargi from Moldavia. She would become the mother of the first Serbian king, Milan I, but also of Alexandru and Dimitrie, the children of Alexandru Ioan Cuza, with whom she had an affair.

Alexander Ypsilantis (1792-1828) as a young man, dressed in a Russian hussar uniform

Encouraged by several great boyars like Grigore Brâncoveanu, Grigore Ghica and Barbu Văcărescu, all sympathisers of the Etería, Tudor Vladimirescu set out from Oltenia to "raise the people to arms" and headed towards the capital. Yet, as he approached the city, most boyars fled to Transylvania for fear of a peasant uprising. Vladimirescu was nevertheless very strict and enforced a firm (even brutal) discipline within his army, so that his militiamen arrived in Bucharest without having caused any disruption. There he met with Alexander Ypsilantis, commander of the Greek force that had arrived from Russia. Sadly, the two men did not agree on the aims of the war: Ypsilantis wanted a Greater Greece, while Vladimirescu only wanted to fight for the Romanian cause. So tragedy struck again – in a way, Ypsilantis, a former adjutant of the tsar, had lied to his Romanian allies by claiming that the Russians would join the war. But the tsar disavowed him, because in the meantime Russia had formed the Holy Alliance, together with the great powers who had defeated Napoleon in 1815, as well as royal France, precisely to defend *against* revolutions. The tsar would not risk supporting a Greek revolution, even if it was directed against the Turks, as that would have meant breaking the commitment he had made to the members of the league of European monarchs, who were meeting at that very moment in the Congress of Laibach (Ljubljana) to discuss an intervention against a revolution in Naples. The tsar thus officially denied any intention of supporting the Greek revolt. The news dealt a severe blow to the morale of the Etería. Tudor Vladimirescu realised that the revolution was lost and entered into secret negotiations with the Turks. The two armies left Bucharest and headed west, following two parallel routes – Tudor marched through the plains and that of Ypsilantis at the foot of the mountains – not knowing how or when to link up again in case of a Turkish attack. However, Ypsilantis intercepted the correspondence between Tudor and the Turkish commander on the Danube. The Greeks captured him in the manor at Golești and, after a pretend trial, murdered him and dumped his body into an abandoned well. It is, however, quite astonishing

Flag of the Etería, which bears the motto "Liberty or death".

that the small Etería unit who took Tudor from Golești did not meet any resistance from his *panduri*. A possible explanation is the excessive harshness – even cruelty – with which he had treated his men; at the time of his arrest, young Urdăreanu (said to be as handsome as an archangel) and another of his captains, both well loved by the troops, were hanging from a nearby tree.

There is one more thing we can learn from the tragic demise of Tudor Vladimirescu: Tudor, who came from a family of free peasants in north-Western Oltenia (a region where there were no serfs, only free peasant villages) did not have a single local "intellectual" by his side in what was ultimately both a national and a social revolutionary movement. An actual "bourgeoisie" had yet to be established in the Principalities. There was a fairly large class of merchants and craftsmen (though many of them were foreigners) who sent their progeny to the Princely Schools, but they did not yet share a sense of belonging to a class that could stake its claims, let alone rule. Politics was for the boyars. In fact, Vladimirescu himself probably believed that if he came to power, he would need the boyars to rule the country. Had he not risen to a lower rank of nobility? Had he not built a fortified manor and allowed himself to be depicted in boyar attire on murals inside

The infamous Pazvantoğlu in a contemporary engraving

Battle between Etería and the Turks in Bucharest

The Holy Alliance, represented in a contemporary allegorical engraving which shows Tsar Alexander I, Austrian emperor Francis I and King Frederick Wilhelm III of Prussia.

The Turco-Egyptian fleet was destroyed at Navarino (modern day Pylos) on 20 October 1827 in the last great naval battle to be fought entirely with sailing ships.

his village church? It seems beyond doubt to me that he hoped to become voivode of Wallachia. He wore a tall white sable hat (Romanian: *işlic*) a colour reserved for the voivode, and let the *panduri* call him "Prince Tudor". The examples of Black George and Miloš Obrenović may well have encouraged him – but then again, there were no Romanians among his lieutenants. Bishop Ilarion of Argeş had been born in Bulgaria; the Macedonski brothers were probably Serbs, but surely from the Balkans; Farmache and Iordache Olimpiotul were Aromanians, as was commander Diamandi Giuvara, *serdar* of the Albanian mercenaries (Romanian: *arnăuţi*).

Following Tudor's death, the leaderless *panduri* dispersed – some continued to fight the war alongside the Greeks, others returned to their homes. The Turks crossed the Danube, defeated the Greeks at Drăgăşani (where the black-clad "Sacred Band" fought heroically, down to the last man) while Ypsilantis fled to Austria, only to be imprisoned until his death.

For at least one year, the Principalities endured another brutal Turkish occupation, marked by reprisals, pillaging and murder. They only left the country after one year because the Western powers forced them to leave.

Steward Tudor Vladimirescu and his panduri, in a depiction that is far removed from the romantic figure we know from Theodor Amman's famous painting, but one that is perhaps better suited to the captain's ambitious nature and manner.

In the meantime, the war continued in continental Greece and in the Peloponnese, where the small town of Missolonghi, defended by Alexander Mavrocordatos, had long resisted the Turks. Due to the prestige associated with ancient Greece, the Greek revolution enjoyed widespread coverage and support in Western Europe, attracting volunteers from France, Britain and Germany – the most illustrious of them, the famous English poet Lord Byron, died of a fever at Missolonghi. As it became clear that they could not prevail on their own, the Turks summoned the forces of Albanian-born Mehmet Ali, the new *bey* of Egypt, who sent his son, Ibrahim Pasha, at the head of a fleet and an entire army. It was then that Russia, Britain and France intervened as allies for the first time – the year was 1827 – as their combined fleets destroyed the Turco-Egyptian fleet at the battle of Navarino.

The intervention of the great powers eventually forced the Turks to grant independence to the Greeks in 1830; two years later, Greece became a kingdom ruled by a king from the Bavarian royal family.

Let us now briefly look at the role played by Aromanians in the Greek reawakening.

The fortunes of Romance-speaking peoples south of the Danube – Aromanians in Greece and the diaspora

As I mentioned before, when speaking about the Slavic deluge that engulfed the entire Balkan peninsula beginning with the 6th century, the Latin-speaking inhabitants who occupied much of what we now call the former Yugoslavia and Bulgaria north of the Haemus (or Balkan) Mountains in Roman times and formed concentrated enclaves further south, in Macedonia – especially along the old strategic route from Durazzo, on the Adriatic coast, to Constantinople – found themselves increasingly isolated, surrounded by a Slavic "sea" to the north and

Romanians in the Balkans (after a map prepared by geographers Simion Mehedinți and Vintilă Mihăilescu for a 1942 school textbook)

interspersed with Greeks and Albanians to the south. Over time, *four* distinct dialectal groups took shape in that region, with those of Northern Bulgaria and Serbia still speaking the same dialect as Romanians north of the Danube – which linguists call Daco-Romanian. From among them hailed the Asen brothers, leaders of the anti-Byzantine rebellion in the late 12th century and founders of the dynasty responsible for the political revival of the Bulgarian tsardom. Today, only a few of their villages remain in north-Western Bulgaria and Eastern Serbia, especially in the Timok Valley.

Aromanian shepherd in traditional costume, photographed around the year 1900

A handful of communities in the Istria peninsula (on the Adriatic seaboard) probably share the same origin. Their dialect, called Istro-Romanian, is nowadays only spoken by a few hundred people.

Further south, on the outskirts of the great port of Thessaloniki, there is a group of settlements where another dialect of Romanian, called Megleno-Romanian by linguists, is still spoken. In that dialect, the name of Thessaloniki is *Săruna*, proof that it comes from the Latin *Salona*, and that it was from the Megleno-Romanians, and not from the Greeks, that the Slavs – Bulgarians and Macedonians – borrowed the name they use for the city, *Solun*.

Finally, the largest and most concentrated group was found throughout the Middle Ages in the mountainous regions of Pindus, Gramos and Olympus. They are known as the Aromanians (Romanian: *aromâni*; Aromanian: *armâni*, though in some regions they also call themselves *rumâni*). Their Slavic and then Greek and Albanian neighbours called all these Latin-speakers "Vlachs" – the same name they used for Romanians north of the Danube.

And there was yet a fifth group of Vlachs in the Balkans, along the Adriatic coast and especially in the port of Dubrovnik (which was a great trading hub in medieval times, even managing to preserve a certain autonomy under the Ottomans). However, modern language experts believe that this Dalmatian dialect, whose last native speaker died on the island of Krk around 1900, was more likely to have belonged to Italian rather than Romanian. The fact that linguists had to ask the question in the first place is an example of how closely related the two languages are.

Eisagogé grammatikés *or* Introduction to Grammar, *printed in Moscopole in 1760*

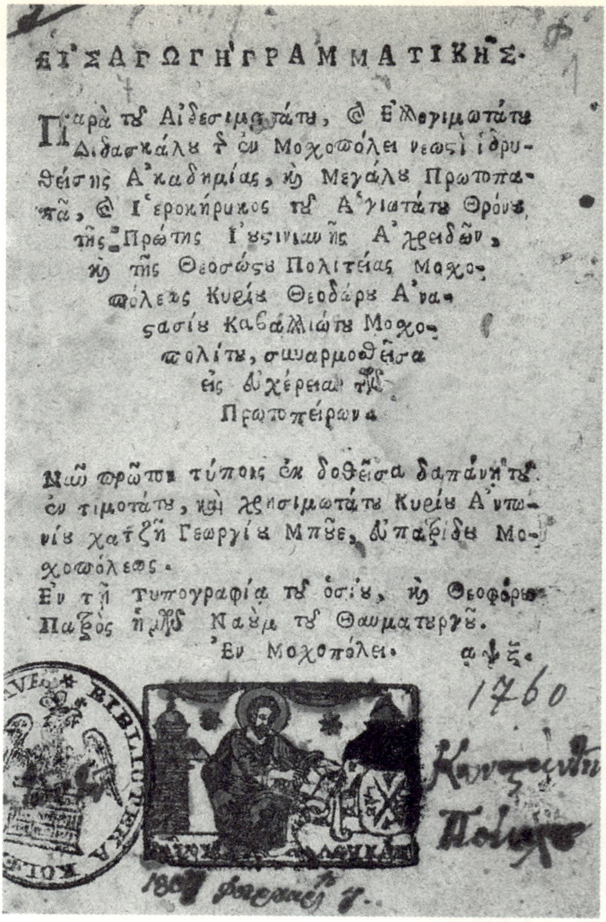
ΕἸΣΑΓΩΓῊ ΓΡΑΜΜΑΤΙΚῆΣ.

Παρὰ του Αἰδεσιμωτάτου, ὁ Ἐλλογιμωτάτου
Διδασκάλου τῆς ἐν Μοσχοπόλει νεωστὶ ἱδρυ-
θείσης Ἀκαδημίας, καὶ Μεγάλου Πρωτοπα-
πᾶ, ὁ Ἱεροκήρυκος του Ἁγιωτάτου Θρόνου
τῆς Πρώτης Ἰουστινιανῆς Ἀρχιδόντων,
καὶ τῆς Θεοσώστου Πολιτείας Μοσχο-
πόλεως Κυρίου Θεοδώρου Ἀνα-
στασίου Καβαλλιώτου Μοσχο-
πολίτου, συναρμοσθεῖσα
εἰς εὐχέρειαν τῶν
Πρωτοπείρων.

Νῦν πρῶτον τύποις ἐκδοθεῖσα δαπάνῃ του.
ἐντιμοτάτου, καὶ χρησιμωτάτου Κυρίου Ἀντω-
νίου χατζῆ Γεωργίου Μπούε, εὐπατρίδου Μο-
σχοπόλεως.
Ἐν τῇ τυπογραφίᾳ του ὁσίου, καὶ Θεοφόρου
Πατρὸς ἡμῶν Ναοὺμ του Θαυματουργοῦ.
Ἐν Μοσχοπόλει. αψξ.

At this point, we should discuss the Aromanians in more detail. Firstly, because they had a role to play in the history of the Balkans; secondly, because many of them emigrated to Romania during the last two centuries and gave the country several notable cultural and political figures; and finally, because their current situation and prospects for the future are a cause for concern.

Because of their geographical dispersion and lack of political will, Aromanians are an ethnic group that has never displayed real unity, nor represented a viable political project. Only once, in the late 14th century and early 15th century, do we find records of an Aromanian family called Buia Spata, who established a duchy straddling Thessaly and Epirus (present day Albania and

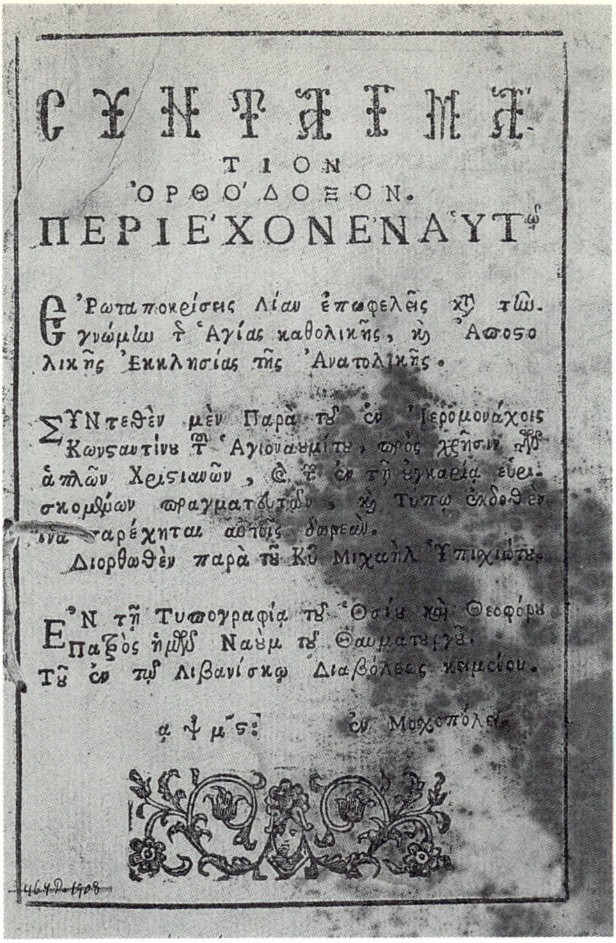
ΣΥΝΤΑΓΜΑ-
ΤΙΟΝ
ὈΡΘΟΔΟΞΟΝ.
ΠΕΡΙΕΧΟΝ ΕΝ ΑΥΤῷ

Syntagmátion orthódoxon *or* Orthodox Compendium, *printed in Moscopole in 1746*

Northern Greece) close to the Balkan Vlachs. This was the source of a long-lasting confusion with Wallachia (north of the Danube) since the Council of Konstanz, where a coat of arms showing the heads of three black men had been thought to belong to a "king" of Wallachia; this misled many heraldry specialists and historians in Romania, among them the brilliant Bogdan Petriceicu-Hașdeu, who believed it to be one of the arms used by the house of Basarab. The mystery has recently been solved by the researcher Constantin Rezachevici: the arms, in fact, belonged to the Aromanian Buia Spata family, of the Balkans.

Aromanians enjoyed a relative autonomy under the Ottomans. They were organised into 12 "captaincies", each

Ioannis Kolettis or Coletti (1773-1847) an Aromanian politician who played a significant role in the Greek War of Independence and twice served as prime minister (1834-1835; 1844-1847).

led by a militia captain (Romanian: *căpitan de armatoli**) responsible for maintaining order. In the 17th century, as the central authority of Constantinople diminished and Albanian Muslims grew more aggressive, Aromanians too began to show signs of unrest: some of their captains became *klephts*, or brigands (Romanian: *haiduci*; Greek: *klephtes*) sworn enemies of the Ottoman power. Documents, as well as folk ballads (both Aromanian and Greek) mention several of them, such as Iani Bucovală, Iani Belu, Nicolo Giuvara and Panu Meitani, whose surnames were then found among the families emigrating to the Principalities. Alongside such early preludes to the Greek revolution, we note the thriving trading activity of these Vlachs. One city in particular made them famous – Moscopole (now Voskopojë, in Albania). After Muslims destroyed this prosperous trade hub in a fearsome raid in 1788, the inhabitants and other Aromanians in the region dispersed to Macedonia, Serbia, Hungary and the Principalities. In Serbia, they would become the nucleus of Belgrade's (and the country's) burgeoisie; in Vienna and Budapest, they gave generations of great bankers and industrialists – Şina, Dumba, Darvari, Belu, Mocioni (or Mocsonyi) and perhaps Karajan. Aromanians would have an even greater impact in the Principalities. It is enough to mention the poets Octavian Goga and Ştefan Iosif from Transylvania, but most importantly, the remarkable figure of metropolitan Andrei Şaguna, reformer of the Orthodox Church, who had been born in Hungary to an Aromanian family living there for several generations. Şaguna's predecessor, bishop Moga, was Aromanian as well, and it was from his family that the poet and philosopher Lucian Blaga was descended on a maternal line.

Aromanians made a crucial contribution to the Greek war of independence. One of the forerunners of the revolution was Constantine Rigas "Feraios" Velestinis (alias Riga Fereu of Velestin – an Aromanian village) the author of the "Greek Marseillaise". Enthused by the ideas of the French Revolution, he dreamed of a great state led by the Greeks, uniting all Christians of the

* The *armatoloi* were a type of gendarmerie, recruited by the Turks from amongst Christian men in the Ottoman Empire.

Balkans. He was executed in Belgrade in 1798, after the Austrians handed him over to the Turks. The most famous of the captains of that war, Kolokotronis, hailing from the Peloponnese, was called "King of the Vlachs" (Greek: *Vlachovasilias*) but historians have not been able to prove that he himself was one. Yet it is certain that another general, Iani Coletti (Greek: *Ioannis Kolettis*) who would later become prime minister, was Aromanian.

Metropolitan Bishop Andrei Şaguna (1808-1873)

As the kingdom of Greece developed in an age of intense nationalism across Europe, speakers of Aromanian felt increasingly marginalised unless they became completely Hellenised and gave up the language of their ancestors. It is true that, for centuries, their elites had adopted the Greek culture in both church and school, and were fond of the country that had always been their home. Thus, most Vlachs who had become wealthy abroad – through banking, industry or trade – such as Şina, Maruzzi, Averoff and many others, were great benefactors (Greek: *evergetes*) of Athens and Greece in general. However, for those who stayed behind, Greek exclusivism became more and more oppressive, leading to serious clashes and bloodshed towards the late 19th century and early 20th century.

The interest that Romania has shown its distant brothers – beginning with Prince Alexandru Ioan Cuza and his minister, Dimitrie Bolintineanu, himself of Aromanian origin – has probably taken a misguided approach: dozens of schools and high schools were opened and maintained across the regions inhabited by Aromanians (first in the Ottoman Empire, then its successor states – Greece, Bulgaria, Albania) but teaching was in Romanian, not the local dialect, which produced the exact opposite of the desired effect: the graduates of Romanian schools, instead of strengthening their own communities, could not adapt to the local environment and were thus only good for emigrating to Romania.

Nowadays, after two Balkan wars and two world wars of great consequence for all aspects of life in the region, the situation of Aromanians in the Balkans is a dire one. If countries in the area are not compelled to establish schools or at least classes teaching Aromanian in the near future, a language that has endured for over two thousand years in the ethnically diverse Balkans will disappear completely, under our very eyes.

V. ROMANIANS IN THE MODERN ERA

The return of local rulers in the Principalities

Ioan Sandu Sturdza, voivode of Moldavia (1822-1828)

Despite its tragic conclusion, Tudor Vladimirescu's revolt nevertheless had beneficial consequences for the Principalities: no longer trusting the Greeks, the Turks decided to pay heed to a long-standing request of Romanian boyars, who sought to be granted a local ruler once more. Thus, the year 1822 marked the beginning of a new period in our history through the election of two local rulers. In actual fact, these were originally appointments by the sultan, but ones he made after delegations of boyars from Wallachia and Moldavia had put forward their proposals. The sultan made Ioan Sandu Sturdza (the descendant of an old Moldavian boyar family) voivode of Moldavia and Grigore IV Ghica (from a family of distant Albanian origins, by now so wholly assimilated by marrying into old Romanian boyar families that they were at the forefront of the "national party") voivode of Wallachia. The modern era began in the Principalities.

It is hard to imagine how people and places looked at the turn of the 19th century, towards the end of the Phanariote era. Certainly, life in the country – especially at the foothills of the mountains, where free peasant villages were more numerous – had not changed in centuries, with work in the fields, vineyards or forests following the rhythm of the seasons. Traditional dress – of both men and women – was reverently passed down from father to son and from mother to daughter, while foreign travellers always noted with surprise how, in such a downtrodden country, even the poorest wore clean, beautifully embroidered shirts. In towns and cities, boyars, rich merchants and even burghers wore Oriental style garments, as was the fashion in Constantinople – or *Țarigrad*, as it was called by the common people, a name that endures to this day in folk ballads. That is why Westerners travelling east – who mostly stopped over in towns – would have already gotten the impression of being in a province of the Ottoman Empire – or, if they travelled from Constantinople westwards, of still being in a Turkish province.

But the differences did not only lie in exterior aspects, such as Oriental attire – sometimes overly "exotic", such as the *calpac* (a huge, pumpkin-like fur hat worn by the boyars, which must have looked quite bizarre to the Western eye). Institutions, customs and the vocabulary (which was "international" only to the extent of the Ottoman world or the Byzantine heritage) were also different, as were mentalities. Therefore, when boyars, clerics and the wealthy and educated began to read translations of French or German novels, or newspapers sent from Vienna and Paris, and when the Turks could no longer oppose our noblewomen imitating Western fashion

Grigore Dimitrie Ghica, voivode of Wallachia (1822-1828)

St Peter's Day Fair in Giurgiu, as illustrated by Auguste Raffet during his travels in 1837. It is from Raffet, who passed through Wallachia and Moldavia on his way to Southern Russia, that we have this and other snapshots of our society at the time.

The upper class, as depicted by Auguste de Henikstein in 1825. The first four figures on the left are great boyars, wearing beards (in fact, the fourth character, sporting glasses, is the future voivode Grigore Alexandru Ghica). The next two are middle-ranking boyars, while on the right we find merchants and lesser boyars.

(with men quickly following suit) and when some of our young men had the chance to travel and study in the West, a veritable revolution took place that would have incalculable consequences for all walks of life. To understand some of the issues Romania is confronted with today, we must emphasise the profound mutations that took place at the beginning of that century and spanning several generations, as we generally overlook this momentous change of 150-200 years ago as if it were somehow shameful to admit that back then, we belonged to a different world than the one we are part of now.

The dominant French influence

French influence started to be felt in the Principalities as early as the Phanariote age, when France enjoyed an enormous prestige across the continent. From Lisbon to Saint Petersburg, the elites of Europe were speaking French. For us, the turning point came during the Russian occupation of 1806-1812. Convinced of the final victory of Russia against the Turks, young noblemen – and most importantly, young noblewomen – all started to wear Western-style clothes, to dance the waltz instead of the ancestral *hora* and to learn French, for French was what they spoke to the Russian invader. This did not prevent some of the older and politically savvier boyars such as the minister of the interior, Constantin Filipescu (who was eventually deported to the Russian Far East)

from plotting against the Russians in favour of the Turks, whom they saw as a necessary defence against Russian expansionism.

When Romanians started to travel to the West seeking the support of a great power against the Russians or Austrians, they would inevitably appeal to the French. This was not only because France continued to be the greatest power in Europe, despite the fall of Napoleon, but mostly because the French language is related to

Reception at the princely palace in Iași in a drawing by Charles Doussault, showing young ladies in European dress alongside boyars in Oriental attire (the year was 1843).

Encounter between a "bonjourist" and an old-fashioned boyar, as described by Ion Creangă: "The younger boyars, raised abroad only with French and German, spoke ill of the past... The speech, attire and customs of their elders no longer sit well with them. Because of this, some of them, in their foolishness, called the elders «rusty old things», «ișlik-wearers», «ghosts» or whatever came to their minds... Of course, some of the elders were just as foolish and scorned the youngsters, calling them «bonjourists», «duel-seekers», «trouser-wearers», «madmen», «arrogant upstarts», «law-forsakers» and «tongue-spoilers»."

Romanian, and both are part of the family of Romance languages. Thus began an extraordinary and peaceful influence by a foreign nation in our country, such that our everyday language consists of mostly French-derived words (some through Italian, which is even more closely related to Romanian) or words borrowed directly from Latin. The fact that young Romanian intellectuals (even those who had not studied abroad) spoke French meant that almost all our modern words would be taken directly from that language. And so we had to change the words taken from Turkish or Greek to serve in our new system of administration, law, politics and the economy: the *ispravnic* became a *prefect*, the *zapciu* became a *jandarm* (French: *gendarme*) and the *vistieria* became the *Ministerul Finanțelor* etc. We would have eventually had to borrow such terms from a foreign language, and this happened to be French. Moreover, this influence has not faded, but has in fact permeated our very ways of thinking and living. We no longer seem to realise how great French influence was in the 19th and early 20th centuries. All Romanian civil society and all our intelligentsia spoke French, while boyars spoke French in the home.

This should not shock or confuse us. It is a universal phenomenon that when a language becomes pervasive in culture, the aristocracies of other countries will take it up without giving it a second thought. If you read Leo Tolstoy's *War and Peace*, you will find that the private correspondence of those Russians who had defeated Napoleon is studded with French phrases. Even more surprisingly, Fredrick II the Great, military genius and the architect of Prussia's rise to power at the end of the 18th century, was so enamoured with the French language (in which he also wrote poetry) that he declared he only spoke German to stable-boys. Finally, an even more revealing (but far less known) example is that of Julius Caesar – great Caesar, true founder of the Roman Empire, whose name became synonymous with "emperor" – and who, having been stabbed 23 times and finding his stepson Brutus among them, is reported to have uttered the words that move us deeply still, two thousand years later: *'You too, child?'* – but said them in Greek (*Kai su, teknon?*) proof that he spoke Greek at home.

Young Romanian boyar around 1830, wearing clothes that were still reminiscent of the old Oriental dress.

Having said that, it should not surprise us that our elites spoke French until very recently.

Consequently, when we began to adopt the science, philosophy, law and, generally speaking, the culture of the West, things changed radically and rather violently in our country – in some ways under outside pressure, in the wake of the wars waged by Austria and Russia against the Turks. We became a theatre of war, which wreaked havoc across the land, but ultimately, also presented us with the opportunity to shake off Ottoman domination.

The Russian occupation of 1828-1834 and the Organic Statute

After yet another war with the Turks (1828-1829) concluded by the Treaty of Adrianople, the Russians occupied the Principalities and imposed on them a new type of constitution that came to be known as the Organic Statute. The irony of it was that the Russians, who were ruled by an autocratic regime, with no civil liberties and no parliament in their own country, imposed on us a system that was actually more liberal than theirs. The

General Pavel Dimitrievich Kiselyov, governor of the Romanian Principalities between 1829 and 1834

liberal movement had appeared in Russia in the early 19th century, and as one of its exponents, General Count Pavel Kiselyov (whose name was preserved in one of Bucharest's main thoroughfares, Kiseleff Boulevard) the Russian appointed governor of the Principalities, along with his entourage, decided to experiment with a relatively more liberal system than the one in Russia, and certainly more liberal than the one previously employed by the Turks. Let us get the terminology straight, however. When I say "liberal", I do not mean to say it was democratic. The constitution was quite aristocratic – only great boyars and some lesser ones could enter Parliament – but it was inspired by several Western European principles, such as the independence of the justice system and the existence of separate executive and legislative bodies; thus, for the first time in our country's history, Montesquieu's 18th century tripartite principle regarding the separation of political powers was being applied (albeit somewhat ineptly) meaning that the executive, the legislative and the judiciary should be separate and independent from each other, so that a country could be ruled in a liberal manner, free from despotism and arbitrary decisions. This principle appeared for the first time in the Organic Statute.

In spite of all this, the condition of the peasants worsened as a result of the new constitution. Through the 1829 Treaty of Adrianople, Russia (but also Britain, who ruled the seas and wanted trade liberalisation) forced the Turks to open up the Black Sea and the Danube to trade. Overnight, trade liberalisation meant that the boyars, who owned most of the land, were much more interested in its intensive exploitation to increase the export of grain. Up to that point, a peasant was relatively free to decide what crops to grow on the boyar's land; a boyar was obligated by law to rent out at least two thirds of his land to peasants, who cultivated it as they liked and gave the boyar one fifth, one quarter or one third of their harvest, but never more than half of it. When boyars were no longer forced to sell their grain to the Turks at a low price, but were instead allowed to sell it to the French or the British on the Danube, peasants began to be much more exploited by the great landowners than they had been before the Organic Statute. This shows us how progress also has its downsides. On the one hand, the first Romanian constitution formed the basis of a Western-style legislative system, while on the other it deteriorated the condition of the peasantry to such an extent that, later on, some socialist thinkers would proclaim that it started a neo-feudal age. Little did it matter that peasants were free (as I mentioned above, serfdom had been abolished since the mid-18th century by the reforms of Constantin Mavrocordat) since the fact that they had to use a boyar's land and pay him half of the harvest (obtained through their manual labour, using their ploughs and their oxen) meant that their situation became progressively worse. Moreover, this happened in the context of a general improvement in hygiene and progress in medicine (the smallpox vaccine, called "smallpox graft" – Romanian: *altoi de vărsat* – had recently been introduced) which led to a boom of the rural population in the 19th century.

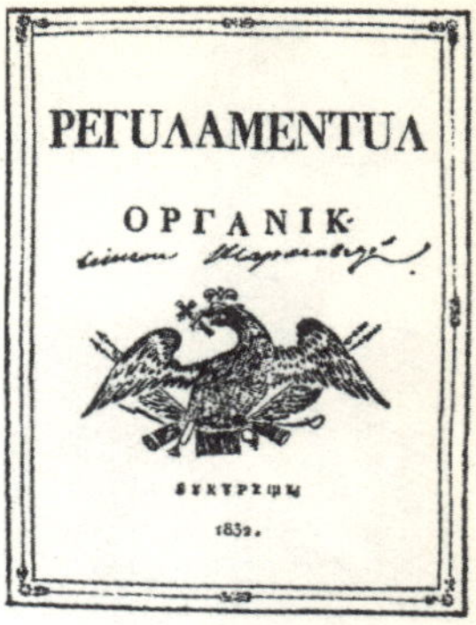

Cover of the Organic Statute of Wallachia (1832)

Politically, the Organic Statute also meant a permanent interference of Russian representatives – Count Kiselyov up to 1834, then the Russian consuls in Iași and Bucharest – in the affairs of the country, which turned the Principalities into *de facto* Russian protectorates. The position of our voivodes – Mihai Vodă Sturdza in Moldavia (1834-1849); Alexandru Ghica (1834-1842) and Gheorghe Bibescu (1842-1848) in Wallachia – was an extremely difficult one, with local liberals accusing them of bowing to Russian pressure on one side and Russian consuls accusing them of bowing to the local opposition on the other. Particularly in Wallachia, Alexandru Ghica was confronted by a fierce anti-Russian opposition. One of the leaders of this opposition, Ion Câmpineanu, travelled to the West, where he hoped to awaken the interest of Europe's great powers in the Romanian question; surprisingly, he was granted audiences by prime ministers such as Lord Palmerston in London and Adolphe Thiers in Paris. Being of great boyar lineage and related to the Cantacuzino and the Cantemir families,

Alexandru Ghica, voivode of Wallachia (1834-1842)

Gheorghe Bibescu, voivode of Wallachia (1842-1848)

Wallachia's National Assembly in 1837. Auguste Raffet gave it a more appropriate name in the legend, calling it the "General Assembly of Boyars", highlighting the aristocratic character of this incipient parliament.

Câmpineanu was introduced to Western political circles by Prince Adam Jerzy Czartoryski, leader of the Polish émigrés and a former advisor to the Russian tsar. Another possible explanation for his success was his links to the Freemasons.

Upon his return, he was imprisoned for a while, as was the young Dimitrie (Mitică) Filipescu, who had become our first Doctor of Laws in Paris, and whose political ideas enable us to think of him as the first socialist politician in our country, despite belonging to one of the most powerful boyar families in Wallachia. Alas, Filipescu died in prison. Incarcerated with him was young Nicolae Bălcescu, who would play a leading role in the revolution of 1848. It was in prison that he contracted tuberculosis (Romanian: archaic. *oftică*) the disease that would eventually strike him down at a young age.

A more able and appeasing man, Sturdza managed to hang on to his throne for longer. Yet for all the faults they were accused of, it can be said objectively that during the government of the three voivodes, both Principalities made significant economic and cultural advances. Entire cities were developed, such as Brăila (for a time regarded by foreigners as more beautiful than Bucharest) and Alexandria (named after Alexandru Ghica); roads were built and the streets of both capitals were paved

Galician Jews in an 1836 drawing by Auguste Raffet. During the previous centuries, a spiritual and religious movement called Hasidism had emerged among them, which also influenced their clothing, among other things.

and equipped with gas lamps. In Iași, Voivode Sturdza inaugurated our first university (Romanian: *Academia Mihăileană*) and maintained a French theatre. Trade flourished in both countries, as a result of the Treaty of Adrianople, which liberalised commercial activity on the Danube and in the Black Sea, and put an end to the Turkish monopoly on grain and cattle. It was during this period that a true Romanian bourgeoisie, made up of traders and lesser boyars, began to emerge. An unexpected consequence was also the increasing immigration of Jews from Galicia, Poland and Russia into Moldavia, attracted by a relatively "pristine" commercial market.

The Revolution of 1848 in the Principalities – aborted in Moldavia, victorious for three months in Wallachia – and the role of Freemasonry

We come now to the Revolution of 1848. But first, we must mention that profound changes had taken place in the economic and social order across Europe after the fall of Napoleon, between the years 1815 and 1848. Industry as we know it today first developed in Britain, with France adopting the British model. I will digress for a moment to address those who feel humiliated by the fact that we needed foreigners for the development of our country, thus giving rise to a complex of inferiority: in France, which had fallen several decades behind Britain

Barricade of the revolutionaries being stormed by French government forces during the 1848 Revolution in Paris.

in terms of industrial development, statistics show that just before the 1848 Revolution, there were no less than 60,000 British workers in the country. The French needed these British engineers and workers to kick-start their own industrial age by building factories, railways etc. If the French did not think it was demeaning to learn from foreigners as they adopted new methods and techniques, then perhaps we should not either. Industrial development brought with it significant new issues across all Western European states. In 1848, the population of Paris rebelled against Louis Philippe – the Citizen King, as he was called – who had been slow to make democratic reforms and had surrendered power to capitalist interests originating more in the bourgeoisie than the aristocracy.

The French Revolution of 1789 had been characterised by populism and bloodshed, but it eventually replaced one class, the aristocracy, with another – the bourgeoisie. Yet in 1848, the people attempted to overthrow the bourgeoisie as well. Interestingly, our young students in Paris joined in the popular revolution with great enthusiasm, despite the fact that most of them were actually sons of boyars; for example, it appears that both the Golescu and the Brătianu brothers took part in the fighting alongside the Parisian rebels. In effect, they were the apprentices of the 1848 French Revolution, which they duly imported to our Principalities, to Wallachia and Moldavia.

Let us now say a few words about a subject that is seldom mentioned in our history books: the role played by a secret society, the Freemasonry, in these revolutions – both the 1789 French Revolution and our revolution of 1848. Our young men studying in France or other Western countries could not have been drawn towards the conservatives – far less concerned with two principalities they considered to be Turkish provinces – but the liberals, eager to spread their ideas of democracy and liberty to the countries of Eastern and Southern Europe, captivated these young Romanians. This, in turn, prompted most of them to join Masonic lodges.

Emblematic image of the 1848 Revolution: young Romanians carrying a tricolor flag with the motto "Justice, Fraternity". On 14 June 1848, the revolutionary government in Bucharest issued an edict declaring it the national flag. The watercolour belongs to Costache Petrescu (1829-1910) one of the first modern Romanian painters.

Hanging the Organic Statute, a satirical drawing from 1848. On the left, alongside the boyars and other representatives of the "reactionary forces", we see the voivode of Wallachia, Gheorghe Bibescu, wearing a plumed hat; to the right, pulling on the rope, are the members of the revolutionary government.

What is Freemasonry? It is a pretty difficult concept to define, because for a long time, Freemasonry shrouded itself in a veil of mystery. During the Middle Ages, the builders of the famous cathedrals, who passed down the secrets of their trade from father to son and from master builder to apprentice, created secret societies to protect their knowledge. In Old French, *franc maçon* meant "free mason". They travelled the length and breadth of the country in "companies" building anything they were commissioned to, but they would only pass on their knowledge to those who had completed considerably lengthy apprenticeships. In the early 18th century, the word "freemason" was adopted by an Anglican pastor who founded a new secret society. The purpose of this society was neither masonry, nor architecture, but the overthrow of a society that had become too dominated by the aristocracy and the Catholic Church. These secret fraternities founded in Britain quickly spread to the continent, aiming to weaken the power of the Catholic Church (which controlled education and had too much influence on governments) but also to destroy the aristocratic monopoly over governments. It appears that Freemasonry played an important role in the outbreak of the French Revolution of 1789 – a controversial matter, but one I believe has a lot of merit, even if the only proof was the fact that all the petitions for reform sent to King Louis XVI from the provinces resembled one another as if written by the same hand, the only plausible explanation being that they had been drafted in Masonic lodges and adopted by Third Estate* deputies (representing the common people) who brought them to Paris. The same thing happened in the Principalities in 1848. Since the archives of Freemasonry were opened to the public, we have had proof that almost all those young men who had studied in Paris were recruited into Masonic lodges and returned to our country as Freemasons, and it was their efforts that brought about the Revolution of 1848, as well as the 1859 Union of Principalities.

The truth must be told if there are documents to prove it. However, later on, Freemasonry degenerated into a sort of clique based on mutual support and the accumulation of power; leftist extremists largely took over the organisation (especially in France) and a great many Jews, eager to break the ostracisation that had plagued them for centuries, joined in. Some of them, having arrived in our country, tried to force the Principalities into immediately granting Romanian citizenship to all Jews who had settled there after 1830, particularly in Moldavia. This resulted in a negative backlash against Freemasonry; Romanian intellectuals were now more reticent and felt that they were being pressured into a direction that no longer served the national interest of the day, as they saw it.

In February 1848, when the revolution broke out in France, some of our young intellectuals, like the Brătianu brothers, found themselves in Paris. They soon returned home, where they began to plot the overthrow of both governments, or the imposition of democratic reforms on the voivodes – Gheorghe Bibescu in Bucharest

Adolphe Crémieux (1796-1880) Freemason and president of the Universal Israelite Alliance, as well as a minister of justice in the French government. In June 1866 he made a visit to Bucharest, where he addressed the members of the government and Prince Carol, requesting the emancipation of Romanian Jews. One week later, a clause that excluded the Jews from obtaining Romanian citizenship was added to the project of the Constitution.

---

* The Third Estate included the bourgeoisie and peasantry. The First Estate were the high clergy; the Second Estate were the aristocracy.

Ion C. Brătianu (1821-1891) as a young man

The Golescu brothers, prominent Wallachian revolutionaries. This photograph shows them in their old age, already senior Liberal leaders.

and Mihai Sturdza in Iași. In March 1848, the plot they were devising in Moldavia was uncovered and immediately thwarted by prince Sturdza. Some of the conspirators were jailed; others managed to escape and fled into exile, so the Moldavian revolution died in its infancy. On the other hand, in Wallachia, where the bourgeoisie was more developed than in Moldavia, the young revolutionaries succeeded in mobilising the population, and even reached the villages through some revolutionaries who hailed from the peasant masses, such as Popa Șapcă. The Revolution began in earnest with the Proclamation of Islaz (9 June 1848) and spread to Bucharest, where the revolutionaries forced Prince Bibescu to organise elections, adopt a declaration of reforms and suppress the boyar class etc. Two days later, realising that there was a risk of foreign intervention to quell the movement, Bibescu abdicated and fled abroad.

The government of these young revolutionaries – of which we have already mentioned Nicolae Bălcescu and Ion Câmpineanu, his nephew Ion Ghica, the Golescu brothers, Christian Tell, Eliade Rădulescu and General Magheru – would last for three months. It immediately began to adopt radical measures. For instance, they decreed the liberation of the Gypsies, who had been enslaved, humiliated, beaten and mistreated for centuries on end, which would explain some of the bad habits they developed. It is not their fault, but that of the hundreds of years of pain and disgrace that they have had to endure. They were, in theory, liberated in 1848, but the failure of the Revolution meant that the decree was not put into practice. Nevertheless, some boyars like Ion Câmpineanu and Prince Mihai Sturdza, had already freed their own Gypsies; the monasteries finally realised that slavery was not consistent with Christian ideology and set theirs free as well, so that around 1850 there were only about 5,000 Gypsy serfs in Wallachia and about as many in Moldavia; these were privately owned by boyars, in whose households they served as cooks, lumberjacks, blacksmiths, tinsmiths and farriers, but also as fiddlers. The complete abolition of Gypsy serfdom did not begin until 1856. It seems unimaginable that

Nicolae Bălcescu (1819-1852) in a portrait made during his lifetime, as was the more "canonical" one, painted by Gheorghe Tattarescu in 1851.

there were still serfs in our country as late as the 19th century, but keep in mind that the United States of America took another 7 years and a civil war to abolish slavery. In this respect at least, we were ahead of the USA.

However, new difficulties emerged with the liberation of the Gypsies: how to integrate them into the country's daily life, how to enable them to become landowners and practice their trades freely etc. Freedom in name only did not solve all their problems.

Let us return to the year 1848. As the government only lasted for three months, its plans were mothballed. For example, talks on land redistribution between peasants and landowners (let us call them "boyars" – although these not only included the boyars of old, but also the nouveau riche of the bourgeoisie) had been in progress for weeks, but that was where things ground to a halt. Russia could not suffer such a revolution, and neither

Battle of Dealul Spirii (13 September 1848) which started from an incident between a company of firemen led by Captain Pavel Zăgănescu and the Ottoman troops that had come to Bucharest to crush the Revolution.

could Turkey, our suzerain power. For once, the two powers agreed to invade the Principalities together – the Russians from the north, the Turks from the south – and put an end to the revolution between September and October 1848. Each occupied half of the territory – even Bucharest was divided in two, just as Berlin would be split between the USSR and the Western Allies after World War II. It was the end of our greatest chance for self-rule yet. Those leaders of the Revolution who had not been captured by the Russians and deported to Siberia fled the country – some to Turkey, but most of them to France. There, they set about an extraordinary propaganda effort that, over time, would transform the opinion of Western governments on the Romanian question.

1848 in Transylvania – Hungarians and Romanians find themselves on opposite sides

At this point, we should mention the events that took place in Transylvania at the same time, where things unfolded very differently. The revolution had started in

Hungary. Some of the revolutionaries in the Principalities, chiefly Nicolae Bălcescu, were considering an alliance with the Hungarians against the common enemy, which he believed to be Russia. Unfortunately, Hungarians (largely represented by their aristocracy) understood their national interest differently. Since the time of Empress Maria Theresa, Hungarian aristocracy had been very powerful, making up a large part of the Austrian army. This helps to explain how the Hungarian revolution managed to resist the Austrians for a whole year. It was even believed they would establish a free Hungary, but the Austrians fought them all the same, calling upon the Russians to help them.

In the meantime, it appears that Romanians in Transylvania had offered Hungarians their support in the fight against Austria, on condition that they would be granted equal rights in the province. Their offer was rejected; on the contrary, Hungarian revolutionaries went even further, proclaiming the union of Transylvania with Hungary. Previously, under the emperor's domination, Transylvania was a separate administrative unit, despite the fact that power lay with the Hungarian Diet. Romanians could not consent to such a union, which would have made them a minority in the newly created state.

Left: *Avram Iancu (1824-1872) in a contemporary engraving.* Right: *Lajos Kossuth (1802-1894) leader of the Hungarian revolutionaries.*

Nicolae Bălcescu met with Hungarian revolutionary leader Lajos Kossuth in an attempt to bring him into contact with Avram Iancu, leader of Romanian revolutionaries, but to no avail. As no pact could be agreed, Romanian peasants rallied around Avram Iancu against the Hungarians, in an unlikely alliance with the emperor in Vienna. The same thing happened in Croatia, and so two of the largest minorities in the Austrian realm sided with the central government in Vienna against the Hungarian revolutionaries. By the time Hungarian revolutionaries finally understood that it was in their interest to ally themselves with the Romanians – signing an agreement with Bălcescu, according to which Romanians would be granted equal rights in Transylvania – it was already too late. The Russian army, under General Paskevich, entered the province and annihilated the Hungarian army.

Although defeated, the Revolution of 1848-1849 served Hungarian interests. The Austrians did not reward the Croats or the Romanians for their support against

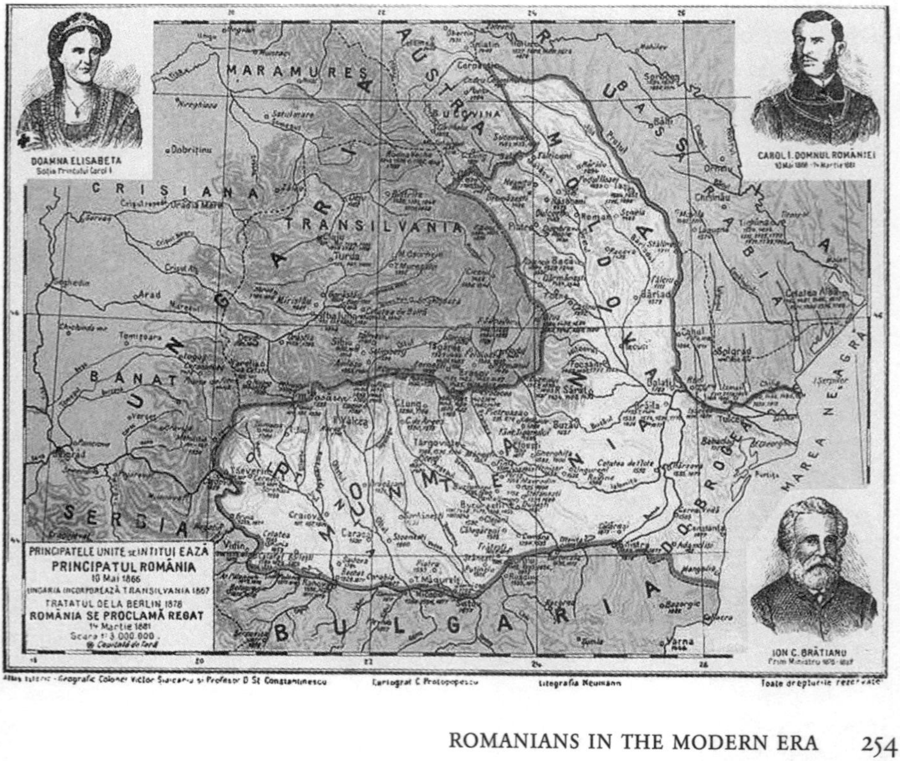

Map of Transylvania from an 1881 historical atlas, depicting King Carol, Queen Elisabeth and Ion C. Brătianu, prime minister of Romania.

the Hungarians, and did not grant them any additional rights. Quite the contrary, less than 20 years afterwards, in 1867, conscious of the fact that the empire could not endure for much longer solely under Austrian rule, they created a new Austro-Hungarian union (Romanian: *Austro-Ungaria*) giving Hungarians authority over the Eastern half of the empire, which spelled disaster for minorities in that territory. The medieval Hungarian Crown was virtually restored, while Hungarians – who were not even the majority population – gained jurisdiction over the Slovaks, the Romanians, the Ruthenians of Western Ukraine, as well as parts of the Croats and Serbs. In the west, aside from Austria proper, the Austrians would rule over Bohemia (present day Czech Republic) South-Western Poland, Bukovina, part of Croatia and the Italian Tyrol. This was the "compromise" of 1867, dubbed the "Dual Monarchy'" with two capitals – Vienna and Budapest – two parliaments, two governments and only the ministry of foreign affairs, the army and several other administrative bodies in common. To Romanians in Transylvania, this amounted to a catastrophe, because as soon as the Hungarians turned into masters once more, they began using any means necessary to assimilate other minority populations.

Lazăr Șineanu (1859-1934) one of Romania's foremost linguists and philologists, born in Ploiești, was in fact Jewish. He was never granted Romanian citizenship.

As an aside, I mentioned above that Jews had immigrated into Moldavia by the tens of thousands after the Treaty of Adrianople. A similar phenomenon happened in Hungary at about the same time. However, Romanians and Hungarians reacted to this in very different ways. Since there had been no bourgeoisie to speak of in the Principalities, our reaction was like that of a seashell closing its plates. We spoke Romanian, they spoke Yiddish, and for decades their integration progressed at a very slow pace. This led to a feeling among many Romanians that they were a foreign body in their country. Hungarians, on the other hand, were clever enough to assimilate the Jews by granting them citizenship. The explanation for this has to do with national interest, as the census showed that only by adding the Jewish population to theirs could Hungarians claim majority in their

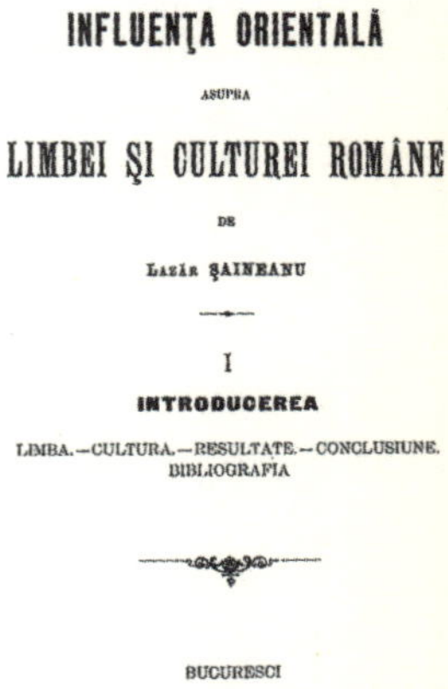

INFLUENŢA ORIENTALĂ

ASUPRA

LIMBEI ŞI CULTUREI ROMÂNE

DE

LAZĂR ŞAINEANU

I

INTRODUCEREA

LIMBA.—CULTURA.—RESULTATE.—CONCLUSIUNE.
BIBLIOGRAFIA

BUCURESCI

Title page of Lazăr Șăineanu's Oriental Influences on the Romanian Language and Culture *(1901)*

own country. The consequences of these different approaches can be felt to this day. Although during World War II Hungary surrendered its Jews to be exterminated in Nazi gas chambers, on the whole, the international Jewish community sympathises more with Hungary than with Romania.

The Principalities between 1848 and 1859 – Preludes to the Union and the Crimean War (1854-1856)

Let us turn our attention back to Wallachia and Moldavia after the events of 1848. Both countries had been under Russian and Turkish occupation for several years. The revolutionary government had only lasted three months in Wallachia, and a new regime, similar to that of the Organic Statue, was imposed. However, the role played by the Romanian diaspora of 1848, both in Constantinople and in Paris, was to prove crucial in 1854, when a new war broke out in the Balkans (started by Russia under the pretext of defending certain rights of Christians in Palestine). This time, Western powers were no longer prepared to accept further Russian expansion into the peninsula, and risk the closure of the straits of

The Romanian Principalities after the 1856 Treaty of Paris, when the counties of Cabul, Bolgrad and Ismail in Southern Bessarabia were returned to Moldavia.

Allegorical representation of the anti-Russian coalition during the Crimean War: Sultan Abdul Mejid I, Queen Victoria and Emperor Napoleon III.

Constantinople. War broke out between a coalition made up of Britain (ruled by Queen Victoria) France (ruled by Napoleon III) and Piedmont (the nucleus of the future kingdom of Italy) in alliance with Turkey, against Russia. This forced the Russians to evacuate the Principalities, which were quickly occupied by the Austrians (who declared themselves neutral) while the hostilities took place in the Crimean Peninsula, where the Anglo-French fleet subsequently landed troops. The fighting lasted for two years (1854-1856) and was very strenuous for the allies, who were disadvantaged by the great distance from their bases; moreover, apart from the Turks, coalition soldiers were unclear as to why they were fighting so far from their homelands. Serious epidemics wreaked havoc, as battlefield medicine was virtually non-existent (the Red Cross would only be founded several years later, at the initiative of a young Swiss social activist named Henri Dunant, horrified by the gruesome spectacle he witnessed during another war, waged by Napoleon III against Austria in 1859, for the unification of Italy).

Nicholas I, tsar of Russia

Fortunately for the allies, Tsar Nicholas I died of pneumonia and his successor, Alexander II, a more pragmatic

Moldavia's Ad-hoc Divan, among whom we note Metropolitan Sofronie Miclescu (middle medallion on the top row) and the future prince, Alexandru Ioan Cuza.

man, who understood that there was nothing to gain from continuing an extremely costly war with the two great Western powers, signed the Treaty of Paris in 1856, which saw Russia concede territories for the first time. The Western powers forced the Russians to return Southern Bessarabia to Moldavia – not out of fairness to the Principalities, but in order to prevent Russian control over the mouths of the Danube. The paradox was that we only got back the three Bessarabian counties where Romanians were in the minority (as the Ottomans had settled Turks and Tatars there for centuries) while the majority Romanian central and Northern parts remained with Russia.

This was, nevertheless a favourable moment for the Principalities: as Russia backed down, representatives of the great powers met again in Paris in 1858 and decided to allow the Romanian Principalities to unite (the lobbying efforts of our young intellectuals in the West were now paying off) on condition that they would still be ruled by two voivodes and only maintain a handful of common institutions at Focșani – all in all, a rather awkward federal arrangement. For once, we were able to take advantage of an opportunity. The great powers also decided to organise two so-called Ad-hoc Assemblies in Wallachia and Moldavia for the purpose of electing voivodes. Unfortunately, elections in Moldavia were rigged by *kaimakam* Nicolae Vogoridi (the Turkish name

Alexandru Ioan Cuza, photographed by Marie-Alexandre Alophe

for an interim governor appointed by the sultan) a Phanariote of Bulgarian origins. The Romanians complained to Napoleon III of France, who succeeded (with great difficulty) in persuading Queen Victoria of England to put pressure on the Ottomans and have the elections declared null and void. Under threat of military action by France and Britain, the sultan accepted; elections resumed in Moldavia, and this time the unionists won by a landslide.

Here we are, in January 1859 – elections took place in Iași, followed by Bucharest and they provide us with a wonderful example of the astuteness of our political class at the time. After much deliberation, those in Iași elected a virtually unknown candidate – Colonel Alexandru Ioan Cuza. Many books have since claimed that he was only elected because he was a high-ranking Freemason. Yet having consulted experts on the subject, who have researched recently disclosed Freemasonry documents in Paris (and specifically those of the lodge who was "making" Romanian Freemasons) I was unable to find a mention of Cuza in any of them. I must therefore apologise for having stated this in one of my French language books, in which I quoted the information I had found in a book of Masonic history. It has never actually been proven that Cuza was a Freemason. But one thing is certain: almost all those young unionists who put his

Alexandru Ioan Cuza attending the opening session of the National Assembly in Bucharest, on 29 February 1860. The political and administrative union of the two principalities was only completed in December 1861.

candidature forward and voted for him were Freemasons, so it would be fair to say that Cuza was a creation of the Freemasons, at least at the beginning. And as we shall see later on, they would also be responsible for his downfall, a mere seven years later.

Alexandru Ioan Cuza became voivode of Moldavia on 5 January 1859. All eyes were now on Bucharest. As I said earlier, a popular movement controlled by the revolutionaries (such as the Brătianu brothers) who had learned how to run a revolution in Paris, had been in existence there ever since 1848. They appealed to the masses, who protested violently in the streets and forced the Parliament to elect the same man, Alexandru Ioan Cuza, voivode of Moldavia, as ruler of Wallachia, on 24 January 1859. We thus presented Europe with a *fait accompli*: both Principalities had elected the same voivode. It took about three years of arduous diplomacy and the support of Napoleon III (whom we may think of as a sort of godfather to Romania) to achieve recognition of the fact that we were ruled by one voivode (or rather *prince*, as the title was known in Europe) but only on condition that the situation be tolerated during his reign of seven years. Also after three years, we were permitted to call our new country (originally named the "United Principalities of Wallachia and Moldavia") by the name "Romania" (Romanian: *România*) a relatively recent creation, derived from the word *român* (meaning "Romanian"). It was also the time when we chose our national flag – a blend of older flags used by voivodes of Wallachia and Moldavia. The blue, yellow and red (Romanian: *tricolorul*) thus became the flag of our country, hopefully for all time.

Barbu Catargiu (1807-1862) the first prime minister of a united Romania. Unfortunately, he was also the first prime minister in our history to be assassinated.

The reign of Cuza

Although he had not been prepared for the role and his election was a rather surprising one, Cuza would prove to be a remarkable ruler. A man of rare kindness and honesty, he enacted extensive reforms during his brief, seven-year reign. Firstly, he attempted something that Russia opposed (because it generally favoured Eastern Churches): the nationalisation of monastery estates. For

First coat of arms of the United Principalities, adopted in 1859 under Prince Cuza. The escutcheon bears the Moldavian aurochs and the Wallachian eagle side by side, topped by a princely crown.

centuries, Romanian voivodes (and many of the boyars) believing that they were making their peace with God before death, had made significant donations to churches on Mount Athos, to those in the Holy Land (Palestine) or to Saint Catherine's Monastery on Mount Sinai, in Egypt. Little by little, it came to be that one seventh of the entire arable land in the country was made up of estates that had been "dedicated" to monasteries on the Holy Mount, for instance; from the time of the Phanariotes, these foreign monasteries had enjoyed the right to send their own abbots to our monasteries, whose role was to survey the accounts and ensure that all the remaining agricultural revenues of these vast estates went to Mount Athos, to Palestine or to Egypt, once the local monks had taken what they needed to support themselves. It had long been remarked within the more enlightened and liberal circles that it was unacceptable for so much of the country's wealth to be sent abroad, even for religious reasons. The first attempt to stop this "haemorrhage" was made soon after the revolution of 1821 (when the father of writer Vasile Alecsandri was the administrator of monastery estates in Moldavia); but just a few years later, under pressure from the Russian

Prince Cuza's visit to Constantinople (September 1860), capital of his suzerain power. Sultan Abdul Mejid I received him with full honours, despite the dependent status of the Principalities.

government, our reformers had to abandon their plans. However, under Alexandru Ioan Cuza, with Mihail Kogălniceanu as prime minister, the decision was finally made during the last days of 1863, taking advantage of the fact that Russia was no longer the unstoppable force it had been prior to the Crimean War. The Parliament voted to nationalise monastery estates. Naturally, this resulted in a wave of protest from the foreign monasteries affected by the new law, as well as Greeks on Mount Athos and everywhere else, who urged Russia and the other great powers to take action against us – but despite this, the Cuza government did not back down. Negotiations to arrange financial compensation failed – Romania had offered 50 million francs in gold, quite a sum for that time – but the proposal was obstinately rejected, so no payment was ever made. Apparently, the former beneficiaries have not forgiven us to this day. When I myself visited Mount Athos, I learned from very trustworthy sources that Greek abbots there still nurture the hope that the estates we "stole" 150 years ago will some day be returned.

Second coat of arms of the United Principalities, which emphasises the union of the two countries under the rule of one prince by displaying the Cuza family motto ("ALL IN ONE") under the quartered shield.

Nationalisation did not only affect dedicated monastery estates, but applied to all lands owned by the Church across the country, which had serious consequences on its independence. Priests, monks and nuns were suddenly turned into paid state employees. Moreover, the government went on to impose new rules regarding canonical life, such as establishing a minimal age for joining a monastery, restricting it to the elderly and infirm – blatantly anticlerical measures, possibly of Masonic influence.

Nationalisation enabled Cuza to proceed with redistributing the land to peasants, but not before he was forced to dissolve the Parliament in order to pass the law. About 2 million hectares were then allotted to over 500,000 families. But as the rural population grew over time, and the plot of land given to each family was too small anyway, Cuza's reform did not significantly improve the situation of the peasantry.

Mihail Kogălniceanu, prime minister of Romania (October 1863 – February 1865). His government passed the law on the nationalisation of monastery estates, and witnessed Prince Cuza's so-called coup, in 1864.

Far more important, from the point of view of long-term consequences, was the adoption of modern codes of law into the Romanian legislation. Largely inspired

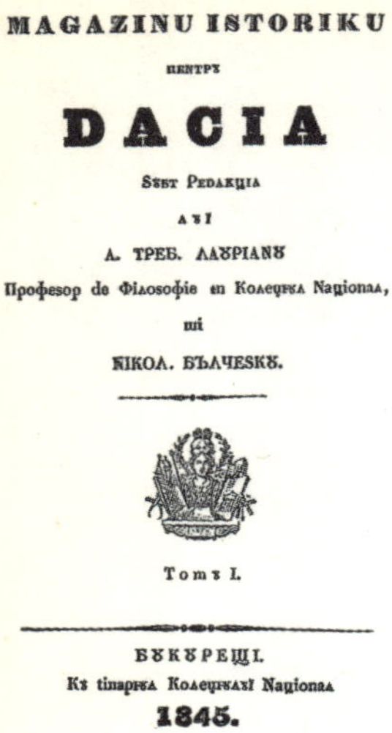
MAGAZINU ISTORIKU

пентрꙋ

DACIA

Sꙋбт Pедакціа

лꙋі

А. ТРЕБ. ЛАꙋРІАНꙋ

Професор de Філософіе ѫn Колеџꙋлꙋ Naціонал,

ші

NІКОЛ. БЪЛЧЕSКꙋ.

Томꙋ I.

БꙋКꙋРЕЩІ.

Кꙋ тіпаріꙋл Колеџꙋлꙋі Naціонал

1845.

Title page of Historical Magazine for Dacia *from an 1845 issue, the first periodical in Wallachia that aimed to publish articles about our history. Note that the text is a mix of Cyrillic and Latin characters.*

by French and Belgian law, new civil and penal codes were created, along with laws on modern education and the use of the Latin alphabet etc. Perhaps not many people know that we have only been using Latin characters since 1863, whereas before that we had been reading and writing in Cyrillic script, just like the Bulgarians, the Serbians or the Russians. In the West, this created the impression that we did not belong to the Romance-speaking family of peoples. Changing the alphabet had long been discussed, but the older generation was reluctant to learn a new alphabet. Therefore, during the reigns of Mihai Sturdza and Grigore Ghica in Moldavia, and Alexandru Ghica, Gheorghe Bibescu and Barbu Știrbei in Wallachia, Latin characters were gradually introduced among Cyrillic ones in official documents and newspapers for over 20 years. This was later called, somewhat ironically, the "transitional" alphabet, as old habits die hard. In the end, under Cuza, the final decision was made to adopt the Latin alphabet in our country – with an orthography that has changed many times since.

Another important decision made during Cuza's reign was the consecration of the Wallachian capital, Bucharest, as the capital of the United Principalities. For the first three years after the double election of Cuza, there had been two separate governments – one in Iași and one in Bucharest. But when the United Principalities became "Romania", one government needed one capital. Yet our otherwise savvy and audacious politicians did not have the courage – political, but mostly economical – to create a new capital in the small border town of Focșani. So they chose Bucharest. Firstly, because Bucharest was the greater city, two to three times more populous than Iași; it was a more important commercial centre, located between Turkey and Austria, comparing to Iași, which is not on the main north-south trade route, but most importantly, if you look at a map, since the loss of Bessarabia, Iași was only 15 kilometres away from the Russian border – nowadays that of the new "Republic of Moldova". Bucharest was thus further away from Russia, the power we feared most.

The overthrow of Cuza

If Cuza's seven-year reign was as important and beneficial as I said it was, then why, you may ask, was he overthrown and replaced with a foreign ruler? Before we answer that question, some explanations are in order. Firstly, there were those who felt that Cuza's reforms happened too rapidly and were not prepared to accept each and every one of the new Western laws; then there were the great landowners who feared that land reform would continue in their detriment; finally, prince Cuza had been criticised for his private life. But, most importantly, a belief that had long been part of the mentality of our 19th century ruling politicians was that our country would never be truly independent in the Western sense, until it would be ruled by a king or prince from a foreign dynasty, thereby putting an end to disputes between our most powerful families – Ghica, Bibescu, Cantacuzino or Mavrocordat. Hence why pleas to be granted a foreign ruler were constantly included in the petitions we brought before the great powers to explain our people's aspirations.

Now, Cuza had pledged not to rule for longer than seven years and to facilitate the election of a foreign prince. As the seven years were coming to an end, Cuza had made no apparent effort, nor taken any steps towards finding and electing his successor. This was the major factor that brought rival politicians into a sort of coalition, to everyone's surprise. The most fervent right-wing

General Nicolae Golescu (left) with Lascăr Catargiu and Colonel Nicolae Haralambie, members of the lieutenancy that assumed power immediately after Prince Cuza abdicated. The lieutenancy was in charge of the selection of a foreign-born prince for the Romanian throne and issued the proclamation that recommended the election (by referendum) of Karl von Hohenzollern as the hereditary "Voivode of Romanians".

conservatives (to use modern terms) joined forces with the most prominent left-wing liberals (C. A. Rosetti and the Brătianu brothers) and became known as the "monstrous coalition". The truth is that this unlikely alliance had been forged by the Freemasons – in fact, they had even created a special lodge dedicated to toppling prince Cuza, joined by conservatives and liberals alike, and which plotted a coup d'état, supported by the commanders of several military units. On the night of 11 February 1866, a group of officers burst into the palace, pistols in hand, and forced Prince Cuza to sign his abdication. Cuza behaved very gracefully, signed the document and left for Austria the next day; he never tried to regain the throne or take any action against the coalition, and always maintained that he too wanted the enthronement of a foreign prince. He died relatively young, in 1873, while still in exile.

How we came to elect a foreign-born prince in 1866

Ion Ghica (1817-1897) the revolutionary of 1848, who became prime minister on the day Prince Cuza was deposed (11 February 1866)

The provisional government, hastily put together the very next day under the presidency of Ion Ghica (the revolutionary of 1848, who would serve as prime minister twice, though briefly, as he did not understand party politics; in his old age, he earned a reputation as one of our great writers through is *Letters* to Vasile Alecsandri) offered the crown of Romania to Prince Philippe, Count of Flanders, second son to the king of Belgium, yet he refused it. He was not interested in ruling a country in Eastern Europe and one under Turkish rule on top of that. We suddenly found ourselves in a dramatic situation: the "guarantor" powers, which had only consented to the Union of 1859 for the duration of Cuza's reign, could use the opportunity to withdraw from the agreement – it was common knowledge that neither Turkey, nor Austria, nor Russia favoured the establishment of a foreign dynasty in Romania. Ion Ghica promptly sent an "emissary of the provisional government" to Paris, a man named Ion Bălăceanu, who petitioned for a foreign prince before Napoleon III. Bălăceanu was chosen because he had previously met the French emperor on the battlefield at Solferino, in 1859, as an envoy of Cuza.

Here is Bălăceanu's version of events (what I am about to recount is still virtually unknown and comes from Bălăceanu's memoirs, which, for various reasons, are yet to be published; I have been fortunate enough to obtain a copy from one of his granddaughters, a French baroness who has since passed away). The French foreign minister gave Bălăceanu a glacial reception, and initially refused to see him – the "agent of a revolutionary government" which had ousted one of the emperor's protégés. Nevertheless, Bălăceanu worked behind the scenes and managed to obtain an audience with the emperor himself. He began by apologising for the overthrow of Cuza and explained the reasons behind the coup. But then he said, "*Your Majesty, the Romanian people want you to give them a prince.*" The emperor was taken aback and asked for time to consider his response. He asked two of his marshals, who refused. I will skip over the details, but as the weeks went by, Bălăceanu was desperately seeking advice, left and right. At the suggestion of an Italian journalist named Ubicini, a great sympathiser of the Romanian cause, Bălăceanu went to see "Madame Cornu", the wife of a French painter and the daughter of a chambermaid to the emperor's mother – they had grown up together, while in exile. As a staunch republican, she was upset with Napoleon III, who had proclaimed himself emperor, but as childhood friendships go, the two had remained close. A while later, Madame Cornu had the idea of proposing prince Karl von Hohenzollern-Sigmaringen, not because he was a distant relative of the Prussian king, Wilhelm von Hohenzollern, but because he also happened to be Napoleon III's nephew on a maternal line. Both of Karl's grandmothers had been French, and closely related to the Bonaparte family. Madame Cornu went to see the emperor and told him, "*Your Majesty, why not put forward your nephew, Prince Karl of Hohenzollern, who is a lieutenant in the Prussian army?*" Napoleon III accepted the suggestion, and although his ministers did not approve of a German candidate, the emperor liked the idea of proposing one of his relatives, and suggested that Bălăceanu contact the

French emperor Napoleon III, to whom Romanians owe gratitude both for his support for the Union of the Principalities and the ascension of Karl von Hohenzollern to the throne of Romania.

Karl von Hohenzollern (Romanian: Carol) in the uniform of a Romanian officer, upon his arrival in the country (photograph by Carol Popp de Szathmári)

Hohenzollern family and the Prussian chancellor, Bismarck. The head of the liberal party, Ion Brătianu, soon arrived to negotiate with the Hohenzollern family, who had not been very keen on the proposal initially. When I say "the family" I mean prince Karl's father – for they were still ruled by a patriarchal system; when Bălăceanu travelled to see the old prince, Anton von Hohenzollern, he found the 26-year-old lieutenant Karl sitting on a stool, at his father's feet. The old prince eventually consented to send Karl to Romania, where a referendum had taken place to see if the people would accept him. His arrival in our country was a real adventure because it was happening at a time of extreme tensions between Prussia and Austria (which had not yet become Austria-Hungary). The two were on the brink of war, and in fact war did break out several days later. Karl of Hohenzollern did not dare to travel openly to Romania, as he risked arrest crossing the whole Austrian empire. He assumed a fake name and used a Swiss passport to board a passenger ship on the Danube, accompanied by a friend and a nephew of Bălăceanu (a cadet in a French military school); Ion Brătianu was also on the ship, which arrived in Romania on 10 May 1866.

And so it came to be that we would be ruled by a foreign-born prince, a distant relative of the king of Prussia but more closely related to the emperor of France. With Karl von Hohenzollern (henceforth mentioned under his Romanian name, *Carol de Hohenzollern*) came a new phase the history of Romania.

Why we needed a foreign monarchy

To those who do not understand why we needed the monarchy, and mostly why we needed a foreign-born ruler, I will simply say this: look at the map of Europe and try to identify all the monarchies still in existence today; almost none of them originate in the countries they rule. In Spain we have a Bourbon king of French origin; the monarchs of England and Belgium are of German ancestry; in Sweden they are again of French heritage and in Norway they are of Danish descent; only in Denmark does the monarchy have local roots – if we disregard the fact that they are related to other foreign ruling families through marriage from previous generations. Therefore, lineage was not important, because once foreign monarchs took power, their new countries became more or less their personal dominions, and they would shortly prove themselves to be more patriotic than the locals. To give an example to the contrary, the only other country in contemporary Europe to have a local monarchy was Yugoslavia, ruled by Serbian kings – which did not bring it much fortune. Instead of keeping the promises he made in 1918, when the "Kingdom of Serbs, Croats and Slovenes" was created, the Serbian king Peter I turned it into the "Kingdom of Yugoslavia", ruled exclusively by the Serbs. If he had been foreign-born, he would have known better than to break the fragile balance that existed between the Serbs, the Croats, the Slovenes, the Bosnian Muslims, the Albanians and all other peoples living together in the new realm. That is why, in the 19th century, it was only normal to have a monarch who was foreign-born, yet understood how to defend the interests of his new country as if it were his own.

Carol heading towards Bucharest, where he was to be sworn in before the Parliament

Sword given to Carol by Sultan Abdul Aziz I during his inauguration visit to Constantinople

Prince Carol I

Only four years after Carol I ascended the throne of Romania, war broke out between Prussia and France. For all his kinship to Napoleon III, our prince was nevertheless a German raised in Germany, a former Prussian army officer who, in his heart, always sided with Germany. But as Romanians supported France, all sorts of hostile movements and tendencies aimed at overthrowing Carol began to emerge. Prince (and later King) Carol had a lifelong affinity for the German Empire, pushing our country towards an entente with Germany and Austro-Hungary.

We must bear in mind that Carol I's 48-year reign – the longest in Romanian history, one year longer than that of Stephen the Great – was immensely beneficial for us. During this time, our country took an astonishing leap forward. Of all modern nations, only Japan experienced progress comparable to that of Romania between the mid-19th century and World War I. Huge economic advances were made, though one generation was not enough to catch up with the West. Most railways outside the Carpathian arc were constructed in the time of Carol I. New roads were built, factories established, and we began the extraction of petroleum – at the time, we were only the third country in the world, after the USA and Poland, to have done that.

Carol being sworn in on 10 May 1866. On the adjacent page we find his oath, countersigned by members of the government: Ioan C. Cantacuzino, Ion Ghica, Dimitrie Ghica, P. Mavrogheni, Lascăr Catargiu, D. Sturdza, C. A. Rosetti and Major D. Lecca.

When it came to domestic politics, King Carol I acted wisely, knowing how to maintain the equilibrium between the two great emerging parties – the Liberal Party (founded by the Brătianu brothers) and the Conservative Party – that resembled the political balance found in Britain.

The vote was not universal, but censitary – only those who paid tax had the right to vote – which may seem undemocratic to us today, but we must not forget that it was the same system used across Europe at the time, with the difference that the degree of illiteracy and the concentration of wealth in certain levels of society made it more restrictive in our country. In addition, the electorate was not politically educated enough to understand that change depended on *them*, which is why the party designated by the *king* to form the new government won the majority in each election.

Under the circumstances, Carol managed to alternate between the two parties every 3-4 years. Only once were the Liberals in power for almost 12 years (1876-1888) under the presidency of Ion Brătianu – apart from a two-month interval when his brother Dimitrie led the government – undoubtedly our greatest politician of the 19th century, who introduced the most fundamental economic reforms, such as the banking system and the industrial establishment, which date back to his mandate.

Commemorative medal with the effigy of Ion C. Brătianu (1821-1891). The reverse mentions the most important moments of his political career: 1848 (his role in the Revolution); 1857 (his return from exile to support the Union); 1866 (his role in electing a foreign-born prince); 1876 (the first Liberal government, which he led) and 1881 (the proclamation of the Kingdom of Romania).

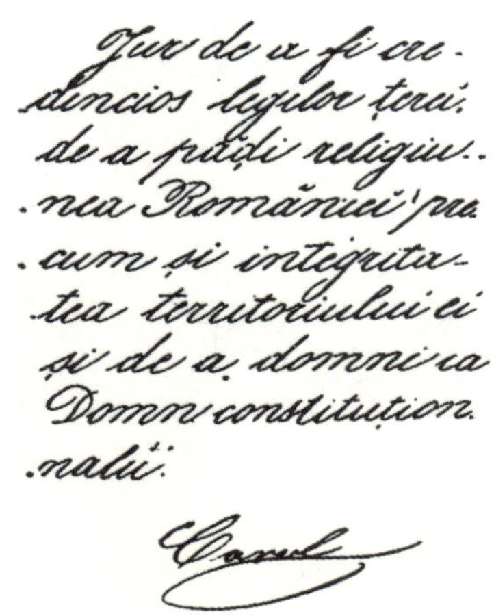

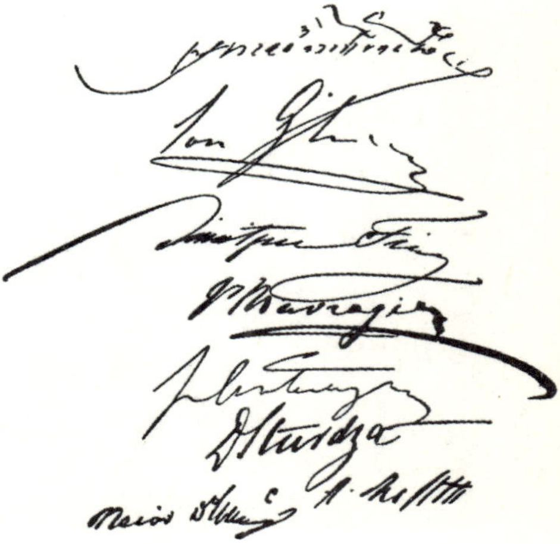

The Romanian War of Independence (1877)

In 1876, rebellious movements by Christian populations in the Balkans against Turkish domination emerged in Montenegro, Bulgaria and Serbia, only to be brutally repressed by the Turks. Europe was outraged by the massacres, but only one country reacted – the one which had a permanent interest to intervene in the Balkans using such pretexts – and that was of course Russia. In the spring of 1877, it presented us with an ultimatum: "*We will be crossing your country to attack the Turks*". Prince Carol, his prime minister, Ion Brătianu and his foreign minister, Mihai Kogălniceanu, had a difficult dilemma on their hands. They held council and realised they had little choice but to accept the Russian transit through our country, but requested independence from the Ottoman Empire in return for our alliance. At first, the Russians were contemptuous and replied that they had no need of our troops – their guarantee not to touch our borders should have been enough. And so the great Russian army began to pour through our territory.

Russian troops passing through Bucharest in 1877, heading towards the Bulgarian front (drawing from The Illustrated London News*).*

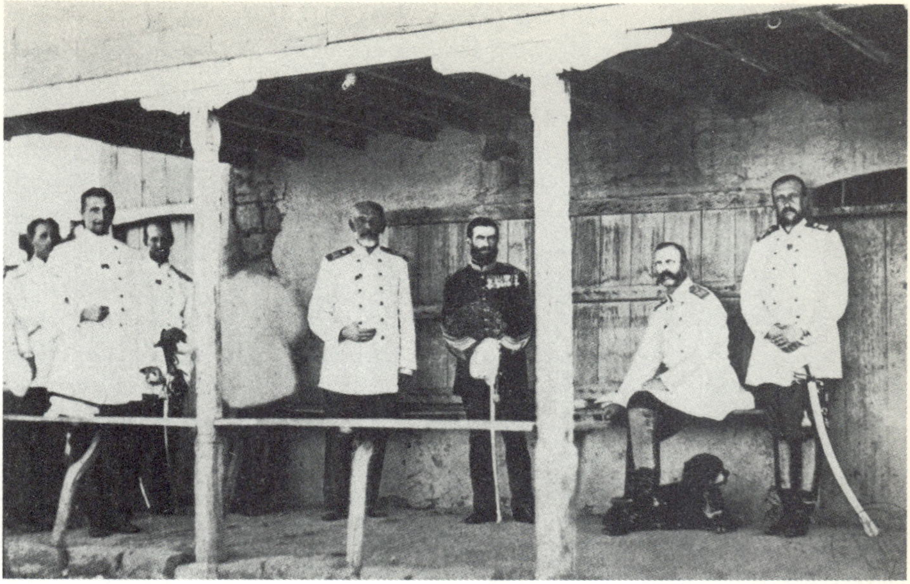

Prince Carol I and Tsar Alexander II at Radenitsa, on the Bulgarian front

The Russians crossed the Danube, but after a few weeks met with such staunch Turkish resistance – especially at Pleven (Romanian: *Plevna*) defended by Osman Pasha, a very capable Turkish general – that they eventually asked us to cross the Danube with our small army of 43,000 men (which had been established in the time of Cuza by General Ion Florescu) now under the direct command of Prince Carol, a former officer in the Prussian army. It is important to remember that this was the first time our principalities were able to assert their military presence and national pride in hundreds of years, since the time of Michael the Brave, when they had been forced to start using mercenaries, or forbidden to take part in any wars directly (with the exception of Dimitrie Cantemir's misadventure in 1711). Therefore, the war of 1877 represents the military resurgence of Romanians in Europe, in the context of an inter-state war. And so bravely did our army fight, that the independence we had proclaimed on the eve of our entry into the war (9 May 1877) had to be recognised after the war ended.

After the fall of Pleven, the Russian advance towards Constantinople was so rapid that Turkey capitulated; in

Osman Pasha, defeated at Pleven and taken prisoner by the Russians, suffered the ignominy of watching the victorious Romanian army march down Podul Mogoșoaiei (renamed Calea Victoriei since 1878) from the balcony of the Boulevard Hotel in Bucharest.

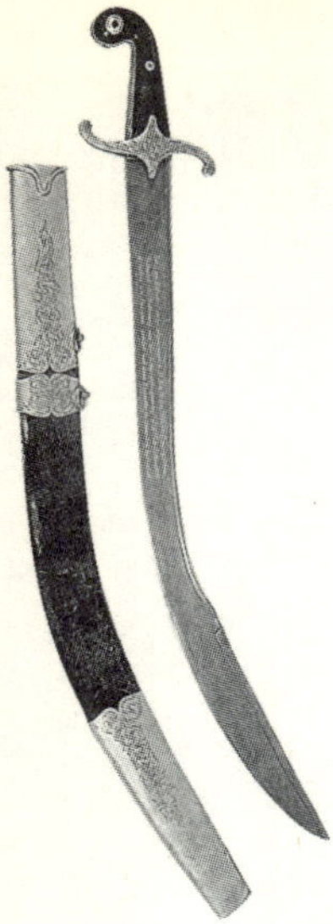

Sword of the Ottoman general Edhem Pasha, surrendered to the Romanians at Pleven (displayed in the National History Museum of Romania).

the small town of San Stefano (present day Yeşilköy) on the Sea of Marmara, an initial treaty was signed between the Russians and Turks creating a sizeable Principality of Bulgaria which extended from the Danube to the Aegean Sea, and giving Russia the right to intervene in the affairs of Christians in the Ottoman Empire. News of the Russo-Turkish treaty caused alarm among the great European powers. Otto von Bismarck, chancellor of the new German Empire and the most influential man in Europe after Prussia's defeat of France in the war of 1870-1871, convened an international congress in Berlin and refused to allow a direct peace between Turkey and Russia. The Congress of Berlin took place in June-July 1878 in an attempt to limit the freedom of the great powers to do anything they pleased in case of victory over another power. Romania was also invited to the Congress, but was "kept in the antechamber" – Ion Brătianu and Mihail Kogălniceanu were only admitted to the conference room once, to put forward our country's point of view. The only ones who took part in the talks were prince Gorchakov, the Russian representative; the Turkish envoy, Karatheodori Pasha; Disraeli, the British prime minister; the French foreign minister, Waddington; and Count Andrassy, the representative of Austria-Hungary (note how only a few years after the creation of the dual monarchy, its foreign minister was a great Hungarian aristocrat). The great powers wanted

Carol I at Plevna, in another photograph by the tireless Carol Popp de Szathmári

Treaty of San Stefano (3 March 1878) when a defeated Turkey recognised the independence of Romania

to force the Russians to backtrack and change the initial treaty of San Stefano, which created Greater Bulgaria as a client of Russia. Of course, we Romanians wanted them to recognise our independence and not lose the south of Bessarabia again, as Russia would have wanted.

But at the behest of Chancellor Bismarck, who was on very good terms with a great Jewish banker in Germany, the great powers demanded that Romanian citizenship be granted en masse to the entire Jewish population in the country, in return for recognising independence. Brătianu and Kogălniceanu did not accept this condition, as they felt that the large numbers of Jewish immigrants, who had settled in Moldavia relatively recently, had nor been sufficiently assimilated and who, they thought, would have hampered the development of the local Romanian bourgeoisie were they to receive equal rights (I mentioned earlier what the Hungarian policy had been on the matter and wonder if it would not have been wiser for us to do the same). Our representatives did not yield, however, and only accepted that Jews be naturalised on an individual, case-by-case

Carol Popp de Szathmári (1812-1887) a pioneer of photography in Romania, who also produced an album on the War of Independence.

basis. The article that was eventually adopted was rather ambiguous, and Brătianu and Kogălniceanu had to return to the country without the certainty that our independence would be recognised. Fortunately, the same Ion Bălăceanu we mentioned earlier, now our envoy in Vienna, managed to obtain the recognition of the Austro-Hungarian government, which had an interest in being the first to have political and commercial ties to Romania. Consequently, Austria-Hungary was the first country to recognise the independence of Romania, which gradually left the other powers with no option but to do the same, despite the fact that we did not meet the conditions set by the Congress of Berlin to the letter. Consider just how difficult was our birth as a state and what diplomatic battles we had to contend *after* we had fought a war to secure our independence.

Romania in 1878, incorporating Northern Dobruja but not Southern Bessarabia, ceded to Russia after the Treaty of San Stefano

The independence of Romania was not the only thing discussed in the 1878 Congress of Berlin – the country's borders also went under scrutiny.

Russia insisted on the return of Southern Bessarabia (which had been given to us after the 1856 Treaty of Paris) to gain access to the mouths of the Danube once more,

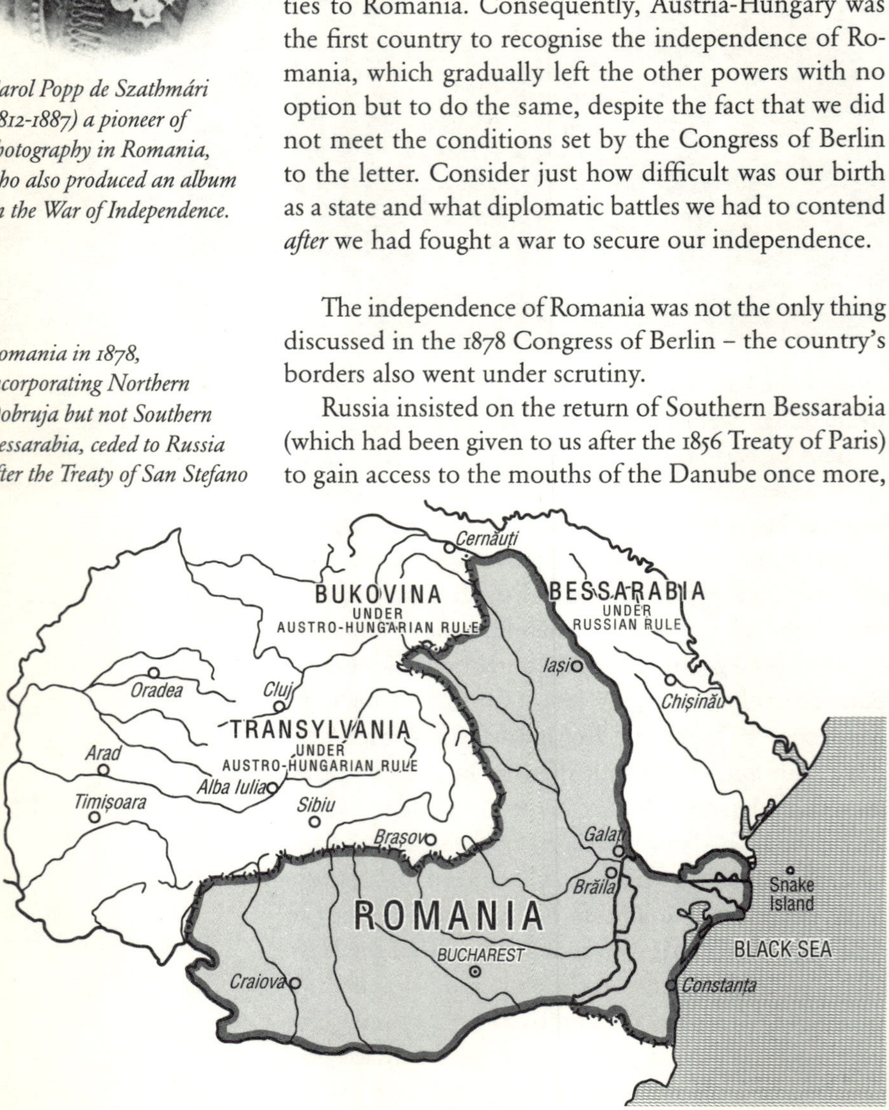

The Steel Crown of Romania, forged from the barrel of a Turkish cannon captured at the Battle of Grivitsa (30 August 1877) was worn for the first time in 1881, for the proclamation of the kingdom.

while as compensation we would be granted Dobruja (Romanian: *Dobrogea*) a territory that had not actually belonged to Wallachia for many centuries. Brătianu and Kogălniceanu were outraged by the loss of Southern Bessarabia, but there was little they could do about it. We had to submit to the pressure of the great powers, and so in 1878 we lost that territory for a second time; in return, we received the two counties making up Dobruja (with the port of Constanța) a province where Romanians could only be found along the Danube, and where Turks, Tatars and Bulgarians formed the majority towards the sea and in the south. Slowly, Dobruja began to be repopulated.

VI. CONTEMPORARY ROMANIA. CAROL I, KING OF ROMANIA

Carol I – Prince since 1866, and our first king, since 1881

Three years after the war of 1878, Prince Carol I took the title of "King" – an act that was accepted by all great powers – which put us on equal footing, protocol-wise, with the other monarchies of Europe. This was a crucial moment for our international status.

Despite the imperfections of the censitary voting system, which I referred to earlier, the political system was fairly balanced, and although the Liberals governed for longer than the Conservatives, the king was shrewd enough to know when it was time to replace them with their rivals, and vice versa. Here are some names of politicians we should take note of: from amongst the Liberals, Ion C. Brătianu and C. A. Rosetti, who was quite the leftist, despite his illustrious name (in actual fact, we know from his letters and various accounts that he was a republican, but did not have the courage to say it outright). After the death of Ion C. Brătianu, the Liberal Party was led by a Sturdza, the descendant of a great boyar family that had given two voivodes of Moldavia, which shows that the Liberals did not only hail from the bourgeoisie, but also from the great or lesser boyars. However, it would generally be safe to say that the Liberal Party favoured the embryonic bourgeoisie, meaning that it was the party of those who wanted to get rich by turning Romania into a modern country, with a developed industry and trade – while the Conservatives was mostly supported by the great landowners. From amongst Conservative Party presidents, we should mention Lascăr Catargi (whose name is borne by a boulevard in Bu-

Proclamation of the kingdom: "Romanian blood, spilled in abundance for the defence and independence of the motherland, has been avenged on this day, 14/26 March 1881. The legislative assemblies, in wishing to provide the Romanian state, born of the union of Moldavia and Wallachia, with an absolute assurance and a glorious manifestation of its individuality, have proclaimed the arrival of Romania among the kingdoms of Europe."

charest) who, truth be told, was an excellent premier. Whenever the Liberals were too hastily pursuing their modernising measures, there came a Conservative government that stabilised the situation through a more austere administration. Catargi remains a model of integrity and efficient organisation. It was said of him that whenever King Carol asked him to implement a measure he did not approve of, Catargi would retort in his Moldavian accent, "*Your Majesty, such a thing can simply not be done!*" (I wish someone could have said that to Ceaușescu from time to time; our politicians clearly had more nerve in those days). I will also mention the great landowner Gheorghe Cantacuzino (nicknamed *Nababul*, meaning "the governor") General Mânu, Petre Carp and later on, Titu Maiorescu, the great literary critic who had

A. Rosetti (1816-1885)
Liberal ideologist and the head of the gazette The Romanian

Ion I. Câmpineanu (1848-1888)
Liberal leader and the first governor of the National Bank of Romania, established in 1880

P. S. Aurelian (1833-1909)
Liberal politician and scholar, president of the Romanian Academy between 1901 and 1904

created the Junimea (*Youth*) movement; finally, Take Ionescu, a democrat who would play a crucial part during World War I and immediately after. So you see, politics at the time was a real mix of intellectuals – even Eminescu and Caragiale had been Conservatives.

All the while, socialist ideas were timidly emerging in publications or through agitation, but were almost non-existent in Parliament, apart from the integration of some overtly socialist members into the Liberal Party. In a country with a nascent industry and a only a minimal urban working class, socialism in its Marxist form could only make slow and marginal progress, especially as it also had to compete with a so-called "populist" movement (Romanian: *poporanism*) which advocated for the development of small and medium-sized agriculture. In this respect, we should evoke the names of two ideologists and political activists, both of whom came from Russia: the "populist" Constantin Stere (a minor boyar from Bessarabia, who would go on to play a role in interwar politics; and the sharp-witted Marxist theorist Dobrogeanu-Gherea.

The dispute between those who regarded industrial development as an absolute imperative for claiming Romania's place among modern nations and those who emphasised protectionist measures for small and medium-sized farmers (leading to the somewhat ironic

motto "*Romania is an eminently agricultural country*") did not only take place at an ideological level, but also unfolded, to a certain extent, in Parliament; of the two dominant parties, Conservatives mainly favoured the agrarian aspects (finding common ground with populists and the future National Peasants' Party) while Liberals were ardent supporters of industrial development.

Petre P. Carp (1837-1919) member of the Conservative Party and the Junimea movement, was twice prime minister and one of the staunchest opponents of Romania's entry into World War I on the side of the Entente.

Take Ionescu (1858-1922) began his political career as a Conservative, but founded the Conservative Democrat Party in 1908. As foreign affairs minister, he favoured joining the Entente in World War I. He died suddenly, one month after he had become prime minister of Greater Romania.

Titu Maiorescu (1840-1917) founder of the Junimea movement and one of the most articulate critics of Romania's hasty modernisation. He served as foreign affairs minister and prime minister of Romania simultaneously.

The beginnings of Romania's cultural heyday

As I mentioned Titu Maiorescu, now is the time to take a quick look at culture, for we have only discussed politics, economics, wars and changes in legislation without referring to cultural life. For it was during the latter half of the 19th century that Romanian culture suddenly blossomed.

When a people adopt a new cultural model, as Romanians did in the early 19th century, it generally takes two or three generations to "digest" it. Take the Russians, for example. Peter the Great's issued his *ukaz* (decree) to westernise the country in 1700, but Russia would have to wait another 120 years for its first great modern literary creations – the poems of Pushkin – and over 150 years for Dostoyevsky, Tolstoy, and the great composers. Things went much faster in our country, to a point where we can safely say that we had first-rate writers from the first generation, such as Costache Negruzzi, or some of the

Queen Elisabeth at Peleș Castle, with composer George Enescu (right). A poet herself, the queen was a patron of musicians and writers.

remarkable mid-century poets like Vasile Alecsandri or Grigore Alexandrescu. However, the real upsurge came in the latter half of the century, when the Romanian language crystallised into its classic, most beautiful form – incorporating all the neologisms in use today, yet still authentic, elegant, with a good balance between the traditional and modern. First and foremost, there was our national poet, Mihai Eminescu; then came many other poets and writers, such as George Coșbuc, Ion Creangă, Alexandru Vlahuță, Ion Ghica, Alexandru Odobescu or Ion Luca Caragiale; the turn of the century was when novelists like Ioan Slavici, Barbu Ștefănescu Delavrancea and Duiliu Zamfirescu made their mark. The next generation gave us great poets – the likes of Tudor Arghezi, George Bacovia and Ion Barbu. This was a time when conditions were ripe for high art to flourish; we had excellent painters, such as Nicolae Grigorescu or Ion Andreescu, as well as sculptors and musicians – the precursors of Constantin Brâncuși and George Enescu, whose genius would be universally acknowledged in the 20th century. Clearly, it only took us one or two generations to assimilate Western culture and reach a level similar to that of the West. This is quite an astonishing phenomenon, and it must be emphasised.

I. L. Caragiale (1852-1912)
Mihai Eminescu (1850-1889)
Ion Creangă (1837-1889)

As to the role of the various Western cultures (French, Italian and German) in our late 19th century "culturalisation" – note that it coincides with Carol I's ascension to the throne – we find that German culture begins to compete with the French influence, especially in poetry and philosophy. At least three of our greatest authors – Eminescu, Caragiale and Maiorescu – were more influenced by German rather than French culture, and the same can be said for philosopher Vasile Conta. Last but not least, let us not forget the great precursors of the Transylvanian School, most of whom had an exclusively German education, but who were also fond of our "sister language", Italian.

This creative drive would continue vigorously into the 20th century, reaching an extraordinary degree of intensity and diversity in the inter-war period, covering all fields of art and science – we produced a number of outstanding scientists, particularly in physics and medicine – but I must avoid enumerating more names for fear of committing some grave omissions. Then came that point in our history when communism brought about a sort of paralysis in our promising evolution, and a relative stagnation of our national creativity. From that moment on, creativity was confined to certain fields that were less vulnerable to the tyranny of political dogmatism, such as poetry and music, or manifested in the work of our brilliant exiles, of whom there were many – both visual artists, as well as writers and philosophers like Mircea Eliade, Eugen Ionescu, Emil Cioran and Ștefan Lupașcu.

Vasile Alecsandri (1821-1890) one of the original members of the Romanian Literary Society (founded in 1866) that would provide the core of the future Romanian Academy. He was one of the leaders of the 1848 Revolution and an advocate of the Union both as a politician and a diplomat.

The old Palace of Bucharest University, designed by architect Alexandru Orăscu (1817-1894). The pediment, decorated by sculptor Karl Storck (1826-1887) has not been preserved, after the Americans bombed the building on 4 April 1944. The crater was only replaced in 1960 by the current building, built in a very similar style to the original.

Let us end this digression and return to the reign of King Carol I. Another positive aspect, still visible today, is the progress made in the architecture and urban planning of the capital. Most of the modern centre of Bucharest dates from this time: the great boulevards Carol, Elisabeta and Kogălniceanu, and almost everything on Calea Victoriei (Victory Avenue); the most beautiful administrative buildings – the Great Post Office (today

Members of the Romanian Academical Society in 1867; the body became the Romanian Academy in 1879.

University of Iași in 1920. The initial design (for the building has been continuously expanded) belonged to Swiss architect Louis Blanc. Many of the late 19th century public buildings were designed by foreign (mainly French) architects.

the National History Museum) and opposite, the House of Deposits and Consignments (now the CEC Bank); the Ministry of Agriculture (perhaps the most beautiful building) and the University; the Palace of Justice on the banks of the Dâmbovița and the former Chamber of Deputies in the Patriarchy courtyard; in the banking district, several edifices such as the National Bank, and the Chrissoveloni and Marmorosch-Blank banks.

Calea Victoriei and the Carol–Elisabeta boulevards were the main axes along which the capital was redeveloped. The rich built more or less elegant residences resembling those being built in Paris and Vienna at the time (some of these are still visible on Lascăr Catargi, Ana Ipătescu and Dacia boulevards, and around Ioanid Park); then there are a number of luxurious little palaces north of Calea Victoriei.

To visitors from the Orient, all of these gave the (rather exaggerated) impression that Bucharest was a "Little Paris". Provincial towns were rather neglected, apart from Iași, which used its own resources to maintain the rank and standards of a former capital – indeed, its University and Administrative Palace (Romanian: *Palatul Culturii*) are more beautiful than their equivalents in Bucharest. North of the Carpathians, the dominant style was that of the Austrian Empire – formal, but somewhat heavyset.

The agrarian question – A great shadow cast over the canvas

Gheorghe Grigore Cantacuzino (1832-1913) nicknamed "Nababul" due to his colossal fortune, especially in terms of land. Overcome by the events of March 1907, he stepped down from the position of prime minister in favour of another great landowner, D. A. Sturdza, who was a Liberal.

In clear contrast to the above, we should now turn our attention to the most sombre aspect of Carol I's reign: the painfully slow approach to agrarian reform.

The rural population was growing – prior to World War II, we had the highest birth rate in Europe – and the small proportion of land that it had been assigned under Cuza was grossly insufficient. Most peasants lived off the labour they provided for their neighbouring landowner, who paid them in cash or in kind. The question of "agricultural agreements" made sporadic appearances in Parliament debates, sometimes with utterly unfavourable results for the peasantry. At the turn of the 20th century, they still made up over 80% of the country's population – yet 1 million peasant families shared around 3.3 million hectares (another 100,000 owned no land at all) while another 3 million hectares were the property of just 6,500 great landowners. This disproportion certainly seems shocking, but there were huge differences even among the 6,500; had they been more or less equal in size, the resulting estate would have only averaged about 450 hectares (which cannot be called a latifundium). In reality, only a few hundred estates covered thousands of hectares.

However, Romania was not an isolated case. The same thing happened in Russia, while in Poland and Hungary this situation would endure well after we had completed the agrarian reform of 1918-1920. In those countries, estates were far bigger: if our largest ones covered about 10,000 hectares, latifundia in these three neighbouring countries could amount to hundreds of thousands of hectares (count Mihály Károlyi, the president of a provisional Hungarian Democratic Republic in 1919, owned over 100,000 hectares).

Even if this system was the norm across Eastern Europe, in our country it had disastrous consequences at an individual level; discontent grew rife among the peasants. Another phenomenon contributed to the widening the gap between small and large estates: since the 1829 Treaty of Adrianople had opened up trade between the Principalities and the West, turning us – almost overnight – into great exporters of grain, relations between peasants and landowners had deteriorated, as I explained earlier. Firstly, the latter were no longer willing to leave large swathes of their land at the will of the tenants, but sought instead to impose on them those crops that were most in demand as exports – wheat, rapeseed etc. – under more favourable terms. Secondly, the ability to travel to the West and a sudden interest shown by rich landowners in practicing liberal professions caused a rise in the use of land leases. Even Moldavian boyars, who famously spent more time in the country than at Court, became increasingly absent from their estates. And so the leaseholder, often a stranger to country life, and sometimes the country itself, armed with short-term lease contracts and no guarantees of stability, proved to be a far harsher "master" and more ruthless toward peasants than the boyar had ever been. It is not surprising that the first acts of violence by rebellious peasants were directed at prominent leaseholders.

The first serious peasant revolt took place in 1888. But the most terrible and tragic of them broke out in 1907 – serving as inspiration for the literary works of Liviu Rebreanu and Panait Istrate – and spread like wildfire from Northern Moldavia down to Oltenia, causing the state to believe it was in peril. The Conservatives, who were in government, conceded power to the Liberals, who did what their predecessors did not have the nerve

D. A. Sturdza (1833-1914) leader of the Liberal Party, who was left with the difficult task of putting down the 1907 peasant revolt after the Conservatives yielded power. The key people in the government he formed on 12 March 1907 were Foreign Affairs Minister Ion I. C. Brătianu and the Minister of War, General Averescu, of whom we will hear more after World War I.

Entrance to the silos of the port of Brăila, where Romanian grain was collected before being loaded onto barges. The docks were built by engineer Anghel Saligny, who also designed the beautiful bridge at Cernavodă.

to do: they used army troops and artillery to stop the peasant march towards the capital. The result was a tragedy – some estimates speak of 12,000 dead. Even if this was an exaggeration (it has never been possible to obtain a reliable, comprehensive report) the shock reverberated through all levels of society and acted as an eye-opener for the political establishment. Measures to protect peasants and limit land leases were taken in the immediate aftermath, as well as the following year. In particular, the Liberal Party manifesto for the 1913 elections featured agrarian reform, which meant the transfer of a large proportion of great estates into the hands of the peasantry. And maybe that reform would have happened had World War I not broken out in August 1914. Meanwhile, new conflicts erupted closer to home.

The two Balkan Wars of 1912-1913, the Peace of Bucharest and the annexation of Southern Dobruja

The "National Momentum" Medal, given by royal decree to all civilians and servicemen who had taken part in the 1913 campaign

In October 1912, a new war erupted in the Balkans – this time, between Turkey and an alliance of Balkan states made up of Bulgaria, Greece, Serbia and Montenegro. Russia did not intervene, as in 1904-1905 it had suffered a surprising and humiliating defeat at the hands of Japan – which had awakened from a long period of medieval isolation just 40 years prior to that, and which, after a formidable modernisation effort, was able to defeat one of the great European powers, both at sea and on land, to the astonishment of the whole world. This unpredicted failure in the Far East had had serious internal repercussions in Russia, with revolts among the Black Sea navy crews in 1905 and revolutionary movements spreading within the working class, as preludes to the revolution of 1917.

Without the support of their great protector, the small states of the Balkans stood alone against an ailing Ottoman Empire, seeking the "natural" borders which none of them felt they had reached.

Romanian troops crossing the Danube on a pontoon bridge, heading towards Silistra, in Bulgaria (13 July 1913).

The First Balkan War pushed back the Turkish border to within miles of Constantinople, but no sooner had the war ended – to the astonishment of Europe – with the victory of the Balkan allies, that frictions began to appear among the four victors. The Bulgarians, a very orderly and disciplined people, who were the best organised militarily (using German military instructors) felt confident enough to claim regions coveted by both the Greeks and the Serbs. For instance, they wanted an outlet to the Aegean Sea, near Thessaloniki, or even the city itself, lands which the Greeks considered their historic heritage; moreover, the Greeks also dreamed of regaining Constantinople, the land route to which would have been severed were they to grant Bulgaria access to the Aegean. Bulgaria would have also wanted the whole of Macedonia, under the pretext that the Macedonian language

Romania in 1913, after the annexation of Caliacra and Durostor, the two counties that make up Southern Dobruja (Romanian: Cadrilater). That was when we acquired Silistra, a port on the Danube, and the beautiful Black Sea resort of Balcic.

Treaty of Bucharest (10 August 1913) attended by the Romanian Conservative elite: the prime minister and foreign affairs minister, Titu Maiorescu, the minister of the interior Take Ionescu and the minister of finance Alexandru Marghiloman.

was closer related to Bulgarian than it is to Serbian, which is true. This was how the Second Balkan War began in 1913, in which tiny Bulgaria promptly defeated both the Serbs and the Greeks. At that point, Romania intervened as a fourth belligerent power to re-establish regional balance, siding with Greece and Serbia against the Bulgarians. Our intervention in 1913 was no more than a military stroll, as the Bulgarians were taken completely by surprise. There was no resistance, so our army did not have to fight the Bulgarians, who capitulated before the three-pronged attack of the Greeks, Serbs and Romanians. The peace was signed in Bucharest, with Titu Maiorescu presiding over the council of ministers. It was a time when Romania saw itself as an important player and arbiter in the Balkans.

I am speaking to the young people of today with a sincerity that is generally not found in our history books, which tell us that everything done in the past was right. It is bewildering for us to learn that, at the time, the Romanian political establishment approved of the government's action almost in its entirety – in fact, we know from speeches, memoirs and other documents of the time that the Liberals' only regret was not being in power, so that the "glory" could reflect on them. I believe we were wrong in 1913, when we were not content only with preventing the Bulgarians from achieving hegemony in the Balkans, but also demanded a portion of their territory in Dobruja, where neither they, nor us – but the Turks and Tatars – were in the majority. Expansion into Southern Dobruja (Romanian: *Cadrilater* or *Dobrogea de Sud*) was not essential for Romania, while the region was vital to Bulgaria, both agriculturally and because the country was smaller. In doing this, we made enemies of a people who had always been at our side throughout history. The annexation of Southern Dobruja from the Bulgarians was a serious political error. We paid for it dearly in 1916, when the Bulgarians fought against us, while some painful consequences endure to this day. There was, however, a caveat to this annexation. Romania got the territory on condition that it would colonise it with Romanians and speakers of Romanian dialects – the Aromanians and Megleno-Romanians – from across the Balkans. It was a poorly contrived project, and an immoral one in my view, because it would have meant uprooting Aromanians from Greece or Albania, and settling them in a region of Bulgaria (or one that was rightfully Bulgarian). In reality, only a fraction of the plan was ever put into practice, involving several thousand families; the tragedy of 1940 forced us to give back

Queen Marie's residence in Balcic, pearl of Southern Dobruja. The light of the beautiful resort was a magnet for the artists of Greater Romania, many of who bought or built themselves holiday homes there.

Three great historians of the inter-war period, each belonging to a different school of thought, with vastly different views of history and the meaning behind researching the past. None of them resisted the temptation to get into politics: Nicolae Iorga (left) was a party leader and prime minister, P. P. Panaitescu was a politician with Legionary inclinations, while Gheorghe Brătianu formed a new Liberal party from a dissident movement inside the party that his illustrious family had dominated for decades.

Southern Dobruja, causing the hasty relocation of the colonists to other areas of the country. Let us be fair: the Aromanian colonisation of Southern Dobruja was a yet another political miscalculation – upsetting the Aromanians themselves – because in return for this territory we gave up trying to force the other signatories of the Treaty of Bucharest to accept an article requiring them to protect the speakers of Romanian dialects where they lived.

Can historians be "objective" about contemporary history?

I now realise that I have not kept my word, my pledge of objectivity implicitly given in this book's short preface; I could not help "taking sides" and expressing critical views on certain political decisions from our recent past. Yet I will not ask for forgiveness, as I am aware that, by the time we get to the present day, I will offend again. This calls for a justification.

When a historian tackles the truly contemporary period, experienced by people who may still be alive today, his point of view changes. Imagine that at the time of these events, in 1913, my father was a grown man, who was drafted into the army. He was called up again in 1916, and died while in service in 1918. As an infant in my mother's arms, I myself crossed Russia in 1917, in the middle of the Bolshevik revolution. This adds an entirely new dimension to the events. One feels directly involved, so the temptation is to pass judgement on what happened, not only give an account of it. A historian's passion to bring the past to life and cast light on it is combined with the political inclinations of someone who is involved in the life of the country and is concerned for its future. It is not possible – whatever one may say – for a historian of contemporary history to refrain from becoming political, meaning "concerned with the fate of the city" (for that is what *politika* meant in ancient Greek – the science and art of governing the city state, or *polis*). Since the beginnings of historical writing, the curiosity to know and understand the past was born out of a desire to better manage the present and choose a path for the future. So you will forgive me if I will not be able to provide an account of events without expressing my views on the main historical turning points, when one decision could have been made instead of another – for I will feel as if the decision rested on my shoulders.

Constantin C. Giurescu was one of Iorga's toughest critics in the realm of historiography. As politicians, however, they shared relatively similar ideas; both of them wore the uniform of the National Renaissance Front during Carol II's royal dictatorship.

Thoughts on the "Seventy-Seven Years' War" (1914-1991)

We now come to the great global conflict that began in 1914. This part may well surprise you, because I will speak of things that are not found in the history books – that is to say, my personal views. You will have been told of the First World War (1914-1918) and the Second World War (1939-1945) whose chief participants were largely the same, only with different line-ups – a bit like arranging chess pieces on one side of the board or the other. Then you were told about the Cold War of the post-1945 era. Well, I believe that in centuries to come, historians will call the period that began in 1914 and ended with the fall of the Soviet Empire in 1991 the "Seventy-Seven Years' War", just as we now speak of the Hundred Years' War between France and England during the Middle Ages, the Thirty Years' War (as the religious

African American soldiers from an infantry regiment that saw action in France. World War I brought the United States into contact with Europe, initially under the guise and with the impact of an expeditionary force.

wars of Central Europe in the 17th century are known) or the Peloponnesian War of Greek antiquity. This too was only one war – the last of a long series – originally fought between the great powers of Europe, and then joined by the United States of America (which was part of the Western civilisation anyway) and Japan. Therefore, if you look at history in the long term, as soon as the Renaissance made possible the rise of the Western civilisation, each of the great European nations nurtured ambitions of hegemony. It began with Charles V, Holy Roman emperor and king of Spain, enriched by the gold and silver of the newly discovered Americas; yet his plans for a "united Europe" were thwarted by France, the richest and most populous country in Europe, through a hegemonic war that began around 1520. Spain will be replaced by France, which attempted to create a French Europe since the time of Louis XIV until the demise of Napoleon's empire. From the 19th century onwards, it was the turn of the Germans to attempt the same – starting with Bismarck and his victory against France in 1871 and ending with Hitler's Third Reich in 1945. The last clash of the great powers for the domination of our civilisation appeared to have ended in 1945 along with the fall of Germany – but that was really only the halfway point. All the great powers of the past – Spain, France, England, Germany, Italy, Austria-Hun-

History exacting its revenge: a Soviet soldier of Asian origin pictured in 1945, in Berlin, the epicentre of a state that had turned racism into a religion.

gary – had fallen. Only the two peripheral great powers remained – Russia, on the one hand, and the USA on the other. The period from 1945 to 1989 was an age of constant tension, when people of my generation anxiously waited to see which of the two giants would triumph and dominate our civilisation. Fortunately, it was the Americans who proved superior, as the artificial construct that was the Soviet Empire collapsed from within. Therefore, from 1991 onwards, there has been only one world power (and *hegemon* of at least the Western world) – the USA. That is broadly how I look at the events that followed after 1914.

The First World War (1914-1918)

For a number of years before 1914, the great powers of Europe had formed alliances in anticipation of a major war, particularly as Germany was vying for hegemony on the continent. Two great power blocks emerged: in Central Europe, Germany and Austria-Hungary (hence the name "Central Powers") were joined by Italy and Romania through treaties.

In the west, a rapprochement between France and Great Britain – after long disputes stemming from colonial rivalry – lead to the so-called "Cordial Agreement" (French: *L'Entente cordiale*). Britain held absolute supremacy over the seas, but had a relatively small army, made up exclusively of volunteers. To have any chance against the Central Powers and outflank them, an alliance with Russia was essential. But the rapprochement between tsarist Russia, the most despotic regime in Europe, and France, the only large republic in Europe, was problematic. Similarly, Great Britain and Russia were bitter rivals over their spheres of influence in Asia, namely over Afghanistan, India, China and Japan (the Japanese fleet that had sunk the Russian fleet at the battle of Tsushima in 1905 had been built and trained by the British). Therefore, the "Allies" were not quite united in 1914.

Poison gas, a horrible weapon of war used by both sides in World War I

Then in June 1914, a fateful accident of history occurred in Sarajevo: the assassination of Archduke Franz

King Carol I with Archduke Franz Ferdinand at Sinaia, surrounded by the members of the Romanian royal family: Crown Princess Marie, Crown Prince Ferdinand, Prince Carol and his other brothers. The assassination of the Archduke by Serbian Gavrilo Princip, on 28 June 1914 was the pretext behind the outbreak of World War I. Carol I passed away on 10 October 1914.

Ferdinand, heir to the throne of Austria-Hungary, at the hands of a Serbian patriot. Why did this happen in Sarajevo? Well, it all began when Austria-Hungary had snatched Bosnia from the Turks at the 1878 Congress of Berlin, hoping to gradually extend its domination over all Serbs. Contrary to this, Serbian irredentists in Belgrade claimed that all Serbs in Austria, Hungary and Bosnia wished to be united with Serbia – which explains the emergence of the secret patriotic movement known as the Black Hand, which murdered Franz Ferdinand in Sarajevo in 1914. Though a tragedy, the assassination could have remained a minor political incident had an agreement been reached, and had the culprits been apprehended and sentenced. The fact is that the Serbs did not accept one of the points of the Austro-Hungarian government's ultimatum, which demanded that the investigation be led by Austrian policemen in Serbia, as they believed it infringed on the country's sovereignty. Backed by a treaty with Russia, the Serbs held firm. The Russians pledged their assistance, while the Germans announced their support for Austria-Hungary; the Russians then ordered a general mobilisation (which could take several weeks due to the size of the empire and the limited railway network). Once Russia's mobilisation was under way, Germany ordered its own general mobilisation, which caused France to do the same – and so, through a fatal chain of events, the greatest war the world had ever seen broke out in early August 1914.

Supremely confident of their military superiority, the Germans believed they would win in a matter of weeks – first against France, then against Russia. To their surprise, however, France (assisted by Britain) put up a fierce resistance; and so the war they thought they would win in four weeks lasted more than four years and ended with Germany's downfall.

To understand our role in this war, we must first call to mind the war of 1877-1878, when the Russians – our alleged allies – stole one of our provinces. Fearing Russia, we concluded an alliance with Austria-Hungary and Germany, at the behest of King Carol I (to which Brătianu contributed extensively; the two men formed a sort of axis of our foreign policy). We signed a treaty with Austria-Hungary, later joined by Germany and Italy, but the agreement remained a secret in our country. Each time the government changed hands, the king would inform the new prime minister of this treaty, which he kept in his personal safe. The Romanian public never knew that our fate had been tied to the Central Powers, and that we would have had to join them in case

Sympathy for the Entente was never unanimous, especially among intellectual circles. The staff of Viața românească *magazine was predominantly pro-German.*

Soldiers undergoing a drill around 1900. However, the war proved how woefully unprepared the Romanian army had been for it.

war broke out. Why was this kept a secret? Because not even King Carol could ignore the people's solidarity with the Romanians in Transylvania, and the fact that the nation's greatest aspiration was to make the country whole by uniting with Transylvania. There was, of course, the issue of Russian-occupied Bessarabia – but at the time that seemed to weigh less on the minds of common Romanians than the Transylvanian question. The day after war broke out in 1914, the king assembled his government and the Crown Council – an exceptional consultative body that was composed of the former prime ministers and a number of civilian and military members – and took out the treaty that dictated Romania's entry into the war on the side of the Central Powers. Ionel Brătianu (son of Ion Brătianu) leader of the Liberal Party and prime minister, as well as the majority of the government and the Crown Council (with the exception of Petre Carp, a former Conservative premier) was categorically opposed to entering the war alongside Austria-Hungary and Germany against Russia. With a heavy heart, King Carol agreed to declare Romania's neutrality. He died several weeks later, in September 1914, deeply affected by his failure to keep the word he had given to the emperors of Austria-Hungary and Germany. Carol I was succeeded by one of his nephews (he had only fathered a daughter, Princess Maria, who had died at a young age, leaving Queen Elisabeth – widely known by her literary pseudonym of Carmen Sylva – unable to bear any more children). The king had adopted the son of his elder brother Leopold and brought his nephew to the country as an adult, where he learned Romanian. He would become King Ferdinand I, our greatest ever monarch. The new king therefore ascended the throne in 1914; he was married to a princess who was half English and half Russian – the future queen Marie of Romania (Romanian: *Regina Maria a României*) granddaughter of queen Victoria of England and tsar Alexander II of Russia, an energetic woman with a good head for politics. It was largely due to her influence, but also because he realised where the true interests of the Romanian people lay, that King Ferdinand, born and raised in Germany, became more Romanian than many of his subjects and took the painful decision to enter the war against his native country in August 1916.

Marie, Crown Princess of Romania, wearing the nurse uniform that endeared her to the people during the war

Romania at war

In August 1916, after lengthy negotiations, Ionel Brătianu signed a secret treaty with the French, the British and the Russians, who promised us Transylvania, Bukovina (annexed by the Austrians in 1775) and the Banat. Once the allies accepted the plan, Romania entered the war on 28 August 1916. We crossed the mountains into Transylvania and initially advanced deep into undefended territory, where we received a

Priest performing the burial service of a Romanian officer who fell in the line of duty in 1917. The High Command estimated the total losses of the Romanian army in World War I to have stood at over 400,000 (killed, injured and disappeared).

Transylvanian volunteers singing the Romanian anthem in the presence of royal family members. Around 8,500 Transylvanian and Bukovinian soldiers and officers chose to fight for Romania between 1917 and 1918.

liberator's welcome from the Romanian population; but the Germans soon deployed divisions from other fronts, led by two of their best field marshals – Mackensen from the south, Falkenhayn from the north– which halted our offensive and drove our small, poorly trained and poorly equipped army back across the Carpathians into Wallachia.

On the Southern front, the Bulgarian and German armies dealt us a crushing defeat at Turtucaia. Little by little, we lost all of Wallachia in what was a full-scale military disaster – despite fierce resistance along the Jiu and Prahova river valleys – and were beaten back to the border between Wallachia and Moldavia by the end of 1916.

At that point, things changed. First, as winter set in, the French managed to send us arms and instructors by way of Russia; the Romanian army recovered during that winter, so much so that it was able to mount a successful defence along the Focșani-Galați front throughout the spring and summer of 1917.

If you look at the map, you will find that the border region between the two provinces, stretching from the eastward bend of Danube to the westward bend of the Carpathians, is a fairly narrow, hilly corridor, where trenches could provide an effective defence. When, in June 1917, the Germans tried to break through Oituz Pass from Transylvania, and at Mărăști and Mărășești from the south, the Romanian army repelled them, supported

Two of the heroic figures of World War I: General Alexandru Averescu and Queen Marie, wearing a uniform of the paramedics service, which she had established and led with great commitment.

by the few Russian troops sent to that front. Those were glorious victories – unfortunately, they would prove to be somewhat in vain.

For several months prior to that, momentous events had been under way in Russia. Already, the revolutionary movement that came to be known as the Bolsheviks had fatally undermined the Russian Empire, weakened after three and a half years of brutal war, whose purpose was not understood by the rank-and-file soldiers and which had already made millions of victims. Communism – whose exceptional leader, Lenin, had been smuggled by the Germans in a camouflaged train car from Switzerland to Finland – succeeded in infiltrating and fomenting revolt across much of the Russian army and the working class.

The great tsarist empire began to falter. Even the soldiers who fought at Mărășești alongside the Romanians mostly deserted and encouraged our troops to do the same, for it was not worth fighting for the capitalists, as they saw it. And so, by the autumn of 1917, despite having held the Focșani-Galați front against the German onslaught, we found ourselves alone and risking encirclement, as Russia almost completely collapsed.

The tsar had already abdicated in March. The new socialist provisional government led by Kerensky had nurtured hopes of establishing a democratic regime, but could not prevent fragmentation. The Bolsheviks, although in the minority, managed to seize power on

Alexandru Marghiloman signing the onerous peace of Bucharest (18 May 1918). The treaty was never ratified by Parliament, nor enforced by the king, and although our allies have blamed us for it, it had minimal consequences during the peace negotiations of 1919-1920. Nevertheless, it did end Marghiloman's political career.

7 November 1917 (25 October according to the Julian calendar used in Russia at the time, hence the name "October Revolution") and immediately began negotiations with Germany. The situation of tiny Romania – whose territory had been reduced to Moldavia and whose entire government had taken refuge in Iași, trapped between the German and Austro-Hungarian might to the west and the Bolshevik revolution to the east – was desperate. Believing the war was all but lost, Prime Minister Ionel Brătianu gave way to those who favoured peace with Germany – first, to Marshal Averescu, one of the heroes of the war, but one who considered that we had lost the war and that we should sue for peace, as the Russians had done just four days before, at Brest-Litovsk. We agreed an armistice on 9 December 1917 and, after several months of negotiations, the government of Alexandru Marghiloman signed the peace in Bucharest, on 7 May 1918.

Again, a few personal remarks: our history books unanimously assert that we had absolutely no choice but to conclude the Treaty of Bucharest – a very painful peace for all Romanians, by which we lost Dobruja to Bulgaria and a significant mountainous strip to Austria-Hungary; the treaty also included extremely harsh conditions, effectively making our country an economic

The armistice between the Entente and Germany was signed in a railway carriage on 11 November 1918, in the forest of Compiègne. Yet sometimes, the vanquished may take their revenge in bizarre ways: in 1940, at Hitler's orders, the carriage of Marshall Foch, which had been kept in a museum, was taken back to the exact same spot in the forest of Compiègne, where it was France's turn to sign its capitulation, on 22 June.

colony of the Central Powers. Yet there was a small minority within our political class (Queen Marie and Take Ionescu among them) who believed that we should not have given in, and instead retreated to Russia with our small army, which was still intact and had fought well. It was not a foolish plan, and it may have just influenced the Russian civil war that followed, in which the Whites fought the Reds. On the other hand, while we were signing the Treaty of Bucharest, the Americans entered the war and, within weeks, completely turned the tide of the conflict in favour of the Western allies. In other words, we made peace in 1918, just weeks before the course of the war changed dramatically.

Starting with July 1918, the Central Powers began to crumble – first on the Western front, then on the Southern (or Salonika) front, where a French-led international force had been deployed. The Austro-Hungarian Empire capitulated on 3 November 1918 and Germany on 11 November. In early November 1918, as the future marshal Franchet d'Espèrey led the French army advance from the south, we took up arms once more and found ourselves alongside the Allies as the war ended.

Arduous peace negotiations at Versailles

Transylvanian politician Alexandru Vaida-Voevod, one of the most resolute diplomats that represented Romania at the Paris peace negotiations

The Treaty of Bucharest in May 1918 made it a lot more difficult to negotiate our position at the peace talks taking place at the palace of Versailles, near Paris. Again, our textbooks often present an inaccurate version of events by implying that France and Great Britain were initially unwilling to make good their promises from August 1916, before we entered the war. This is somewhat true, but there is no mention of the reason why: it was because, from a legal point of view, we were accused of disregarding the agreement we had made in August 1916, which clearly forbade us to make a separate peace – which we had done. The dramatic circumstances we had found ourselves in during November 1917 were not seen as a sufficient reason to justify our capitulation. The Allies drew parallels with the attitude of Serbia, which had been occupied in its entirety, but which withdrew its army through Albania to the Adriatic, from where it had been transported by French and English ships to fight on the Salonika front. Our delegation at Versailles was therefore in a precarious position as it tried to persuade the Allies to respect the clauses of the treaty agreed in 1916. This was compounded by a dispute between us and the Serbians regarding our border in the Banat, where preference was given to Serbian claims. Finally, the Romanians were very reticent in accepting the various proposals on guaranteeing the rights of minorities. Ionel Brătianu left the conference and left it to other parties to conclude negotiations.

The signing of the peace treaty in the Hall of Mirrors at the Palace of Versailles (28 June 1919). Undoubtedly, this was not a random choice, for it was in the same room that Kaiser Wilhelm I had proclaimed himself emperor of Germany on 18 January 1871, after its victory in the Franco-Prussian War.

The Great Union of 1918

In the meantime, important events were happening on the ground. An extraordinary series of circumstances converged in that historic moment: on the one hand, the Bolshevik revolution enabled Bessarabia to break away from the Russian grip, as the National Assembly in Chișinău voted in favour of the union with Romania on 27 March 1918; on the other hand, after the collapse of the Dual Monarchy, the Great National Assembly of Romanians in Transylvania, Banat, Crișana and Maramureș voted for unification with Romania on 1 December 1918. The National Council of Bukovina had done the same three days before. This was how, in almost miraculous fashion, the country was made whole, both to the east and to the west.

Another unforeseen event occurred during the extended negotiations at Versailles (1919-1920): in March 1919, a communist government led by Béla Kun took power in Hungary. The country's collapse had been dramatic – having suffered a military disaster and with a territory reduced to less than half its previous size – which made it an ideal target for communism spreading from Moscow across the world, after the victory of the revolution in Russia.

Iuliu Hossu, Greek Catholic Bishop of Gherla, reading out the resolutions of the assembly that had decided the union of Transylvania with Romania, on 1 December 1918 in Alba Iulia.

Coronation ceremony of Ferdinand I, the first king of Greater Romania, on 15 October 1922 in Alba Iulia. The king is wearing the Steel Crown of Romania, while the queen donned a gold crown, similar to those worn by the consorts of Romanian voivodes in church frescoes.

The Béla Kun government was not content with simply transforming the country into a communist state, but also ordered the Hungarian army to attack Romania in an attempt to reclaim Transylvania and – according to some sources – link up with the Bolshevik troops on the Dniester. The Romanian army entered Hungary, despite a Franco-British warning not to advance; for once, we did not heed the great powers and occupied Budapest (4 August 1919).

To this day, honest Hungarians will admit that we saved them from communism in 1919 and that it was due to our three-month occupation of the capital that a relatively democratic government was able to take charge, under the leadership of admiral Miklós Horthy, who was named regent – that is, a provisional chief of state in the absence of a king (since the Romanians, Slovaks, Serbians and Croats had not allowed the new Hungary to become a kingdom under the former emperor Charles IV, who had succeeded his uncle Franz-Joseph in 1916). By occupying Budapest and ousting Béla Kun, we prevented communism from taking hold in Central Europe for over twenty years. This is a great accomplishment of the Ionel Brătianu government and something worthy of remembering.

The extraordinary creation of Greater Romania in December 1918 was the embodiment of a centuries-old dream of the Romanian people: to be united, from the Banat to the Dniester. Greater Romania would be forged with great efforts, for it meant that people who had never been ruled by the same authority suddenly had to come together and work side by side. What united all Romanians was the fact that they spoke the same language. As I mentioned before, we are perhaps the only large country in Europe whose national identity is exclusively based on a common language, spoken "*from the Dniester to the Tisza*". This is not the case in other countries, where the national ethos was gradually built for many centuries around a common history. Our "mortar" is the *language*. In my opinion, the Great Union we achieved in 1918 was exceptionally well carried out. Considering the difficulties that the Czechs and Slovaks encountered in trying to maintain a single state, or the drama of former Yugoslavia (not only recently, but also during the inter-war period) we must appreciate that this unification of Romanians, the first in their history, was nothing short of a miracle. Here is just one example to illustrate this: Prime Minister Ionel Brătianu enjoyed enormous prestige and had the full confidence of King Ferdinand (their 13 years in power were some of the most flourishing in our history). But he understood that it would take a Transylvanian to cement the union and represent us in Paris – at a time when we faced

French geographer Emmanuel de Martonne (1873-1955) was the author of field studies on the physical geography of Romania. As an expert participating in the Paris Peace Conference, he established the concept of "border viability", due to which Romania's Western borders were drawn several kilometres to the west.

Signing of the peace treaty with Hungary at Trianon, on 4 June 1920

serious difficulties because of the peace we had concluded in Bucharest – and accepted a Transylvanian prime minister, Alexandru Vaida-Voevod. Therefore, it was a Transylvanian who negotiated on our behalf at Trianon, not a Wallachian. It was a very liberal way of doing things, which later enabled us to integrate the previously separated provinces in a straightforward manner.

The peace with Hungary was not signed in the palace of Versailles (the former residence of the "Sun King", as Louis XIV was known) but in the Trianon, a smaller palace on the same domain; this only happened on 4 June 1920 because of endless disputes regarding borders and the rights of minorities etc. We had already signed the peace with Austria in Saint-Germain (on Bukovina) and Bulgaria in Neuilly (on Dobruja) both near Paris, in December 1919.

Agrarian reform and the domestic situation in the early days of Greater Romania

The new country, double the size of pre-war Romania, incorporated provinces that had never been ruled together

Greater Romania, the maximum extent of territory ever held by Romanians. According to the 1930 census, 5 million of a total of 18 million inhabitants belonged to an ethnic minority, the most numerous of which were the Hungarians, the Germans, the Jews, the Ruthenians, the Russians and the Bulgarians.

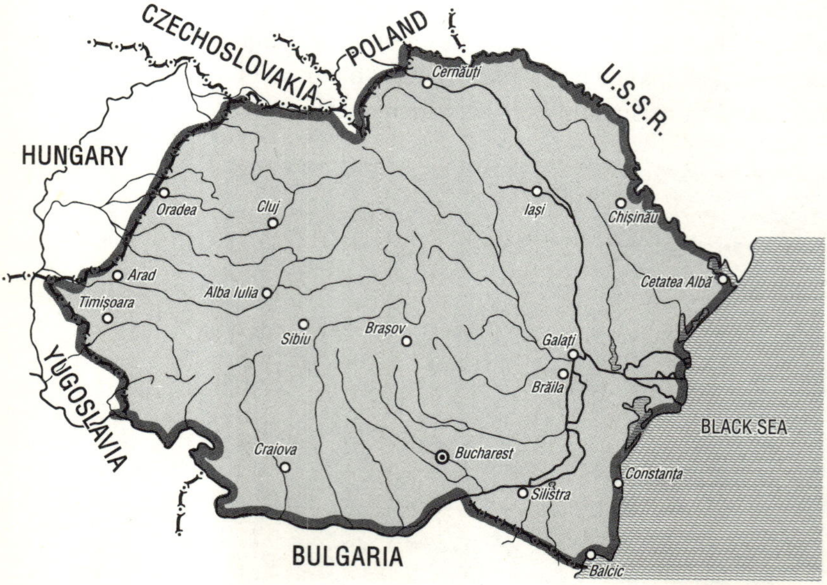

in the past – the "Old Kingdom", the Banat, Transylvania, Crişana, Maramureş, Bukovina and Bessarabia; ethnic minorities represented 28% of the population, which posed new and difficult problems for the government.

The question of minorities, or rather that of the guarantees they were supposed to be granted by the new or re-established states (such as Czechoslovakia and Poland) or those which had been significantly enlarged (like Romania and the future Yugoslavia), had been one of the most hotly debated issues at the Versailles peace negotiations.

The difficulty of putting these guarantees in practice is still an issue today, 80 years later. Let us not forget the state of affairs in 1918: after the unification of the country to the north, west and east, if we were to put together all the minorities within our borders – Hungarians, Germans, Ukrainians, Gagauz, Bulgarians etc. as well as the Jews, Armenians and Gypsies who wanted their own representatives in Parliament – then one citizen in four was not of Romanian origin. Keep in mind the scale of this problem that Greater Romania had to face almost overnight.

Agrarian reform had been part of the Liberal manifesto even before the outbreak of the war. Then, in the midst of war, in April 1917, King Ferdinand aimed to encourage the peasant soldiers by declaring that the

Thrasher at work in Gottlob, a Swabian village in the Banat region (1938). In other regions of the country, farming was sometimes practiced using the ancestral ox-drawn plough.

Dimitrie Gusti (1880-1955) one of the first sociologists to carry out field research in Romanian villages, at the head of a substantial and diverse team of experts. He also created a program of education for rural inhabitants.

lands of great estates would be redistributed after the war was won, so post-war governments were obligated to put the king's solemn promise of reform into practice. I must emphasise that this agrarian reform (which began in 1918 and ended in 1922) is still the most comprehensive of its type ever put into practice by a civilian government – or, in some cases, by the great landowners themselves; having researched the entire universal history, the only precedent I came across was in 10th century China, but in that case reform was triggered by a revolution and its effects were short-lived. If we look at European history, there was, of course, the massive confiscation of lands during the Russian revolution, however that was not done to redistribute them to the peasantry, but to create the state collective farms (Russian: *kolkhoz*). A peaceful redistribution of land, such as the one we achieved with a parliament made up almost entirely of landowners, is a unique achievement in history.

And so it came to be that, in the inter-war period, our country had achieved a land distribution ratio similar to those in France or Sweden, where 20% of the land belonged to owners of over 50 hectares, while the rest belonged to medium or small farmers. However, it can be argued that the economic consequences of the reform were less than favourable, though perhaps there was not enough time for the benefits to emerge. The initial results were poor: before the war, the relatively forced labour of the peasants enabled the cultivation of wheat on large estates, making Romania an important exporter of grain; after the war, however, our country was barely able to export anything at all. Quantitatively, the overall level of production decreased, partly because small farmers lacked the means, and partly because modern agricultural technology was ignored. On the other hand, being a prolific nation meant that small properties were fragmented even further as land lots got divided between heirs, right from the first generation; as a result, it is fair to say that the situation of small farmers was anything but prosperous before the outbreak of World War II. Nevertheless, we must add that "halfway" through

Team of sociologists teaching children about beekeeping. Dimitrie Gusti believed that sociologists, once in the field, also had a socio-cultural function to fulfil.

the inter-war period (between 1929 and 1931) came the biggest economic crisis the world had experienced since the beginning of the industrial age; the Great Depression had started in the United States as a crisis on the stock exchange (paradoxically, caused by over-production) and spread across the world at an alarming rate (proof that the economy had already become global). Food prices dropped sharply to less than half (I remember this period as a child) so that producers were barely making ends meet. None of the reforms planned by the Liberals or the National Peasants' Party (which included the establishment of a rural cooperatives system and bank subsidies for modernisation) were able to take off before the start of World War II.

Old parties, new parties and political life in the inter-war period

New political parties appeared after World War I, while the Conservatives faded away, largely because it had been the Liberal government of Ionel Brătianu that made those crucial decisions – universal suffrage and land redistribution – democratic reforms that had changed the makeup of Parliament. As the Conservative Party disappeared, some of its politicians were recruited into the new People's Party (PP) formed around marshal Averescu, one of the heroes of the war, who went into

50 bani coin from the first issue of Greater Romania

Ferdinand I, king of Romania (1914-1927) called "the Loyal" for Romania's entry into the war on the side of the Entente, or "the Unificator" for having created Greater Romania after the war.

politics at the end of the conflict. His party, nevertheless, did not make much of an impact on the country, and only governed when Ionel Brătianu saw fit to concede his place. In the first years after the war, it was the Liberals and the People's Party who were the most powerful; but it was not long until the National Party from Transylvania (led by Iuliu Maniu) merged with the Peasants' Party from Wallachia (led by Ion Mihalache) to form the National Peasants' Party (PNȚ). The word "national" meant that the party had roots in the Transylvanian party that had struggled for the emancipation of Romanians and against Hungarians, now allied with a peasant party further to the left on the political spectrum, which advocated in favour of a more radical land reform and emphasised social aspects. This union gradually became the largest party in all of Romania, surpassing even the Liberals. The pre-1914 alternation between the Conservatives and Liberals now became one between the Liberals and the PNȚ.

But tragedy befell the country when, in 1927, both King Ferdinand and Ionel Brătianu, the greatest Romanian politician of the 20th century, died. That was when the country's troubles began. King Ferdinand, allegedly advised by Ionel Brătianu, had disinherited his son, Crown Prince Carol, as both of them felt that he was not worthy of becoming the next ruler of the country. Prince

Michael became king on 20 July 1927, when he was not yet 6 years old. This photograph shows him on his way to the coronation ceremony, accompanied by his mother, Elena, wearing mourning dress, Patriarch Miron Cristea and Prince Nicholas, members of the regency alongside Gheorghe Buzdugan and, after his death in 1929, Constantin Sărățeanu.

Carol had done something unthinkable: in 1918, he had fled the country to enter a morganatic marriage with his sweetheart, a woman named Zizi Lambrino, who descended from a Moldavian boyar family; the couple were wed in Odessa, Russia. In the eyes of Brătianu, this reckless adventure did not bode well for the maturity of the prince – and rightfully so. When King Ferdinand died in 1927, Prince Carol was legally disowned and the throne passed to his 6-year old son, Michael. The tragic and unexpected death of King Ferdinand left the country in a very difficult situation, with a child on the throne and a regency made up of three politically inexperienced people – namely Miron Cristea, the country's Orthodox patriarch (we had had a Patriarchy since 1925); Gheorghe Buzdugan, president of the High Court of Cassation and Prince Nicolae, Carol's younger brother. Yet by 1930, amid the economic and political crisis affecting the country, there were growing calls among the general public, as well the as political parties, to put Prince Carol back into power. On 6 June 1930, Prince Carol returned to the

Ion I. C. Brătianu (1864-1927) was initially a railway engineer. He went into politics and became the leader of the National Liberal Party in 1909.

Political Carnival, a caricature by I. Anestin. The character in the centre is Prime Minister Constantin Argetoianu; around him are Virgil Madgearu, Alexandru Averescu, Gheorghe Tattarescu, Dinu Brătianu, Nicolae Iorga, Alexandru Vaida-Voevod, Iuliu Maniu and Octavian Goga – almost every leading politician of the inter-war period.

Iuliu Maniu (1873-1953) president of the National Peasants' Party and prime minister of Romania during the years of the Great Depression

country by aeroplane and, with the aid of several accomplices, organised a coup – at a time when Iuliu Maniu was prime minister. The timid Maniu resigned and left the decision to Parliament, which promptly confirmed Carol as king of Romania. Young king Michael I (Romanian: *Mihai I*) had to make way for his father, who began his reign as Carol II, with Maniu back in power several days later.

Nowadays, it is difficult – particularly for people my age, who have lived through that period – to be entirely objective and tell right from wrong in relation to the reign of King Carol II. The man was intelligent and cultured, and the choices he made in terms of foreign policy were later proven to be correct; yet he was utterly immoral and incapable of reining in his passions, allowing himself (early on into his reign) to be surrounded by a group of profiteers and businessmen, which public opinion nicknamed the "royal *camarilla*" (a term from Spanish history).

To better understand the dramatic reign of Carol II, I will attempt a brief description of the political situation in Europe and our country at the time.

The political situation in 1930's Europe and the rise of far-right parties

One of the most ominous aspects of that period was the emergence of far-right movements across most of Europe. On the one hand, they emerged as a reaction against Bolshevism, while on the other, they were a result of the discredit of the parliamentary system in many countries, seen as being plagued by corruption and incapable of ending the economic crisis. The risk of experiences similar to that of Béla Kun in Hungary, and the situation in Germany, Spain (both of which had powerful communist parties) or Italy in the early 1920's, gave rise to nationalist movements preaching the abolition of the multi-party parliamentary system and rule by a single, anti-communist party. The first example is from 1922,

Hitler, as chancellor, and Hindenburg, president of the German Weimar Republic. After the death of the marshall in 1934, Hitler also assumed the duties of the chief of state. Carol II had already become chief of state on 8 June 1930. He needed a party for his one-party state, which he created in 1938: the National Renaissance Front. Even so, comparisons with Nazi Germany are far-fetched.

when Benito Mussolini, founder of the Fascist movement, came to power in Italy (the name comes from the Latin *fasces*, a symbol of authority in ancient Rome). Authoritarian regimes then emerged in countries closer to ours: in 1926, Marshall Józef Piłsudski imposed his dictatorship in Poland; in 1927, King Alexander seized power in the "Kingdom of Serbs, Croats and Slovenes", which he renamed "Yugoslavia" in 1929.

An event with far more serious consequences happened in 1933, when Adolf Hitler came to power in Germany as head of the National Socialist German Workers' Party (German: *Nazionalsozialistische Deutsche Arbeitspartei*, hence the term "Nazism"). It is worth mentioning that it was Marshall Hindenburg, president of the then German Weimar Republic, who appointed Hitler chancellor after his party had obtained a relative majority in the parliamentary elections.

In 1936, the dictatorship of General Metaxás took hold of Greece. That same year, a long and bloody civil war started in Spain, between the Popular Front communist government and General Franco's nationalists, ending after three years with the victory of the latter – while Franco remained dictator (Spanish: *caudillo*) until his death in 1975. So let us not be too harsh on King Carol II for imposing a personal dictatorship in 1938 – Romania was, after all, the last country in this part of Europe to adopt a dictatorial regime, having enjoyed a relatively more democratic rule than any of our neighbours in the inter-war period. Even in Western European countries with democratic traditions such as France, there were two or three far-right movements that held an unexpected level of political sway.

The Legionary Movement (Legion of the Archangel Michael or the Iron Guard)

A. C. Cuza, professor at the University of Iași and the ideological and political mentor of Corneliu Zelea Codreanu. In 1927, Codreanu left Cuza's National Christian Defence League and formed the Legion of the Archangel Michael. Cuza's party fused with Goga's National Agrarian Party in 1936, forming the National Christian Party.

The most prominent far-right party in our country was the Legionary Movement. I feel compelled to explain what this movement stood for, as its ideology still appeals to some people to this day. And it is not an easy thing to explain. First of all, it was not a copy of Nazism or Fascism, as its adversaries have said. The Legionary Movement was a homegrown movement, born out of anti-communist student groups, one of which was led by a man named Corneliu Zelea Codreanu. Things took a turn for the worst during a trial in which Codreanu stood accused of sedition by the prefect of Iași, when Codreanu took out his revolver and assassinated the prefect. In truth, the prefect had severely mistreated him and several students he had arrested (the use of entirely despicable and reprehensible interrogation methods such as beatings and torture did exist before the communist era, but on an infinitely smaller scale). This murder was the first political assassination in our country since that of Prime Minister Barbu Catargiu in 1863, during the reign of Prince Cuza – in stark contrast to Balkan "habits" (to this day, the assassin is still not known, but it was most likely the work of Cuza's supporters, since the premier opposed the prince's reforms). In fact, this is one of the most serious accusations laid against the Legionnaires (Romanian: *legionarii*): that they introduced assassination into our political landscape, something that had not previously been part of our "tradition".

Thus began the persecution of these young men, who wanted radical changes in the country's political

Corneliu Zelea Codreanu (centre) and his comrades from the early days of the Legion: Ion I. Moța, Ilie Gârneață, Radu Mironovici and Tudose Popescu

practices. Having been acquitted of the prefect's murder by a popular jury, Codreanu and several of his associates created the Legion of the Archangel Michael (later also called the Iron Guard) amid an atmosphere of religious mysticism. The Legionnaires claimed that they would cleanse the country of "vile political practices" and "eradicate the poisonous, cosmopolitan influence of the Jews and Freemasons"; they dreamt of returning to a traditional, mythical past, and sometimes used slogans that seem naïve to us today – for example, "*Let us build a country as holy as the sun in the sky*" etc. Codreanu himself (also referred to as *Căpitanul* or "the Captain" by his acolytes) would walk through villages wearing national dress, sometimes mounted on a white horse, like a fairy-tale hero. There was a certain archaic appeal to their behaviour, but in those times of severe economic crisis and political uncertainty, with very high unemployment among young intellectuals, their somewhat childish enthusiasm proved so contagious that a large part of the country's students – but also priests, craftsmen and workers – became affiliated to the Legionary movement in a very short time.

Our world today – and in particular the more committed of democrats – can no longer fathom the idea that men of the intellectual stature of the philosopher Nae Ionescu, the quality of Mircea Eliade, Emil Cioran and so many other figures of exceptional erudition and morality could have become attracted to this movement.

General Gheorghe Cantacuzino (nicknamed "the Sentinel") and Nae Ionescu, at the Bucharest North Railway Station, waiting for the funerary train that had carried the remains of Ion Moța and Vasile Marin around the country; the two Legionnaires were killed in the Spanish Civil War, where they had gone to fight against republican forces (11 February 1937).

From a social point of view, even if the initiators of the movement hailed from the common people, Legionary recruitment eventually permeated all levels of society, so that its leadership included a staggering number of people bearing "historic" names such as Cantacuzino, Ghica, Sturdza, Mânu etc. It was a sort of collective blindness. Only later – much later, after the traumatic experience of the war – did we realise that any movement that entailed single party rule would inevitably lead to brutality and murder. This makes the revival of the Legionary movement in the context of our world today an all the more anachronistic and dangerous aberration.

After Hitler's victory in the 1933 parliamentary elections in Germany, the Legionnaires prepared to stand in

Cortège of Legionnaires Ion Moța and Vasile Marin, heading towards the Green House (the Legion's headquarters in Bucharest) where the two were given a martyr's burial (13 February 1937). The king and politicians were both impressed and concerned with the magnitude of the event.

the upcoming elections on such a violently fascist, anti-Semite and anti-Western manifesto, that the liberal prime minister I. G. Duca, charged by King Carol II with their organisation, banned the Iron Guard from taking part. Three weeks later, a death squad of three Legionnaires assassinated him on the platform of Sinaia train station. An even more unjustifiable assassination took place in 1936, when a death squad of ten Legionnaires (all of them theology students) shot the dissident Legionnaire Mihai Stelescu in his hospital bed, and then hacked his body to pieces with hatchets while dancing around the corpse (leading some ethnologists to believe this unimaginable scene was reminiscent of the ancient rites of the Cabeiri).

Nevertheless, the Legion became more and more popular, especially after a unit of Legionnaire volunteers went to fight alongside the Francoists in the Spanish civil war; two of these men, Moța and Marin, who had died in combat, were solemnly buried in Bucharest in January 1937, demonstrating the extent to which the movement had spread. Then in 1937, Gheorghe Tătărescu, appointed prime minister by King Carol II after Duca's assassination, failed to win a majority in the elections (with only 36% of the vote instead of the 40% required by law).

Carol II, a king in love with ceremony, and his son, Michael, Great Voivode of Alba Iulia, on their way to Easter Mass. Behind them, donning the uniform of the National Renaissance Front, the archetypal political villain, Constantin Argetoianu.

The imposition of royal dictatorship

The Liberal electoral failure was partly due to a "non-aggression pact" between Iuliu Maniu's PNȚ and the "Everything for the Country" Party (the electoral name of the Legion; Romanian: *Totul pentru țară*). The result was that the king had to include the leaders of two smaller far-right parties into the government, but not from the Legion – the poet Octavian Goga and Professor A. C. Cuza, the leader of a party focused exclusively on anti-Semitism.

It could be argued that the king only co-opted them into power to discredit the far-right and, amid external pressure and a new economic crisis, to provide himself with an excuse to dissolve Parliament and impose a royal

Banknote with the effigy of King Carol II on a banknote from 1939, the heyday of Romania's economy

dictatorship (February 1938); later that year, he invented an entirely artificial party called the National Renaissance Front.

Compared to the rest of the dictatorships that were to follow – the brief Legionary experience, then General Antonescu's dictatorship, and of course, the 45 years under a communist regime – it would appear that the royal dictatorship was less harsh. Moreover, a year or two after he assumed the throne, Carol II had profited from a revival of the world economic situation, which had beneficial consequences for our country, making his reign a time of relative economic progress (featuring great public works in Bucharest and the first asphalt roads in the country). Unfortunately, this economic "boom" was overshadowed by suspicions regarding illegal profits made by the "royal camarilla", which included the king's mistress, Elena Lupescu – a very unpopular woman, for whom the king had divorced Queen Elena (a member of the Greek royal family).

Let us return to the fate of the Legionnaires during the royal dictatorship. In November 1938, during an official visit to Hitler's Germany, Carol II did something

The rich and the poor during the golden age of Bucharest: a well-to-do lady and a humble flower seller at the intersection of C. A. Rosetti Street and the new boulevard built during the reign of Carol II (5 May 1937). The boulevard, lined with buildings designed by great modernist architects such as Horia Creangă and Rudolf Fränkel, is nowadays neglected, as if intentionally.

Another snapshot of urban life during the booming inter-war period: the sisters Suzana and Gabriela Mihalescu, daughters of a Bucharest lawyer, wearing the mandatory school uniform of the day.

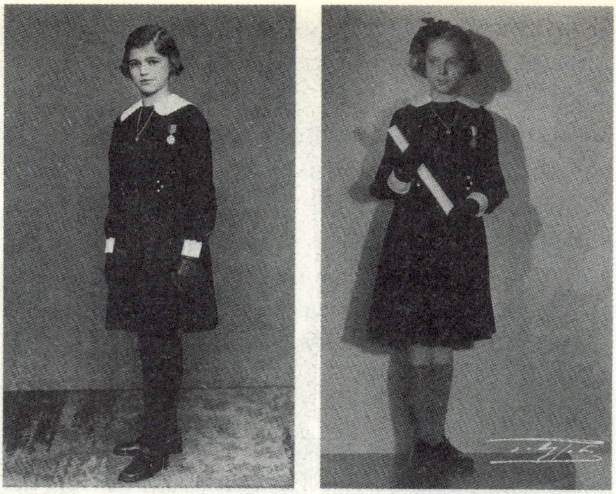

unacceptable for a sovereign (or any ruler for that matter): he "rid" himself of the "charismatic" Codreanu by ordering his assassination (the Legionary leader was strangled along with all thirteen of I. G. Duca and Stelescu's assassins during an alleged escape attempt staged from the prison where Codreanu had been jailed after a political trial).

The liquidation of the "Captain" and the subsequent arrest of the movement's leadership left the Legion in disarray and prompted the rise through the ranks of a mediocre conspirator named Horia Sima. Ten months after Codreanu's assassination and just a few weeks after World War II broke out in September 1939, the Legionnaires took their revenge by murdering Prime Minister Armand Călinescu.

The king's men reacted with near-medieval methods: they summarily executed the culprits, leaving their corpses to rot in the streets for days, and then carried out hundreds of seemingly random executions in the provinces, sending the country into a spiral of violence.

The Molotov-Ribbentrop Pact (23 August 1939) and the outbreak of World War II

Adolf Hitler and Arthur Seyss-Inquart, the man who surrendered Austria to the Nazis without putting up any resistance (March 1938).

Just as the royal dictatorship was being imposed on the country, the world was moving towards the outbreak of World War II, which everyone knew was approaching year after year since Hitler had come to power in 1933. He had reoccupied the Rhineland (a German border region "demilitarised" by the Treaty of Versailles) in 1936; this was followed by the annexation of Austria (known as the *Anschluss*) which he considered German, in March 1938; and on 29 September that same year, after a tense diplomatic crisis between the Berlin-Rome Axis on one side and the Franco-British on the other, the latter accepted the dismantling of Czechoslovakia through the Munich Agreement as they felt unprepared for a military confrontation. Germany annexed about a third of the Czech territory (which it called the Sudetenland) inhabited by a large German population, Hungary received the south of Slovakia, while Poland was given the Zaolzie region; on 15 March 1939, Hitler invaded the rest of Czechoslovakia. The Czechs found themselves living in a German protectorate, while Slovakia (having lost Carpathian Ruthenia and the south to Hungary) became theoretically independent. The Franco-British failed to react on either occasion.

The Little Entente (an alliance consisting of Czechoslovakia, Romania and Yugoslavia) had not come close

Vyacheslav Molotov signing a non-aggression pact that lasted less than two years, but which, for Romania, meant the loss of Bessarabia and Northern Bukovina. Directly behind him is Joachim von Ribbentrop, the German foreign affairs minister, standing beside a smiling Stalin, to his left, content at the deal he thought he had struck with the Nazis (23 August 1939).

Polish refugees crossing into Romania in September 1939 were given a warm welcome by the locals and authorities. Our government allowed the transit of tens of thousands of Polish troops towards the Middle East, from where they continued fighting alongside the Allies.

to becoming a real military power since its creation in 1920 and was now a thing of the past. Before the unstoppable advance of the Third Reich (meaning "The Third Empire", as Nazi Germany had styled itself) our country was forced to sign a commercial treaty that made us a quasi-exclusive client of Germany.

On 23 August 1939, the world learned with stupefaction that Germany and the Soviet Union, which everyone thought of as mortal enemies, had signed a non-aggression pact (later revealed to include the partition of Poland and the German consent for the Soviet invasion of Bessarabia). It came to be known under the names of the two foreign affairs ministers who signed it, as the Molotov-Ribbentrop Pact. No later than a week afterwards, on 1 September 1939, Nazi Germany invaded Poland without warning, fielding a formidable military machine. The pretext was the recovery of the majority German port of Danzig (Polish: *Gdańsk*) and the corridor that separated it from Germany. In accordance with the treaties that bound them to Poland, France and Great Britain declared war on the Germans (3 September 1939). Thus began World War II, which would last longer than the first and claim tens of millions of victims.

The French and British were unable to launch an attack on Germany straight away because of their aerial inferiority and the presence of a defensive system of reinforced concrete fortifications along the entire Western German border (the Siegfried Line). Germany was able to continue its *blitzkrieg* (German for "lightning war") against Poland, which put up a heroic resistance, but was eventually overwhelmed after the Soviets attacked from the east; the two aggressors divided the country between themselves on 28 September.

Suddenly, Germany appeared to be an invincible power. What should we, Romanians, have done under these circumstances? We too had received guarantees from France and Great Britain, but they hardly seemed to be worth anything.

The Germans attacked the Franco-British forces on 10 May 1940, avoiding the French defences (the Maginot Line) by violating Dutch neutrality and crossing Belgium from north to south. Shockingly, France succumbed within a matter of weeks.

The Soviet ultimatum (26 June 1940) and the Second Vienna Award (30 August 1940)

The consequences for us were almost instantaneous. Just one week after the French armistice was signed on 17 June 1940, Romania received an ultimatum from the USSR which demanded the immediate handover of Bessarabia and Northern Bukovina. It was an extremely dramatic moment. As he no longer had a parliament, King Carol II was forced to revive an old institution and summoned the Crown Council, which hastily assembled 21 members. We had been given 36 hours to reply to the ultimatum. How could we have defended a 650-kilometre border against a power 20 times greater than Romania? The Council promptly telephoned the German foreign affairs minister, asking him to intervene with the Russians on our behalf and arrange for negotiations. But at that point, the Germans and the Russians were allies. Hitler replied that we should give in, then and there. Several hours later, during the second meeting of the Crown Council, only six of the 21 members argued that

Nicolae Titulescu, foreign affairs minister of Romania, had created a system of regional alliances during the inter-war period. However, all alliances and international guarantees proved futile in the summer of 1940.

Mihail Manoilescu, foreign affairs minister of Romania, signing the Second Vienna Award, which lost us Northern Transylvania (30 August 1940). Almost a year before, Hungary had annexed a portion of Slovakia through another such arbitration.

we should resist no matter the consequences – the historians Nicolae Iorga and Ștefan Ciobanu (a Bessarabian) among them.

Decades later, I still ask myself – now that we know what followed, and about the secret clause of the Molotov-Ribbentrop Pact (including the German consent for the Soviet advance to the river Prut) – whether it was not those six men who were right after all. Would it not have been better to declare our resistance on that day? We would have lost the war in eight days and several tens of thousands would have died, but it would have been the *Germans* who occupied the country – something that could not have escaped our politicians at the time – because they could not have allowed the Russians to seize the Ploiești oil fields while they prepared to go to war against the USSR. This was a well-known fact – Hitler himself had written about it years before in his book, *Mein Kampf* ("My Struggle" in German). It was therefore obvious that, had we allowed the Germans to occupy the rest of our territory, we would have been in the same situation as Poland – occupied by the two aggressors throughout the war, but with our *honour* intact. There is one principle we should have never strayed from: never surrender an inch of land without a fight. In my opinion, this was probably the greatest political error we have made in the past 50 years. We should have fought the Russians in 1940, even if we would have only lasted for eight days. For after surrendering Bessarabia and Northern Bukovina to them, we also had to relinquish Northern Transylvania. The Germans slammed their fist down on the table, forcing us to give up half of the province to Hungary (the Second Vienna Award or the "Vienna Diktat", as it is known in Romania) and Southern Dobruja to the Bulgarians. Thus, within a few months, we effectively lost a third of our territory without having fired a single shot.

Again, it is my firm belief that we should have fought, firstly because we *had* to fight; secondly, we could argue in retrospect that the consequences to our country would have been less catastrophic. We would have lost infinitely less men than we did during two major campaigns – first in Russia, all the way to Stalingrad and the Caucasus, then in the west, all the way to Prague – but, most importantly, we would have projected a far nobler image onto the world, which is of vital significance to the national *psyche*. From the moment we yielded (27 June 1940) it could be said that everything went against us and that we gave everyone cause for condemnation: the Serbs and the Greeks, our old friends and allies, can blame us for allowing the Germans to use our territory to attack them from the rear; our traditional Western allies will not

Territorial losses during the summer of 1940

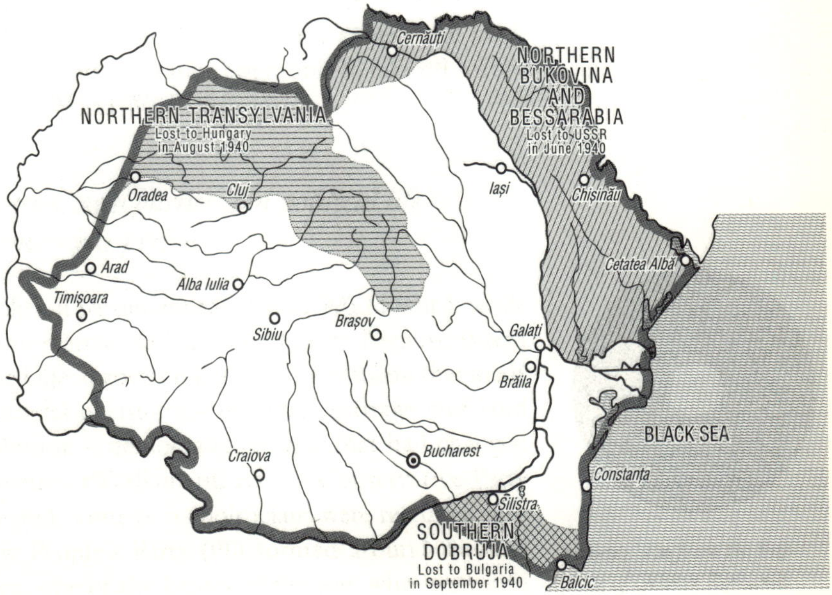

forget that we allied ourselves with Germany to take back Bessarabia and Bukovina; the Russians will not forgive us, a minor power, for having dared to set foot in "Holy Russia" and march to the banks of the Volga; while the Germans can harbour deep resentment for our "betrayal" of 23 August 1944. In other words, we lost face before all sides because of one fatal error we made on 27 June 1940.

I am often told that such interpretations have no value. One cannot rewrite history or guess what might have happened *if*... and that is only fair. But historians have no other means of assessing the merits of a decision in the past other than to imagine, in the most rational way possible, what could have happened if a different decision had been made (a logical technique by which one imagines circumstances contrary to what has actually occurred, called "counterfactual conditional" in Anglo-Saxon philosophy).

General Antonescu and the "National Legionary State"

Let us return to the facts: after the country's humiliating triple "amputation", King Carol II had to abdicate and fled abroad, and thus, General Ion Antonescu assumed power. Antonescu was a bold, resilient and honest man, but he was only able to form a government with the

Ion Antonescu, Conducător *("Leader") of the National Legionary State proclaimed on 14 September 1940 and Horia Sima, leader of the Legionnary movement, on one of the many rallies held during the several months of their strained cooperation.*

"King Carol II" Guards Barracks riddled by bullets, in the aftermath of the Legionary rebellion of 21-23 January 1941. Not far from it was a depot of the Bucharest Tram Company, which had been infiltrated by a very powerful branch of the Legionary Workers' Corps.

help of the Legion (or what was left of it); this led to the establishment of the "National Legionary State" in 1940, with General Antonescu as prime minister and half of the government made up of Legionnaires.

Needless to say, we had to ally ourselves with the Germans and even allowed them to deploy troops to Romania, supposedly to train our army – but in fact, mainly to prepare the invasion of the Balkans and the attack against the USSR from our territory. After just a few months, General Antonescu found it impossible to work with the Legionnaires, who had behaved unacceptably – they had created a parallel political police; they had unleashed violence against the Jews and confiscated their property, dividing it amongst themselves under the pretext of "Romanianisation"; and they had murdered a large number of former ministers and dignitaries (no less than 60 of them killed in Jilava prison in November 1940). The assassination of the great historian Nicolae Iorga caused the greatest consternation and from that moment on, it was clear that General Antonescu would break with the Legionnaires. A two-day "civil war" ensued in late January 1941, in which the army defeated the Legionnaires. Yet this only happened after Antonescu secured the neutrality of the Germans, who had spent a few months observing Romania's internal situation and decided that, on the eve of their attack on the USSR, the military discipline of General Antonescu would serve them better than the Legionary chaos. Some Legionnaires escaped to

Two of the victims of Legionary vengeance: Armand Călinescu was shot dead on 21 September 1939, while Nicolae Iorga was murdered on the night of 26-27 November 1940, along with Virgil Madgearu and 64 former "Carlist" dignitaries jailed at Jilava.

Germany, while the rest were interned in camps, imprisoned or marked for removal later on, in one way or another – for example, by having them sent to the front line when we entered the war, which we eventually did. It was the end of Legionary domination in our country.

Antonescu's dictatorship, however, would prove to be even more ruthless towards other political, social and ethnic categories. After the start of the war against the Soviet Union, under the pretext that the Jews of Bessarabia and Bukovina had generally favoured Soviet occupation and had even engaged in criminal acts against the Romanian army, Antonescu decided to deport all the Jewish population of those provinces across the river Dniester. Yet without explanation, more groups of Jews from the rest of the country suffered the same fate, as did a significant number of Gypsies (unknown to this day). The mass deportation was estimated at about 150,000 people, who were literally abandoned in the steppes, with no infrastructure in place to receive them. As Transnistria was a war zone and the German army was notorious for the brutality of its advance, evaluating the definitive number of the dead and disappeared is nigh on impossible. This terrible tragedy is a crime now attributed not only to Antonescu and his government, but also to our entire nation. I, for one, swear that I had not the slightest knowledge of this atrocity at the time.

One of the two freight trains that had left Iași, a city that had to be "cleansed" of Jews, at Antonescu's orders. Over 4,000 people were crammed into the death trains, one of which reached Călărași; the other stopped in Podul Iloaiei, Iași County, on 30 June 1941, when this photograph was taken. In total, the Iași Pogrom of late June 1941 resulted in no fewer than 13,000 victims.

However, it must be said that Marshall Antonescu changed his attitude towards the Jewish minority during the following years (1942-1943) when he repeatedly refused to surrender our Jews to the Germans, despite insistent requests from their government to do so; he even supported the rescue of some Jews from the West or from Hungarian-occupied Northern Transylvania, unlike the Hungarian government, which gave in to Nazi demands in the spring of 1943 and surrendered all its Jews in Hungary proper (again numbering around 150,000 individuals, few of whom survived). Antonescu's actions of 1943 are little known in the West, yet even so, it does not absolve him of what he did in 1941.

The war in the East (June 1941)

Germany attacked the USSR on 22 June 1941, and we found ourselves on the side of the Germans. I too was on the front line – from day one. We were all young and full of enthusiasm at the thought of erasing the shame of the previous year and regaining Bessarabia and Bukovina. With the German army alongside, we thought it would

Commemorating one year since the loss of Bessarabia (21 June 1941). Portraits of Mussolini, Hitler, King Michael I and Antonescu are hanging from the façade of the "Carol I" University Foundation building. The next day, Romania entered the war. Our troops advanced into enemy territory, retaking Bessarabia after fierce battles. The anti-Soviet campaign would later turn sour after the great tragedies at Stalingrad and the Don Bend in 1942.

Column of Romanian soldiers captured by the Soviets at Stalingrad (November – December 1942). The "Tudor Vladimirescu" and "Horia, Cloşca and Crişan" divisions, infamous for having taken part in the post-war Sovietisation of Romania, were made up of Romanian prisoners who had switched sides and joined the enemy.

be an easy war to win; quite to the contrary, it was a highly dramatic war, because Antonescu (promoted to marshall at the start of hostilities) was not content with Bessarabia and Northern Bukovina, and did not stop at the border, as the Finns had done; he wanted to go further with the Germans, for if they won the war, at least part of Northern Transylvania might be returned to us, their faithful allies. On the basis of this political gamble – yet another miscalculation – we continued to fight on, until our troops reached Stalingrad, the Volga and the Caucasus Mountains. And when the tide of the war turned at Stalingrad, where the German armies (as well as the Romanian divisions) were dramatically surrounded, we suffered the greatest military defeat in our entire history. We lost hundreds of thousands of men – killed, wounded, frostbitten or captured. It was a national tragedy, for they were never recovered. The Germans blamed us for the encirclement of the city, and we had no means of our own to retreat. It gradually became obvious that Germany was losing the war and that we needed to get out of it.

Mihail N. Georgescu, a young military doctor who was used with tragedies. He escaped the Don Bend encirclement, and worked as a paediatrician after the war.

Every lucid politician understood that Germany could no longer win the war. The most perceptive of them had come to this realisation a year before, when the United States had entered the war, provoked by the Japanese attack on Pearl Harbor. The entry of the world's principal industrial power into the war alongside Great Britain and the USSR meant the beginning of the end for Hitler's ambitions. But dictators are – by defini-

tion – blind. Overnight, America turned its formidable industrial potential into an equally formidable military machine, which decided the fate of the war (the thousands of trucks that transported the Soviet army to Stalingrad were American, as were the tens of thousands of warplanes that turned German cities to rubble). Early into the American intervention, when I myself heard of President Roosevelt's declaration that they would be producing 1,000 planes every week, I remember thinking it was sheer boastfulness. A year later, the United States produced 52,000 planes per year, and one Liberty Ship (as their cargo vessels were called) every 10 days.

One of the thousands of Studebaker US6 trucks, made in the United States and sent to the Soviets as part of the Lend-Lease programme, entering Bucharest on 30 August 1944. A part of the population naïvely greeted the Soviets with cheers and applause.

After the fall of Stalingrad (February 1943) both the Antonescu government and the opposition led by Iuliu Maniu (with the secret support of King Michael I) began to test the waters – first with the Allies, then with the Soviets. By May 1944 we were provided with the last of the Soviet conditions for our capitulation. Yet Marshal Antonescu could not make up his mind, not even when – with half of Moldavia occupied – the Soviets broke through the Germano-Romanian front on 20 August 1944.

On the one hand, he was reluctant to break the soldier's oath he had given Hitler, while on the other, he was waiting for more favourable strategic circumstances to take the step. The opposition, however, feared that any further delay would hurt our chances of regaining Northern Transylvania from the Allies and the USSR when peace was concluded.

Antonescu's arrest and the changing of alliances (23 August 1944)

With the support of the recently established National Democratic Bloc (Maniu's PNȚ, Dinu Brătianu's Liberals, Titel Petrescu's Social Democrats *and* Lucrețiu Pătrășcanu's Communists) King Michael I organised a kind of "palace coup" on the afternoon of 23 August 1944. As Antonescu was still refusing to sign an armistice with the Soviets, the king relieved the marshall of his duties as prime minister and arrested him; he then ordered the army to stop fighting the Soviets and asked the Germans to leave the country. But as the Germans refused to leave and attacked the capital with anti-aircraft units stationed

One year since the royal coup (23 August 1945). Portraits of British Prime Minister Atlee, King Michael I, Soviet leader Stalin and US President Truman are hanging from " the façade of the "Carol I" University Foundation building, bombed by the Germans on 26 August 1944.

in Ploiești, we had to take up arms against our former allies. It was a painful thing for the army to do, but the king's orders were carried out without hesitation. From that point on, we fought another war in the west, which cost us several more hundred thousand men – but we took Northern Transylvania back. We marched through Hungary and got as far as Czechoslovakia. We were *de facto* allies of the Soviets and the Westerners, yet we were refused co-belligerent status, which would have given us certain rights during the peace negotiations. At the same time, Romania was occupied by the enormous Red Army, which thought it could do whatever it wanted in our country. A new era in our history began: because we had lost the war against the Soviets, we were now forced – despite promises of protection from the Allies – to adopt a regime imposed by Moscow.

The Yalta Conference (February 1945) and the international situation after 1945

To understand what happened in our country during the past 50 years, we must take another look at the international situation. World War II ended in August 1945, after the Americans dropped atomic bombs on two Japanese

Winston Churchill, Franklin D. Roosevelt and Joseph Stalin at Yalta, on 11 February 1945.

Nicolae Rădescu, the Democratic prime minister who was forced to resign on 28 February 1945, after prolonged unrest instigated by the Communists in the capital. The photograph is taken while in exile, where he founded the Romanian National Committee alongside other émigrés, and continued to work against the Communist regime until his death in 1953.

cities, Hiroshima and Nagasaki. In 1945, after three years of Allied aerial bombardment, which had left it completely destroyed, Germany was divided between the Russians (who occupied the east) and the American, British and French allies (who took over the west). But along with East Germany, the Soviets also occupied all of Eastern Europe – meaning Poland, Hungary, Czechoslovakia, Romania and Bulgaria. In February 1945, the three "greats" – Roosevelt, Churchill and Stalin – signed the Yalta agreement in the Crimea, which stipulated that free elections would be organised in the countries liberated from German hegemony. How the Soviets understood the notion of "free" elections is well known. Slowly but surely, they created artificial political movements. At the time of the Soviet invasion, the Romanian Communist Party (PCR) numbered a mere 900 members – as the party itself was illegal. But it had been outlawed because it was the instrument of a foreign power that wanted to take Bessarabia away from us; it was only common sense for inter-war governments to ban a party that was under the direct control of a large neighbouring country that coveted one of our provinces. It could therefore be argued that the PCR's clandestine status was the reason why it had so few members. Yet as soon as Soviet power took hold of our country, thousands and thousands more Communists sprouted from the ground. They may have supported the party before then, but most of them became Communists only to be on the side of the winner, and of those who held power. Fictitious popular movements organised street protests, demanding that the government step down, and for the briefest of times after 23 August 1944, we believed that normal parliamentary life could resume. However, on 6 March 1945, King Michael I was forced to replace the government led by General Nicolae Rădescu, an opponent of Antonescu. The Soviet deputy foreign affairs minister, Andrey Vyshinsky (who was of Polish descent) travelled to Bucharest, slammed his fist down on the table, surrounded the royal palace with tanks and forced the king to accept a prime minister designated by the

Soviets: Petru Groza. A bourgeois banker from Transylvania, Groza nevertheless supported the PCR and seemed a decent enough man – but in actual fact, he was but a fool (excuse my language) who allowed himself to be manipulated by the Communists. He was the one who helped them seize power between March 1945 and the end of 1947. During those three years, King Michael I tried to resist Soviet pressure (with theoretic Anglo-American help) but in vain. The government slid more and more into the hands of the Communists, who made unilateral decisions to confiscate land, create agricultural cooperatives, nationalise industries etc.

On 14 March 1945, after one week of "democratic rule" imposed by Andrey Vyshinsky (left, wearing glasses) and General Ivan Susaykov, vice-president of the Allied Control Commission (right) Petru Groza and Gheorghe Gheorghiu-Dej took part in a rally in Bucharest, celebrating the return of Northern Transylvania.

Some might say that the Anglo-Americans failed to protect us at Yalta, that they "sold us" to the Soviets. To them I will present a rather different point of view from those which have been circulated in the press and political literature for years: let us not forget that the great Western democracies are neither led by dictators, nor do their governments enjoy absolute power. In 1945, the idea of going to war against a former ally – even one

Iuliu Maniu in the dock, waiting for the sentence to be pronounced after his show trial (November 1947). He was given life in prison and died on 5 February 1953 in Sighet prison, where almost all former great Romanian dignitaries were jailed.

that was committing abuses in Europe – was inconceivable to the British or American public, especially after 5 years of war in Europe, Africa and the Far East. On the other hand, Western leaders agreed to organise free elections at Yalta. Even if those elections were rigged (as was the case with our 1946 elections) they could not see that as sufficient cause to declare war on the USSR.

Our politicians at the time – chiefly Iuliu Maniu and the king – were at first surprised and then outraged by the reaction of the Allies towards the ever more serious and unashamed abuses of the Soviet occupation, in complete violation of their international commitments. While our troops fought alongside them on the Western front, back in Romania the Soviets behaved as if they were in conquered territory. They deported tens of thousands of Romanians from Bessarabia and Bukovina, along with tens of thousands of Germans and Swabians from Transylvania and the Banat; they exploited our mineral resources to depletion (especially uranium, which they needed for building the atomic bomb); and for years, they controlled the Romanian communist government from behind the scenes, using Soviet advisors which they had placed in every key position of government. The most obvious accusation we can bring against the Anglo-Americans is that they did not even have the courage to be honest with Maniu and the Romanian opposition about their inability to help and their calculated, categorical decision no to intervene at that point, given the risks involved. That way, needless sacrifices could have been avoided.

Believing that the great American power, alongside the West, would prove superior to that of the USSR, many Romanians hoped that salvation would come in four or five years. Yet it would only come 45 years later, when the USSR collapsed from within, as communism was unable to build a viable economic system. That is how history works – in the long term, mercilessly treading over individual destinies.

Emblem of the "Tudor Vladimirescu" Division, part of the Soviet military, formed in 1943 in the USSR from Romanian prisoners of war.

The forceful establishment of the communist regime

The period that began with the Soviet occupation completely overturned the values of Romanian society. A great part of our intellectual and political elite was wiped out in prisons, sent to the labour camps along the infamous Danube-Black Sea Canal (known in Romania simply as "the Canal") or forced into exile. The regime imposed a system of terror that is hard to imagine for anyone who did not live through it. People thought one thing and said another. To use a psychiatric term, it was a kind of national schizophrenia that lasted for 45 years.

REZULTATELE PARȚIALE calculate până în prezent constituie

Scânteia

O VICTORIE HOTĂRÎTOARE

A DEMOCRAȚIEI ASUPRA REACȚIUNII

Blocul Partidelor Democrate singura forță politică a țării care poate vorbi în numele POPORULUI ROMÂN

Capitala a dat 424.826 voturi listei Nr. 1 în frunte cu GH. GHEORGHIU-DEJ

Participarea masivă a cetățenilor a făcut ca votarea să continue și în timpul nopții de Marți spre Miercuri

REZULTATUL OFICIAL al votului în Capitală

Comunicatul Ministerului de Interne asupra desfășurării alegerilor

Primele rezultate oficiale din țară

Sediul Comisiei

Scânteia ("the Spark") *the main newspaper of the Romanian Communist Party, proclaiming victory in the elections of November 1946. The results of the ballot were forged and the victory fabricated.*

Of course, the communist regime did have its achievements: illiteracy was considerably reduced; but when the entire education system is in the service of a foreign pseudo-ideology and the freedom of thought is savagely repressed, does that not cancel out any gains made through the reduction of illiteracy?

The network of asphalt roads was extended, although the roads themselves were of sub-mediocre quality; the railway network doubled in size; more importantly, the great number of factories built during this period accelerated the industrialisation of the country and led to a precipitous, very low-quality urbanisation – in short, everything was ill done. The claim that none of these achievements would have been possible without the communist regime is ridiculous. For example, the Americans promoted their famous Marshall Plan (named after General George Marshall, the former US Army Chief of Staff and Secretary of State – meaning foreign minister) to rebuild Western Europe after the terrible devastation of the war. The economic aid plan was spread across

Nikita Sergheyevich Khrushchev, among his counterparts from the Soviet Union's satellite states: Chivu Stoica (first on the left) Gheorghe Gheorghiu-Dej, János Kádár (Hungary) and Todor Zhivkov (Bulgaria).

several years and enabled that part of the continent to return to normality. When countries in the Soviet sphere of influence – such as Czechoslovakia – manifested their interest in the program, the USSR was categorically opposed. Imagine what our country could have become had it been able to take advantage of this veritable manna from heaven. Meanwhile, the Soviets bled us dry with their infamous SOVROMs and forced upon us a Soviet-style planned economy and an inherently flawed industry.

The height of economic fallacy was reached under Nicolae Ceaușescu, who succeeded Gheorghe Gheorghiu-Dej at the helm of the party and the country. Though less brutal than his predecessor at first – for it was during the time of Gheorghiu-Dej that the upper social classes were systematically destroyed (affecting not only the intellectual elite, but *anyone* who was better off, even in rural areas) following Lenin's precepts; tens of thousands died in prisons, along the Canal or were deported – Ceaușescu lost any sense of measure over time. An uneducated, yet cunning and ambitious man, he used his political abilities both domestically – to consolidate his dictatorial powers – and internationally – to create the impression that he was trying to shake off the Soviet yoke, in the eyes of renowned Western politicians such as General Charles de Gaulle or President Nixon. However, he never went so far as to give his masters in the Kremlin any real cause for concern. On the contrary, with their consent, Romania became one of

The cult of personality at its peak: a medal trying to accredit the notion that Nicolae Ceaușescu had entered politics as a child (January 1988).

21 August 1968, the day Ceaușescu seduced an entire people when he condemned the invasion of Czechoslovakia by Soviet troops. Both at home and abroad, he was tipped to become the man who would open up a breach into the Socialist block.

the satellite states through which the Soviet Union maintained contact with countries that had become their enemies – such as Israel, Albania or China – while at the same time, behind his feigned independence, Ceaușescu allowed his "special" services to score spectacular hits in the West, which could only have served the Soviet secret services. The dictator was assisted and spurred on by incompetent opportunists without scruples, who provided the inspiration behind his most ludicrous development plans – such as the decision to build gigantic steelworks in a country that lacked both the raw materials (iron and coal) and the energy required for production, at a time when international demand for steel was in free-fall, on account of recent technological breakthroughs. Moreover, alongside other catastrophic errors in economic planning, Ceaușescu ordered pharaonic construction projects in the capital, following the example of other megalomaniacs in the communist world, such as Mao Zedong or Kim Il Sung. How many

Banknote issued in 1966, displaying the Soviet-style emblem of the Socialist Republic of Romania (which had been called the People's Republic of Romania between 1947 and 1965).

Ceaușescu visiting Kim Ir Sen, his North Korean counterpart, in June 1971. Soon after, undoubtedly impressed by the "delights" of the personality cult, he launched the famous ideological theses that put an end to any cultural détente, forcing writers and artists to dedicate their work entirely to him and to socialism.

schools, hospitals and roads could have been built with the billions spent on the merciless demolition of an entire quarter of old Bucharest and the erection of the monstrous "House of the People" and the luxury boulevard leading to it (longer and wider than the Champs Élysées in Paris)? Communist propaganda trumpeted all of these "achievements", but a healthy economic growth like that of the inter-war period would have taken us further and served us better. To my mind, however, these major blunders of economic policy that sowed the seeds of the dramatic crisis we are facing were not the most tragic heritage of the communist regime. The most tragic consequence of that half-century was that it destroyed our *soul.*

It would have been impossible for a regime in which lying became an instrument of government, in which terror revealed the cowardice of most and foolish heroism of some, in which denunciation was considered a virtue, in which stealing – not only from the state, but from one's own neighbours – appeared legitimate because of the permanent deprivation and the examples of fraud that came from above, not to leave a lasting mark on mentalities and behaviours. This collective mentality is now the single most crucial impediment we face in our attempt to integrate into a new world. The evil seems to have gone so deep and become so generalised, that the generation of young people today may not be able to eradicate it. For

Enei Church in Bucharest, alongside the Dunărea building, half collapsed after the earthquake of 4 March 1977. What tectonics failed to achieve, Ceaușescu completed: the church was damaged on his orders, then immediately razed to the ground. Another 19 churches in the capital, some of which were hundreds of years old, suffered the same fate as a result of his "systematisation" policy.

a tarnished morality is more difficult to mend than old factories. It may only be the future generations who will find the balance again, if they would only be resolute enough to establish a culture of honesty, of respect for commitments made and for those around them.

Politically, I put my confidence in the development of a civilised parliamentary system. Some may say that parliaments and politicians are of ill fame. Winston Churchill himself once said that democracy is the worst form of government... except for all the others that have been tried. My hope lies in our integration into the great European community – the great family of united Europe that has brought phenomenal advances to the countries that joined it 15-20 years ago. I have seen it with my own eyes: Greece today is unrecognisable from that of 20 years ago. Even larger, richer countries such as France have been transformed economically since they created this Union (despite great domestic reticence) 50 years ago. Therein lies the future of our country too.

This does not mean we should naïvely idealise the West. But the genius of every people lies in its ability to combine its own heritage with the integration into a wider ensemble. I believe that, in time, our political ability will help us not only join this great continental entity, but also play a leading role within it. This is my conviction. But it is up to the future generations to make it happen.

CONTENTS